A GOURMET TOUR OF FRANCE

Translated from the French by Kerrin Rousset (chapter text)
and Carmella Abramowitz-Moreau (recipes)
Design: www.atelier-champion.com
Copyediting: Penny Isaac
Typesetting: Gravemaker+Scott
Proofreading: Helen Woodhall
Color Separation: IGS, France
Printed in China by Toppan Leefung

Simultaneously published in French as *Les plus belles tables de France*
© Flammarion, S.A., Paris, 2011

English-language edition
© Flammarion, S.A., Paris, 2011

87, quai Panhard et Levassor
75647 Paris Cedex 13

editions.flammarion.com

11 12 13   3 2 1

ISBN: 978-2-08-030171-0
Dépôt légal: 04/2011

Gilles Pudlowski & Maurice Rougemont

A GOURMET TOUR OF FRANCE

Legendary Restaurants from Paris to the Côte d'Azur

Flammarion

Contents

Restaurants to Dream About

If we were being biased and narrow-minded, we might say that nowhere else—not in New York, London, Tokyo, or Sydney—will you find more splendid establishments, more creative chefs, more delectable dishes, more accurate tributes to tradition, or more convincing hymns to the art of fine living. But it's nearly impossible to draw up a categorical list of "best" restaurants from the breadth and variety found across the globe and within France itself. Nevertheless, in this book we have selected restaurants from throughout France that allow us to dream a bit, to experience a touch of myth and legend on every level.

To extend this idea for a moment: one goes to a restaurant to enjoy a dream-like moment, not just to indulge in the pleasures of the palate. Part of it is about participating in the myth surrounding that place, about going on an adventure, discovering a new idea, family, story, or region. The Parisian restaurants covered here, in and of themselves, tell stories about the capital's culinary history. After all, Lasserre was once only a small wooden pavilion at the Universal Exposition, Ledoyen a little café on the Champs-Élysées, Pré Catelan a restaurant/casino in the Bois de Boulogne, and the Grand Véfour just a café under the arches of the Palais-Royal.

In fact, some of these restaurants are more famous than the cities to which they geographically belong. Paul Bocuse is better known than Collonges-au-Mont-d'Or, Troisgros than Roanne, the Haeberlin family's Auberge de l'Ill than Illhaeusern, or Georges Blanc than Vonnas. Some places change chefs, but their reputation remains. We love and will always love the Auberge des Templiers, the Bézards' venison empire in the Gâtinais, or Les Crayères, an elite table in the heart of Champagne, or L'Huîtrière, the top seafood restaurant in France, located on Rue des Chats-Bossus in Lille, no matter who the chef in those kitchens may be.

On the other hand, this book contains creative chefs whose reputation, madness, and passion wildly outpace the history of their restaurants. Régis Marcon singlehandedly created his property in Saint-Bonnet-le-Froid, like Michel Bras, who bravely and daringly set up on his own by Laguiole on the heights of the Aubrac, and Michel Trama, who fearlessly settled into his stone country house of Puymirol. Pierre Gagnaire carried his ingenious ideas from Saint-Étienne to Paris with resounding success, and Alain Passard created Arpège, with unparalleled brilliance, in the building of the Archestrate restaurant where he was trained.

There are also those peripatetic chefs who fascinate us because they have breathed new flavors into the restaurants of famous luxury hotels. They include Alain Ducasse, the globe-trotting chef at the Plaza Athénée and Louis XV, Éric Briffard, whose unusual genius became apparent at the George V, Yannick Alléno, who reinvents Parisian cuisine at the Meurice, and Éric Fréchon, who gathers the whole political scene from the top down at the Bristol.

There are those who, in being loyal to their *terroir*, identify themselves so closely with the region that their name automatically comes up when invoking the tradition that has given rise to them or shaped them. So, there is Burgundy according to Marc Meneau, Jean-Michel Lorain, or Patrick Bertron with the stamp of Bernard Loiseau; the Lyonnais style of La Mère Brazier, revisited by young Mathieu Viannay; the North by Marc Meurin; the Crocodile's Alsace of yesterday with Emile Jung, or of today with Philippe Bohrer; the Landes region according to Michel Guérard; Jean-André Charial's Provence at Baumanière; Gérald Passédat's Petit Nice, one hundred percent Marseille; Jacques Chibois at La Bastide Saint-Antoine amid the olive trees; and the Dombes in the manner of Alain Chapel, as channeled by Philippe Jousse.

Finally, there are those who haven't been cited here and who seem to operate on their own terms (though we could probably put them in one or other of the above categories): Bernard Pacaud, the solitary maestro of L'Ambroisie; Anne-Sophie Pic, who achieves culinary feats in Valence; Guy Savoy, friend of all mankind, and the most subtle chef there is, just a couple of steps away from the Arc de Triomphe; Taillevent, the ultimate Parisian club; and La Tour d'Argent, the live incarnation of a myth, still standing despite time and the dictates of fashion.

And this is what leads us here: Maurice Rougemont, my travel companion of thirty years, with his sharp eye, and I, the unrepentant gastronome, both have big hearts. We love the Kleins' marvelous Arnsbourg in Baerenthal in the very secret region of the Bitche, as much as we love Alain Dutournier's Carré des Feuillants on the edge of Place Vendôme and the Tuileries gardens. But we really wanted to put the spotlight on all the places here, and show you restaurants that tell the story of French culinary tradition, then and now; restaurants that make us dream. We hope these will fascinate you too. So go on, turn the page. It's time to sit down for a meal.

Gilles Pudlowski

Divine
Arnsbourg

AT THIS OTHERWORLDLY PLACE IN THE LORRAINE REGION OF FRANCE,
WITH A HOTEL ANNEX THAT LOOKS AS IF IT WAS DESIGNED BY A SYLVAN LE CORBUSIER,
YOU'LL FIND ONE OF THE BEST RESTAURANTS IN THE WORLD.

Our favorite restaurant meal (by "our" I mean that of Maurice Rougemont, the photographer, and me, the journalist) is not included in the usual English-language newspaper rankings of the world's best restaurants. In a clearing in Untermunthal, by the Moselle in the Lorraine region, on the border with Alsace, there is an inn. It looks like a modern chalet with a double-sided wood-paneled dining room; there is an exotic entrance with flowers, slightly Thai-looking sculpted doors, and, just across the way, up a set of sandstone stairs, is the contemporary hotel. Another world? No doubt about it.

Twinned with the "K," a hotel annex in a woodsy Le Corbusier style that is affiliated with the Relais & Châteaux brand, this gourmet's paradise amid a backdrop of greenery has brought itself up to date without losing its sense of tradition. The Kleins are very attentive and see to every guest's individual needs. Nicole is at the hotel and Cathy reigns over the dining room, while Cathy's brother (and Nicole's husband) Jean-Georges is the magical genie of the place. As shy as he is discreet, he twirls around the kitchen, creating and dazzling his clients with pleasure. It would not be an exaggeration to say that his grand tasting menu is a gift, considering the plethora of beautiful things he offers, and that the basic menu offers superb value for money, the epitome of the finest creative cuisine currently available.

The succession of delectable hors-d'oeuvres includes the pairing of cream and Transmontanus caviar, raw langoustine with curry and Granny Smith apple, and the "perfect" egg, where the yolk is cooked like the white (a technical feat), served with pearl barley and wood sorrel. There is sea bass with pine nut risotto and a rice emulsion in a miniature barrel and a "virtual landscape" of foie gras, but where the foie gras is quite real, cooked in a terrine and accompanied by pralines and caramelized squash seeds. It is substantial and at the same time inventive and delicious.

When one has experienced a meal consisting of thirty-seven novelty tapas at Ferran Adrià's El Bulli in Catalonia, regularly cited at the head of the world's best restaurant rankings in English publications, a meal at L'Arnsbourg starts to look like "classical" dining. One bites into something and feels warm as well as cold. It may be surprising, but it is also satisfying. After working front of house for a long time, Jean-Georges took over the kitchen from his mother, Lilly, who had obtained the restaurant's first Michelin star in 1989. Jean-Georges recognizes the debt he owes to the great Ferran Adrià, in whose kitchen he worked.

But Jean-Georges has not forgotten that his inn, dating from 1900, was originally a woodsman's cabin, later renovated into a coal-miner's and lumberjack's lodge; nor that it was transformed into a family hotel by his grandmother, Rose Donnenwirth, in the 1950s. After hotel management school, he worked twenty years at front of house before his sister Cathy encouraged him into taking over his mother's kitchen. Self-taught, and now in his 50s, he has become an outstanding technician. And the old woodsman's cabin, with its light wood moldings and big bay windows opening out onto the forest, is now a sophisticated restaurant.

The cuisine is eclectic: half cosmopolitan, half focused on the Lorraine region at its finest. There is substantial genius at work here: mozzarella gnocchi in a tomato consommé; grilled foie gras with a Melba-style peach and elder bouillon; blue lobster with garden pea bonbons, yuzu, the Japanese citrus, and verbena; cornetto of black olives that resembles caviar; pigeon breast with corn puree; and sour cherry mille-feuille.

We can still taste the blackberry and kumquat duckling, and the desserts that are consistently and brilliantly executed by a pastry chef recently arrived from the Amphitryon in Lorient. There is souffléed tomato with yuzu confit and thyme ice cream, magical and so easy to digest, wild strawberry confit with lemongrass honey and pine bud sorbet, as well as a light and exquisite piña colada (pineapple, rum, and coconut), barely sweet and so fruity.

And we must not forget the great Alsatian wines (Ostertag or Albert Mann Muscat, Hengst or Brandt de Josmeyer Riesling, Humbrecht's Clos Saint-Urbain Pinot Gris) or the Burgundies (magnificent Bonnes-Mares or superb Chambolle Musigny les Cras George Roumier) recommended by an expert sommelier, perfect in his role who, by his mix of competence and experience, adds vigor to a young and exceedingly dynamic space.

Jean-Georges's young Japanese assistant, Yoshiko Takayama, works with him with great poise and charisma, and all here (the average age being 30) contribute to a team full of unmatchable enthusiasm. As far as we're concerned, this may well be the best restaurant in the world!

L'Arnsbourg

18, rue Untermuhlthal

57230 Baerenthal

Tel: +33 (0)3 87 06 50 85

www.arnsbourg.com

Hôtel K.

Tel: +33 (0)3 87 27 05 60

For recipes, see pages 173–174

Blue lobster with garden pea bonbons, yuzu, and verbena (page 8). Sommelier Yoshiko Takayama officiates in the dining room (below). Facing page, clockwise from top left: The whole Arnsbourg team is at the restaurant's windows. The cellar, in which another sommelier picks his wines, is visible through a glass pane. Soft-boiled egg with truffle, pigeon breast, and souffléed tomato.

The Sun over
Baumanière

IN AN ENCHANTED VALLEY, HIDDEN BETWEEN ROCK AND GREENERY, LIES A SOLITARY PLACE,
AN ODE TO PROVENCE. IN THE HEART OF THE ALPILLES MOUNTAIN RANGE,
FRENCH CULINARY TRADITION IS PERPETUATED THROUGH A SUN-DRENCHED CUISINE.

It is unlike anywhere else, "a reward" as Frédéric Dard calls it. A fan of Baumanière, he saw it as "an exceptional experience that must be earned." Perched on the peak of the Alpilles, across from the Crau desert plain, is the village of Baux, which Frédéric Mistral, nineteenth-century lexicographer and champion of the Provençal language of Occitan, wanted to make his Provence capital. Craggy hills surround the vale known as Hell's Valley, and the houses look like a myriad of small gems amid the stone and grass.

When he founded the Oustau de Baumanière, Raymond Thuillier imagined it had an etymology meaning "elegant manners," as well as "the art of living and of greeting both people and life with an acute sense of joy." There are several buildings where guests can stay, the Guigo and the Manor, as well as the Oustau's little sister, known as the Cabro d'Or, with its friendly service, delicious restaurant, spa, and the Carita equestrian school. It is a paradise-like retreat with luxurious housing and a gourmet restaurant for those seeking calm and relaxation.

Arles is only a stone's throw away, Camargue a short distance, Saint-Rémy-de-Provence and Glanum's Roman ruins just at the foot of the hills; Avignon, Marseille, Aix, and Nîmes are neighboring beacons. But it is at the Oustau, just below Baux, nestled on its rocky spur, that the art of relaxation and sumptuous dining in the shade is celebrated. Born in Chambéry in 1897, Raymond Thuillier was raised by a mother who ran the buffet of the Privas

train station in Ardèche. She promised him a better future ("you will never do such slave's work"), and so he first worked in insurance; he was the director of the Union Life Company.

But when he discovered the ruins of a fifteenth-century manor house at the foot of Baux-de-Provence in 1938, everything changed. Little by little he transformed it into a modern hotel. He gave it medieval-style rooms, a dining room with huge vaulted ceilings, and a vast swimming pool, where sun and blue skies were reflected. He opened the establishment in 1945, received a Michelin star as early as 1946, and a second star in 1949. His style of cuisine showed a sense of tradition and loyalty. He didn't wear a chef's coat but a long white doctor's or inventor's shirt, as if he were healing the world's wounds or inventing new reasons to believe in the existence of beauty.

His signature dishes were veal sweetbreads in pastry, red mullet with tapenade, and Alpilles roast lamb in a crust. Queen Elizabeth II of England and General de Gaulle, among many others, came to enjoy the surroundings, to honor his restaurant by their presence, and to recharge their batteries. The third Michelin star finally came in 1990, about three years before Thuillier died. In 1993, his grandson Jean-André Charial followed in his footsteps. An alumnus of the HEC school of management, Jean-André was passionate and self-taught when it came to cooking, like his grandfather. Together with his wife Geneviève, he renovated the house with a style that was both contemporary and Provençal. Rooms were added in the Manoir and La Guigou, in addition to those redone at the Ostau, all with a design element and jewel-like gardens. There was also the bistro on the square in Maussane-des-Alpilles and the new-wave Prieuré in Villeneuvelès-Avignon.

A businessman and multifaceted and inquisitive hotel owner, former intern with Troisgros, Bocuse, Chapel, and Haeberlin, friend and spiritual son of Michel Guérard, Jean-André brought a breath of fresh air to the cuisine. Truffle ravioli with leeks, raised to new heights by the subsequent addition of foie gras, became the new signature dish. Talented chefs came later to assist him. The Wahid brothers, two young alumni of the Ducasse school, added a dazzling ray of sunshine to the already modernized Baumanière tradition, with Sylvestre doing savory and Jonathan doing sweet dishes.

Seared red mullet with tomato, basil, and thyme flower in lukewarm vinaigrette and bitter herbs, and a frothy hen's egg and green asparagus with black truffle fumet *en chaud-froid* are their new "classics," deftly brought out by black-tie service that is both correct and enthusiastic. A dish of wide pasta covering a stew of green peas, asparagus, broad beans, and lettuce, all of it rubbed with truffle shards, displays the richness of the vegetable garden. The roasted and lacquered Costières pigeon with turnips and beets, deglazed with lavender sap, or the legendarily tender lamb roast infused with purple garlic and skewered with anchovy, then spit-roasted, offer incredible opportunities for carving and serving prowess at the table.

The cheese comes from La Mère Richard in Lyon. The colossal wine list showcases new wines of Provence and the Rhone Valley, with a particular penchant for Châteauneuf-du-Pape, but also the coastal wines of Nîmes and of the Baux Valley. Desserts are fresh and light, and honor local fruit. Strawberries in a chilled essence with a crunchy meringue and sugar sablé; or wild strawberries on a shortbread crust with a crushed basil emulsion and Château d'Estoublon olive-oil ice cream are some of the sweet delights you may expect here.

In the summertime, there is the terrace under trees that are hundreds of years old, and the vaulted rooms in the fall and winter; this is the theatrical stage set at Oustau, just below the deserted village. When one leaves the house at night, at the end of a feast, the light seems to spill over the surrounding rock, as if Baumanière is spreading its magic over this eternal landscape, laying out its bounty for the taking.

L'Oustau de Baumanière

13520 Les Baux-de-Provence

Tel: +33 (0)4 90 54 33 07

www.oustaubaumaniere.com

For recipes, see pages 174–175

Chef Jean-André Charial entering his domain, where the red mullet with basil remains one of the great classics (pages 12–13).
For dessert, cream is poured on the souffléed crêpes Baumanière (below).
The maitre d'hotel carves tableside under the gaze of the chef (facing page, top left). A unique dish: hen's egg and green asparagus with black truffle fumet en chaud-froid (bottom, left).

"La Vie en
Blanc"

GEORGES BLANC IS LIKE A DISCREET AND GRAND ORCHESTRAL CONDUCTOR,
OVERSEEING MULTIPLE PROPERTIES IN HIS KINGDOM-LIKE VILLAGE AND
MAJESTICALLY EMBODYING HIS REGION AND HIS LEADING INGREDIENT.

He is the prince of Vonnas, the king of the Bresse region, who watches over his village as if it produced the only AOC (*appellation d'origine contrôlée*—origin-controlled) poultry in the world. A happy man? Without a doubt.

He has created a mini-empire for himself, the capital of which is an abundantly flowered village. He has garnered nothing but praise since obtaining three Michelin stars in 1981, the only person to do so that year, as well as in the two following years.

Georges Blanc is descended from "la Mère Blanc," his grandmother Elisa Gervais, who was named the "world's best high-society cook" in 1933 by Curnonsky, the prince of gastronomy, after she obtained two stars in her modest village café. Blanc is unlike any other great chef.

Cook, hotel manager, businessman, and winemaker, he turned an average rural town into the "first gourmet village in France," confirmed by a sign at the town's entrance. In the town's main square, which, incidentally, is as gorgeous as a theatrical backdrop, almost all of the houses belong to or were redecorated by him. There is the Ancienne Auberge (Old Inn), recreated from his grandparents' café, which offers such dishes as pigs' trotter carpaccio, snails in a light stew, sautéed frog, and chicken in cream sauce.

There are also two shops, one with ingredients and the other focused on decoration, the Résidence des Saules, and of course, the already large main house made even larger. Some of the rooms, close to the vast sauna and swimming-pool complex with a Carita beauty spa, have views of an arboretum. Such is the magic of Blanc who, like a Walt Disney of cooking, has managed to combine the needs of both body and mind for gourmets who have seen it all elsewhere and want to rest and feel revitalized by visiting him.

One cannot help but be impressed by his large inn with a view of the river, the two elegant dining rooms, and the attentive service, supervised by Marcel Perinet, who has been there for forty years. There is also his sumptuous cellar, one of the biggest and best stocked in the world, with more than one hundred thousand bottles overseen by the Meilleur Ouvrier de France (Best Craftsman in France) winner, sommelier Fabrice Sommier. Nevertheless, one quickly feels at ease there, as if grandmother Elisa's simple village café had just naturally evolved over time.

The kitchen strikes the same delicate balance between tradition and modernity. Pigeon supremes and lobster on a bed of eggplant lasagne, "ochre velvet" of sweet bell peppers and coral oil, poultry medallions with oysters and white beans, and crab Chartreuse with osetra caviar, all play the role of appetizer with equal grace and aplomb. Sea bass marinière with olive oil, Chardonnay, and tomato and herb fondue is a miracle of lightness that reduced Michel Guérard, the apostle of light cooking, to tears when Georges first created it twenty-five years ago. The dish continues to be astoundingly avant-garde today.

Agile and flavorful, light and refreshing, exciting and so palatable, his chicken from Bresse, like the region itself, which is so ardent and sunny without being overbearing, is a big contrast to the region's antiquated reputation for rusticity and provincialism. There are variations on regional products originating between Bresse and Dombes: lukewarm "scramble" of frogs' legs, artichoke, and garden herbs; and potato Vonnassian crêpes luxuriously wedded with salmon and caviar, served with butter whipped with kaffir, the lime from Réunion.

A Chassagne-Montrachet by Niellon would be marvelous on top of this, but the wine list is so vast that one inevitably misses it. We still have some wonderful memories, though, such as Francois Faiveley's Mazis-Chambertin, fabulously fruity, round, supple and long, and a perfect accompaniment to the emblematic Bresse chicken with confit garlic cloves, Parmentier crêpes and chicken liver with artichoke, dressed in a cream and foie-gras sauce. Upon being served such a combination, it is tempting to give up as a food critic, having been left with practically nothing to criticize. The cuisine here is both an act of devotion and one of lust for the exciting pairings that can be achieved between great wines and high-quality artisanal ingredients.

Georges Blanc, who has told his life story through many anecdotes and short stories (*La Vie en Blanc*, GSL Editions), seems to have come full circle. He may be an innkeeper (Le Saint-Laurent), modern and alert, on a major waterway at Saint-Laurent-sur-Saône across from Mâcon and the river; the owner of a brasserie in Lyon (Le Splendide), across from the Brotteaux train station, and another in Bourg-en-Bresse (Chez Blanc); and even a winemaker in Aze in the Mâcon region. But it is in Vonnas that one must rediscover him. Be sure not to miss the "Bresse panouille," the most delicious of any caramel vacherin, the apple and vanilla mille-feuille, or purple figs and butter sablé with a green tea mousseline cream and honey-orange ice cream.

One must not rush to Vonnas; it's important to take the time to stop on the shores of the flower-lined Veyle River and to be open to the pleasures of this symbolic and exemplary place in the heart of France.

Georges Blanc

Place du Marché

01540 Vonnas

Tel: +33 (0)4 74 50 90 90

www.georgesblanc.com

For recipes, see pages 176–177

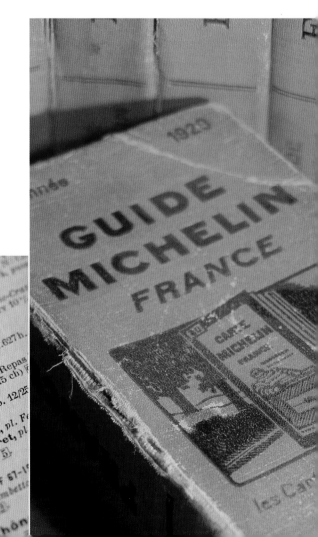

The spectacular dish on page 16 is pigeon supremes with lobster.
Georges Blanc champions his region with the Bresse chicken he proudly holds in front of his restaurant (page 17).
In the 1923 edition of the Michelin Guide, there is already one star for La Mère Blanc.
Facing page, counterclockwise from top: Georges Blanc chooses a bottle, and offers a light tempura of frogs' legs en chaud-froid *and a chocolate and prune pavé.*

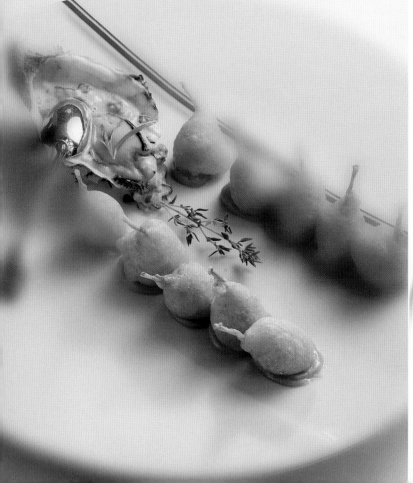

Paul Bocuse
France

What's Cooking,
Bocuse?

It is the story of an eternally young man who refuses to grow old, who celebrated his eightieth birthday having marked more than forty years with three Michelin stars. At the peak of the gourmet universe, he never abandoned his family inn at Pont de Collonges, which he'd bought back so many years ago to turn into a temple dedicated to his family's glory.

Paul Bocuse is everywhere, at home in Lyon: on the famous Lyonnais mural in the city center, and at the Halles de la Part-Dieu market, where his portrait sits in prime position behind the main stands. The queen of butchers, Colette Sibilia, proudly stands by him in the portrait, dry sausages in hand like war trophies. Mother and daughter Renée and Renée Richard, both elite cheesemongers and grand priestesses of all things Saint-Marcellin and Saint-Nectaire, have created a veritable picture gallery dedicated to Paul, to whom they are absolutely devoted.

Early in the morning at Val-d'Isère, the chefs hold endless discussions across from Les Halles, beneath the portraits of Paul and his cousins, the first one having died, the second retired. Like an apostle with his followers, the emperor on his throne, Paul Bocuse dispenses justice and hands out advice. There isn't a single young chef who sets up shop between Saône and Rhône without asking for "Mr. Paul's" advice.

In spite of all this, the easy-going Bocuse avoids his image and laughs at his own myth. One may think he is on a restaurant consulting trip in New York or Tokyo, and then find him at a motorcycle rally in Dayton, Ohio, or at a friend's snowmobile race on the slopes of the Canadian mountains.

These days he appears relaxed, serene, and rejuvenated. His private life, like Mitterrand's before him, is no longer a mystery. His son Jérôme, who was a ski instructor in the U.S., poses in a chef's hat on the day of the Bocuse d'Or competition, the major event, held every two years in Lyon, that brings together the entire gourmet world in the Rhône-Alpes region. Jérôme is now fully part of the family tradition.

Across from the bridge over the Saône, the restaurant in Collonges sparkles like never before, with its new coat of red paint and its gallery of chefs praised by the renowned intellectual television presenter Bernard Pivot. The restaurant's service team, run like clockwork, is supervised by François Pipala, winner of the Meilleur Ouvrier de France (Best Craftsman in France) in the maître d' category in 1993. In the kitchen, chefs Roger Jaloux, Christophe Muller, and Christian Bouvarel, all MOF (Meilleur Ouvrier de France) as well, and beyond faithful to the end, ensure that the restaurant's reputation continues unfailingly.

Jean Fleury, the boss's right or left arm (no one knows for sure), oversees the communication between the kitchen and the front of house. Along with the sensible Roger Jaloux, Fleury sees to it that the menu is adapted with each new season. He flies from one table to another when the boss isn't there—which is rare—and also ensures he keeps an eye on the annexes: the East, the North, the South, and the newest one, the West, in a large loft across the Saône, which all belong mostly to Paul and in part to his assistants.

From the moment it opened, the North on Rue Neuve was a success, with its reasonably priced old classics of brasserie cuisine. The South is often full, offering a vibrant cuisine in which items such as delicate pizzas (salmon and caviar, or onion and tomato in the manner of a pissaladière), tagines, couscous, and cod stuffed with mushrooms are the stars in a cheerful yellow and blue setting, offset with light stone. With a hundred and eighty covers at each service, the success of these was such that Bocuse and his team, as if in defiance of the economic crisis, opened the East in the Brotteaux train station, specializing in "travel cuisine," as well as the West, focusing on a modern take on fusion cuisine.

Meanwhile, the main restaurant in Collonges is always full, thanks to its generous menus and a local clientele who, though they love to eat and accept change readily, are also happy to find their usuals. That means the red mullet dressed in crisp potato scales with tomato coulis and garlic clove confit, bass with basil and stuffed artichokes, delicate frog cream with borlotti beans, watercress, and sorrel, and tender and juicy Bresse pigeon, simply spit-roasted and served with buttered potatoes. Then there are the cheeses of the wonderful Mère Richard, Chevenet's goat cheeses from Hurigny, crème brûlée as a homage to Sirio Maccioni, his pal from Le Cirque in New York, and the desserts, which were updated without losing the quality of the "desserts my grandmother used to make" (floating islands, freshly hand-churned vanilla ice cream, shortcrust tart with fruit). On top of all this is a Côtes-du-Rhône picked by sommelier John Euvrard (do you know the amazing Cornas of Colombo?). And so this establishment of traditional haute cuisine has a mission to keep sophisticated French taste current.

Paul Bocuse reigns over his house like a protective father. A dash poetic and a touch philosophical, he collects aphorisms, making him the last thinker of his profession. "One can only make good ends with very good beginnings." (Although, in fact, this is a quote from Prosper Montagné.) Or, "The great are the great, and the small are small," which the sorely missed, most faithful and perceptive of his disciples, Bernard Loiseau at Saulieu, loved to repeat. There is also, "Cream, butter, and wine, that is the trilogy of Lyon's regional cuisine." And lastly, "Nouvelle cuisine is nothing on the plate, it's all in the check."

They tried to call him a know-it-all, always giving lessons, a polemist, an obstacle to the work of critiquing, when he is in fact a merchant of happiness, above all. "We are sons of the poor who live like the rich." Listening to him is almost as enjoyable an experience as eating his poultry roasted on a spit with the legendary macaroni gratin.

The only mystery left is as to what magical potion he could have imbibed to seem to be living life in reverse. He appears to be gifted with eternal youth. We await the new Bocuse for the year 3000.

The truffle soup V.G.E. invented for President Valéry Giscard d'Estaing remains one of the legendary dishes (page 21). Red mullet with crispy skin (above) and the magnificent fish in a puff pastry crust, presented in a superb, traditional manner (facing page, bottom right).
Here, the show is always in the dining room, especially when Paul Bocuse takes part in the service. Loyal Daniel Abdallah has been making sure everything runs smoothly for years (facing page, top left). In the kitchen, all dishes are still made in beautiful copper pots (top right).

L'Auberge du Pont de Collonges

40, rue de la Plage

69660 Collonges-au-Mont-d'Or

Tel: +33 (0)4 72 42 90 90

www.bocuse.fr

For recipes, see page 178

Bras
A Touch of Warmth in the Aubrac

ONE OF THE WORLD'S BEST CHEFS IS DEEP IN THOUGHT AND SERENE IN HIS TRANQUIL SURROUNDINGS. THAT WOULD BE MICHEL BRAS WITH HIS SON SÉBASTIEN, ON THE PLATEAU OF FRANCE'S AUBRAC REGION.

The Aubrac hides among the cumulus clouds; wind and rain blows over the plateau. We put off our planned walk of the upper ridges toward the cow herders' old stone shelters. Above 4,000 feet, winters are harsh. The countryside was hibernating, and it is now ready to open up.

At home, Michel Bras watches and waits. He has not changed over the years; he still rubs his eyes behind his glasses, he still writes short, evocative texts to introduce dinner feasts. At home, on top of the Aubrac plateau, across from the windy forests, no one says, "the chef," but simply Michel.

That said, he removed his first name from the menus. It's just "Bras" now; total restraint in line with the decor of stone, glass, and slate. In this spaceship ready to take off, he is relieved by his son Sébastien, back from his lessons with Guérard and Gagnaire, who has now embraced his father's ideas. It is all too easy to forget that the young lad Michel, born in 1946, is over sixty years old.

Michel is self-taught, yet learned good manners from his mother (who still stirs the aligot—potato and cheese puree—in the kitchen behind the commis cooks, who make the most modern of dishes). He seems to be fleeing the rest of the world's forward march. It would be an understatement to say that he doesn't resemble his contemporaries. It is easy to imagine, in his round glasses and dreamy discretion, that he is related to Woody Allen, or the German film director Wim Wenders.

He maintains the air of an intellectual marathoner with a threadlike silhouette, while hiding his anxieties or his serenity under the most angelically simple terms. His menu reads like a poem. It may be called "Discovery & Nature" or "Escape & Earth," and these are merely the titles. The dishes are carefully titled: there is "In Memory" for the divine Luc veal rib, grilled on embers. The "Classic Today" for the famous Feast of Fall Vegetables, which is not merely a selection of vegetables picked that day, but admirable in its purity and biblical simplicity.

A founder of the school of herbs (along with Marc Veyrat in Veyrier, Jean-Paul Jeunet in Arbois and his alter ego and neighbor Régis Marcon in Saint-Bonnet-le-Froid, who followed in his footsteps), he is above all a singular poet who takes care to instill his brand and leave his mark. He may be a man of the mountains, a foraging cook, a poet of the high paths, but he is first and foremost a creator who does not flinch in the face of asceticism, who only accepts that which has reached a sufficient level of perfection, meaning, to his eye, a sort of Zen degree of abundance.

Copied, adored, and revered, Michel Bras is one of the best chefs in the world. He knows it, even if he seems not to care. His lukewarm cake of flowing chocolate (he registered the trademark for "chocolat coulant") has been copied and pillaged a hundred times over; mutilated by mediocre chefs or faithfully imitated by admirers. One comes to him nowadays to discover the "original version" or the multiple variations he has done on a theme of fruits.

But Michel Bras, who successfully launched a collection of products, oils, spices, and condiments, is on a constant mission to renew his palette—like an artist. We can't get enough of the variations on the Aveyron truffle, which he presents crumbled in a crust, on top of sweet onion confit, in olive oil vinaigrette, and with a shred of sautéed asparagus. We revel in his soft-boiled egg to which a splash of black olive oil is added and which is served with wholegrain toast. Jumbo langoustines are dressed with mushrooms and salad burnet, a nod to his "cousin" Olivier Roellinger in Cancale, and slices of duck foie gras are served with chutney-style peppered strawberry confit ("strawberry is not a fruit" says the menu, as if it were an idea of Magritte's).

A meal at Michel and Sébastien Bras' restaurant is a feast of the palate as well as of the mind. One comes to taste the best new wines of the great Southwest, picked by Sergio, the most clever of Francophile Argentine sommeliers (do you know the Côtes du Marmandais Chante Coucou d'Elian da Ros?), and to bite into the lovingly married vegetables (the confit or grilled eggplant with raw bream). Do not forget to save some room for the most refined desserts in the world, which evoke childhood memories (like the potato waffle with brown butter cream and salted butter caramel).

On return visits, one does not forget those delicious things which come and go, symbolic of his thought process, like the whole beefsteak tomato, cored and sliced at the top, with fragrant basil and licorice-tasting dried black olive on breadcrumbs, the whole taking on the air of a manifesto; or pork terrine complete with snout; guinea-fowl terrine with pumpkin puree; and sole cooked in butter, sliced and served with a Chinese amaranth leaf, milk skin, fragrant hazelnut bread, and meltingly tender chestnuts.

There is also his seemingly simple masterpiece—but isn't simplicity a tortuous adventure in itself?—that is the sumptuous white and creamy Beauvais potato soup, with fragrances of black truffle, almond milk, and a dash of olive oil. Warm liver with quince compote; a puree of small, sweet Cebe onions with truffle vinaigrette; turbot with sugar snap peas in a cilantro-egg vinaigrette like a light Hollandaise sauce; juicy pigeon breast spiced with juniper berry, pepper, and orange; and tender lamb with orange-flavored eggplant—all are of the same high caliber.

Bras

Route de l'Aubrac

12210 Laguiole

Tel: +33 (0)5 65 51 18 20

www.bras.fr

For recipes, see pages 178–179

The transition between Michel Bras and his son Sébastien (both on pages 25 and 27) has been smooth. The famous Feast of Fall Vegetables (page 24) is always on the menu in this architecturally astounding restaurant over the Aubrac. The saddle of Allaiton lamb roasted on the bone (right) and the beefsteak tomato (facing page, bottom right) are worth a detour to Laguiole.

His desserts also play on the "return to your roots" idea, with the lightness, freshness, and innocence of childhood: lukewarm and crispy cookie (shortbread dough and meringue) opening onto a flow of blueberries, rhubarb paired with milk skin and walnut butter confit. They are all exquisitely delicious, and transport us back, in an instant, to a childlike sense of enjoyment.

The setting too takes us back to more innocent times. This modern inn with clean lines plays the role of a beacon of purity. Like a UFO made of concrete, glass, mixed woods, and soft beige, white, and gray tones, the building stands solitary on the vast plateau, like a temple of the sun or of nature dedicated to the worship of herbs and vegetables. There are twelve spartan rooms, with their bay windows a mirror on the Aubrac; a corridor between them calls to mind the paths on the surrounding mountains. A restaurant? A hotel? This is something else. We are at Michel Bras'.

The Fréchon Era at
Le Bristol

A NATIVE OF PICARDY AND NOW LIVING IN PARIS, ÉRIC FRÉCHON'S
HEAD MAY BE IN THE CLOUDS BUT HIS FEET REMAIN FIRMLY ON THE GROUND.

He was a night laborer, the kind who worked proudly for others without ever making waves. Long a henchman of Christian Constant at Paris's luxurious Hôtel Crillon, he created meals fit for kings. Originally from Corbie in the Somme department of France, he apprenticed at the Homard Bleu in Tréport, then came up to Paris to work at La Grande Cascade. Emboldened by his experience, he became the chef at La Verrière, across from the Buttes-Chaumont, where he was overlooked by the Michelin Guide.

Though a little late, his talent has finally been recognized. He awaited these accolades impatiently, especially upon seeing some of his neighboring colleagues honored, even though they were no more deserving than the Bristol. Nicolas Sarkozy and his wife Carla Bruni are regulars. The capital's gourmets love this civilized place, for its discreet bar, beautiful wood-paneled winter room, and the big glassed-in summer lounge looking out onto the fabulous tree-lined garden.

There is also the impeccable service, eloquent menu, lovely glassware, and immaculate table setting. And the cooking? It's the cherry on the cake: precise, delicate, and light, even intelligent. A man of the North, from the coast, Éric Fréchon adds dynamism, great subtlety, and even a touch of genius to a piece of whiting, mackerel, or herring. He transforms the Roscoff pink onion into the most stunning composition imaginable for spaghetti carbonara, and serves a quail egg pan-fried with lentil and bacon jelly. In short, he has an innate sense of what constitutes an interesting mix of roguish and chic, like him, and of how rusticity can be matched with refinement. He has a propensity for aesthetics that never compromises good taste.

He is unlike some of his fellow chefs who know how to make dishes that look pretty but don't actually taste good. He combines red mullet with zucchini flower in an arrangement where the deboned fish, stuffed with condiments and matched with cumin and a yellow pepper coulis, transports one across the Mediterranean without becoming too much of a fusion dish. With the mullet tasting like mullet, and the zucchini and its flower full of pure vegetable flavor, Fréchon gives new meaning to Curnonsky's old saying which goes, "Good cuisine is when things taste like what they are." No more, no less.

For a first meal at the Bristol, we might suggest that a gourmet tries the seasonal menu, which is truly a bargain. In it, the truffled endive with ham and aged Comté cheese is a nod to the most trite of old home-style meals. But for a feast with friends, it would be hard to turn down sharing the admirable Bresse chicken with crayfish cooked in a pig's bladder and served with a selection of variety meats, truffles, and foie-gras cream. With the thigh meat shredded in a most delicious consommé, this may be one of the most astounding dishes currently available in French cuisine.

We'd like to add a hymn to the desserts, which have always represented a moment of majesty. Mikan Mandarine, frosted,

With his tricolored collar as Meilleur Ouvrier de France (Best Craftsman in France), Éric Fréchon was born to reign over the Bristol's large wood-paneled dining room (page 28). Meticulous in the kitchen and passionate about good ingredients, he picks the best truffles from a vendor (far right).
He pairs delicate egg mousseline (page 29), red mullet with zucchini flower (facing page, top), sea urchins in their shells with tongue and foam, and dazzles us with his litchi in snowy meringue (facing page, bottom left).

honey-poached, or with Grand Marnier soufflé, or chocolate in many ways (dark cream with crispy sablé cookie and crunchy toasted hazelnuts, with a caramel emulsion, as liquid cocoa, or as a milk mousse with iced Jivara milk chocolate) are some examples of the astounding choices available here, like cardinal sins, or the finishing touch to a royal feast.

Under Fréchon's rule at the Bristol, located next to Place Beauvau and the Elysée Palace, nothing is out of place; everything fits together. Whether it's the bread selection (poppy seed and rye bread are excellent, as is the crispy mini-baguette), Marie-Anne Cantin's seasonal cheeses, or anything else, under the baton of this pitch-perfect conductor, the music is immaculate and the symphonies sublime.

Le Bristol

112, rue du Faubourg-Saint-Honoré

75008 Paris

Tel: +33 (0)1 53 43 43 00

www.lebristolparis.com

For recipes, see page 180

The Gascon of Paris at the
Carré des Feuillants

ALAIN DUTOURNIER, ORIGINALLY FROM CHALOSSE IN THE LANDES REGION OF FRANCE, WAS WON OVER BY THE CHARMS OF THE CAPITAL YEARS AGO. NOW LOCATED ON THE POSH SIDE OF TOWN, HE HAS RETAINED HIS CHARACTER AND GAINED IN TALENT, WITHOUT LOSING HIS ROOTS.

We adore Dutournier. Born in the village of Cagnotte, he is passionate about the great unbridled Southwest and is happy to cross over the Pyrenees to find inspiration, giving Parisians a craving for this "southern flair." He is at home at Pinxo, on Rue d'Alger, where his pupil Fabrice Dubos creates excellent tapas. He keeps an eye on the Trou Gascon, his first restaurant on Rue Taine, which maintains its charm and drive, and where he still serves the best cassoulet in the city and a ham worth swooning over.

Yet the Dutournier to whom stylish gourmets give three heartfelt stars, is to be found on Rue de Castiglione, at Carré des Feuillants, made chic, restrained, and minimalist by artistic designer Alberto Bali. There, the great Alain rewrites his beloved cuisine with brilliance, creating an entire festival around the truffle. Oxtail raviolo in a truffled bouillon, chestnut cappuccino with grated Alba truffle, Jerusalem artichoke cake with foie gras and truffles: here is a perfect ode to the black or white diamond in all its forms. Add to that the variations on Aquitaine caviar

with crisp monkfish, cabbage lasagna and horseradish aroma, or divine oysters in seawater jelly and seaweed tartar in a creamy foam. It is all so good that one cannot help but think something special is happening in this gastronomical space hidden between the Tuileries and Vendôme.

The most beautiful products in the world are enhanced with passion, talent, and creativity; this is what the maestro Dutournier boldly proposes. Only the highest praise can be sung over the subtle plays that are the Souvaroff guinea fowl in a Dutch oven, veal sweetbread medallion with mushroom macaroni, or oven-baked rack of lamb from the Pyrenees, its shoulder braised in a clay pot. All dishes a Gascon grandmother could hardly have imagined.

The service is cheerful, brisk, and friendly. The wine list reveals classy finds from the Bordeaux region, and desserts (a marvelous pistachio-infused "Russe" with red berries, and a nod to the vacherin with splendid hazelnuts, cocoa nibs, and Tahitian vanilla) are top class. How can you not adore Dutournier?

Carré
des Feuillants

14, rue de Castiglione

75001 Paris

Tel: +33 (0)1 42 86 82 82

www.carredesfeuillants.fr

For recipes, see pages 180–181

In the gorgeous, chic, and understated dining room, the world's most beautiful ingredients are served, like wild jumbo prawns in "Crème de Tête" with melon scoops in chutney and saffron-scented gazpacho (page 32) or wild turbot fillet with Aquitaine caviar, rice in squid ink, green asparagus, and girolles (above). After a fig and nut dessert (facing page), the chef may propose an aged Armagnac from the cellar.

It is obvious that these young cooks, copper pots in hand and surrounding Alain Dutournier in his kitchen, are going to amaze us.

Chapel's
Images of Mionnay

On the shores of the Dombes, a region of southeastern France, not far from Lyon, there is a sweet, happy, and unique place.

The highway looks pristine in the fog. It is a misty and magical road toward the Dombes ponds. A bird flies up high, carried by the wind. It is dawn, and dogs are barking in the distance.

Philippe Jousse carries on as he always has. He has already been here twenty-five years. It was here in this famous house, long ago, that Alain Ducasse had the idea of making ingredients the star, of describing each dish like an elegy.

A fall meal here would be hen pheasant with foie gras in aspic and hot toasts; scallops and porcini mushrooms in a Paimpol coco-bean cream; sea bass fillet on its skin with truffled vegetables; or young boar chop and sausage, accompanied by Dauphine potatoes resembling Bressans dumplings, filled with chestnuts and juniper berries.

It feels as though an angel has passed by. The meal is accompanied by a vintage Raveneau Montée de Tonnerre Chablis (ah, the 1996!), a wonderful biodynamic, aged Côte-Rôtie or a thick Fonsalette red. And followed by a selection of the local herders' cheeses and Renée Richard's runny Saint-Marcellin. It is already seventeen years since Alain Chapel passed away, prematurely, to join chef's heaven, yet his shadow still looms protectively over the restaurant.

After lessons in the kitchens of some well-reputed friends, Alain's son, Romain, born in 1983, came home to help out. The Chapel spirit still permeates Mionnay, in the multiple tributes to the best ingredients in the world, with dishes like a delicate vegetable tart over crab rillettes, warm foie gras with turnip confit, or veal breast with pumpkin ravioli. A young and motivated staff continues the grand tradition of fine French artisanship.

The beautifully wood-paneled sitting room, a few bedrooms with charmingly rustic decor, and the dining room with wood beams, stucco walls, and polished floor tiles are all simply enchanting. As are the desserts: blackberry tart topped with caramelized chiboust cream and served with "strawberry tree" honey ice cream, aged dark rum baba and vanilla-infused fruit skewers, and a mille-feuille of chocolate meringue and crisp praline. They are simply some of the best desserts in the world.

If Alain Chapel were still with us today, the joy would remain, but without a shadow. "Images of Mionnay," he would say, adding, "happy images."

Alain Chapel

60, route de Bourg

01390 Mionnay

Tel: +33 (0)4 78 91 82 02

www.alainchapel.fr

For recipes, see pages 182–183

The monument that is the millefeuille of chocolate meringue and crisp praline, with Suzanne Chapel looking on (pages 36–37). Hen pheasant with foie gras in aspic with hot toasts (above) and the crab with vegetable marinière (facing page) are served in the museumlike dining room overlooking the fairy tale garden. Alain Chapel's shadow still hovers over this establishment, carried on by his son, Romain (facing page, bottom left).

Jacques Chibois
Portrait of a Modest, Hardworking Chef

THIS ASSIDUOUS NATIVE OF FRANCE'S LIMOUSIN REGION,
A CONVERT TO THE OLIVE OIL OF HIS ADOPTED VILLAGE NEAR CANNES,
HAS TURNED INTO AN INCONSPICUOUS GREAT CHEF OF THE GOLD COAST.

The building is stunning, a country house in the middle of an olive grove. It is like a dream, of a modest Limousin child, lost on the French Riviera. Rest assured, almost all the great chefs there come originally from somewhere else. Jacques Chibois trained under famous Auvergnat chef Roger Vergé in Mougins, and under Louis Outhier at La Napoule. He then became a chef under Michel Guérard in the Landes, before taking over the reins of the Royal Gray on the Croisette in Cannes. Chibois is truly unique.

He was never a braggart like Maximin, a megalomaniac like Ducasse, or a tough guy from Marseille like Passédat. This old sage in a young quintagenarian's body, Buddha-like in his seriousness and sense of origin, is nothing more than a calm builder. In his splendid *bastide*, or Provençal country house, which borders the olive groves of Grasse, he replanted his own trees, built a first-class Relais & Châteaux property, and established his domain.

The *Michelin Guide* considers it first and foremost a restaurant, and bestowed upon it only two stars and four red forks. There are twelve "elegant bedrooms" according to the guide; in fact they are some of the loveliest on the coast. There are red floor tiles, marble in the spacious, practical bathrooms with separate shower stalls, and private toilets. There are cozy lounges, a beautiful entrance with a shop alongside it, Provençal and stucco furniture, and impeccable service. The sommelier's recitation of his script is perfect and the receptionist smiles upon greeting guests.

It would be wrong not to mention the organization in the kitchen of this quiet cook, who can be a rigorous taskmaster: he is a man of sense and order above all. While so many others suffered the fallout of their excessive investments, he, having been a hotel employee (at the Gray d'Albion in Cannes, where he was the first to get up in the morning to go to the market in Forville), refused to open bistros and annexes (except for the Mirazur in Menton, of which half belongs to him) and paid everything off rapidly in six years.

In fact, his *bastide*, which is carefully updated as the years go by, and which hosts several movie stars during the Cannes Film Festival each year, has never been so resplendent. With carefully selected staff, an immaculately maintained garden, a cloud of olive trees, views over Grasse's countryside, a dining room made to look like a friend's home, warm and cozy sitting rooms, a terrace overlooking vast open spaces, a clever wine list, and enticing menus, it strikes the perfect chord with the modern gourmet who wants to feel loved, taken care of, and nourished, without being weighed down. In short, it's about being pampered with exemplary skill. And everything that the Limousin man offers reflects his adopted land and embodies pure sophistication.

Cook and inn-keeper, Jacques Chibois opens the doors to his magnificent bastide where he treats us to zucchini and truffles (pages 40–41). Roasted pears with caramelized honey nougatine and licorice cream (facing page).

La Bastide Saint-Antoine

48, avenue Henri-Dunant

06130 Grasse

Tel: +33 (0)4 93 70 94 94

www.jacques-chibois.com

For recipes, see pages 184–185

Some examples taken from the tasting menu, which can also be served all at once in small, delicate portions: truffle, artichoke, and purslane salad; green asparagus with beetroot leaves and mustard greens with almond petals; golden langoustine served with spiced chickpea puree and zucchini Matignon with Vitelottes potatoes; mini red mullet with paprika, small fava beans, sage, and rosemary, served with sautéed lemon fennel; the unusual but successful duo of salt cod and skate with black olives, truffles, and Jerusalem artichoke; a whole truffle with rice, ravioli, pesto, and scallops with a dry fennel and walnut-oil sauce; and the caper-roasted veal with marinated or slow-roasted eggplant.

Sheer madness? Undoubtedly, though Jacques Chibois, native of a butter-worshipping region, having become a grand specialist of olive oil, uses the latter to make all of this go down without the slightest hiccup. After this, there are still the desserts, and in this realm Michel Guérard's former pupil reveals himself to be a master, with creations such as a mandarin-quince "ball," wild strawberries and geranium juice, or a delicate minestrone of spiced fruits and vegetables with basil, mint, and iced olive candy. After such a feast, you will sleep like a baby, and then wake up refreshed the next morning to enjoy the best breakfast on the coast, with out-of-this-world jams, heavenly breads, and mouthwatering pastries.

In spite of it all, Chibois stays modest. Here's a question for the *Michelin Guide*: When will this modest chef receive his third, well-deserved star?

The Glory of
Le Cinq

In a grandiose setting,
Éric Briffard restores a touch of genius to Le Cinq.

The neo-Louis room, a bit hoity-toity with its large rectangular or round tables, isn't necessarily meant to please everyone. But there is something chic about the place. Under the direction of Éric Baumard, ranked second-best sommelier in the world, and of Patrice Jeanne, who used to be at the Régence at the Plaza Athénée, the service is classy and cheerful.

The novelty in what is undoubtedly the best, most elegant, and, in spite of its pomp, one of the most discreet hotels in Paris, is the presence of Éric Briffard. This genie from Auxerre, modest and straight-shooting, trained by Robuchon, was the last cook at the Plaza before Ducasse. He is one of those chefs who researches and experiments endlessly, and is probably one of the most brilliant at that.

He dazzled us not long ago, at the Elysées du Vernet, with dishes that were occasionally so overloaded they felt as rich and heavy as someone else's entire meal. There is something of a more bourgeois Gagnaire in his manner, but this worthy heir to the great Joël Robuchon is primarily a technician who prizes pristine, high-quality ingredients above all else.

He has polished his style, refined his combinations, and eliminated any unnecessary risks. The resulting brilliance is seen in his lavish version of deep sea abalone from Brittany in chicken broth with squash, seaweed butter, and watercress meunière sauce, or in his fabulous truffle galette, much like his other delicate truffle and sweet onion mousse tart, or in lemongrass-scented John Dory cooked on the bone with green melon, accompanied by glazed cuttlefish and black rice with sea cucumber (which the Catalans call *espardeñes*).

A specialist of rare ingredients, Briffard also revisits and embellishes classic dishes such as the "Rennes Coucou" hen, roasted with crayfish in a jellied mousse, according to an old southern tradition, and served with watercress and aged Comté macaroni and a lemongrass broth. Astounding!

Desserts redefine tradition with the same brilliant and fresh style. Hence the fabulous iced coffee Viennetta with Piedmont hazelnut nougatine. The wine list, meanwhile, is one of the capital's finest, under the direction of the other Éric (Baumard). It is notably filled with the finest *terroirs* and some top-notch—though not unreasonably priced—unknowns.

Even if you have already been, the restaurant merits rediscovering. The "small" lunch menu entitled "Freedom" extends a tempting invitation. It's time to crown the genius, Briffard.

Le Cinq

31, avenue George V

75008 Paris

Tel: +33 (0)1 49 52 71 54

www.fourseasons.com

For recipes, see pages 186–187

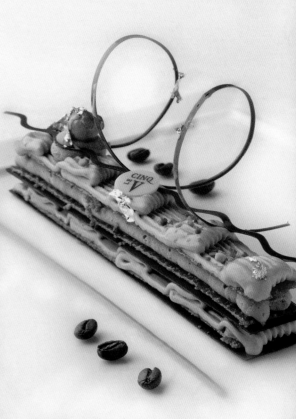

The dining room is majestic and the table setting suggests a historical performance (page 44).
Lemongrass-scented John Dory cooked on the bone with green melon (page 45).
Éric Briffard in action (top). He captivates us with his fabulous iced coffee Viennetta with Piedmont hazelnut Nougatine (far right) and his sumptuous variation on deep sea abalones (facing page, top right).

The Delight of
Les Crayères

A MAJESTIC DWELLING IS FOUND IN REIMS, WITH TOP-NOTCH SERVICE AND A CHEF
WHO IS BOTH A FEARLESS INNOVATOR AND A DISCREET REINVENTOR.

Reims, capital of Champagne, and the city of kings and coronations, is worthy of a regal dining experience. Les Crayères, with its aristocratic past, its gastronomical glory, woodwork, high ceilings, theatrical staircase, and grounds enlivened by beautiful trees, is that place. It first belonged to Louise Pommery (of the Champagne family) in 1885, who passed it on to her daughter and son-in-law, the Marquis of Polignac, and finally to her grandson Melchior, a member of the international Olympic committee and a well-known Parisian man-about-town between the two world wars.

In 1940, it was taken over by the Germans, who built a blockhouse on the grounds. It then housed the headquarters of the Royal Air Force (and the vineyards were bombed), and later of the US Army, who turned it into a rest and recreation center, transforming the terrace into a dance floor. After this checkered history, it reverted to the Pommerys after the war. It was inhabited by Prince Guy de Polignac, chairman of Pommery, Bailiff of the Order of Malta, and his mother, Princess Henri, until 1980. It was then purchased by the Gardinier family that same year, who renovated it with interior decorator Pierre-Yves Rochon, transforming it into a luxury hotel and restaurant managed by Gérard and Éliane Boyer. The restaurant became famous when it received three Michelin stars in 1983. A native of Égliseneuve d'Entraygues in Auvergne, Gérard Boyer, who was trained by one of the great chefs of yore, became the star of his

adopted region at La Chaumière where, until 2003, he produced classical fare, impressing high society with traditional offerings. His utterly charming way was half rustic and half refined, as demonstrated in dishes like porcini cream soup; the emblematic pig's trotter stuffed with foie gras and served with pink lentils; sea bass with fatty bacon and a potato emulsion with milk; or hen cooked in champagne.

After two years under the direction of Boyer's sous-chef, Thierry Voisin, the Gardiniers (who had purchased and improved Château Phélan Ségur in Saint-Estèphe in the meantime), returned to manage the property. Taking the advice of Alain Ducasse, they hired the ebullient Didier Elena. Born in 1971, this Monaco native had intended to go into medicine when he just happened to meet the maestro of the Louis XV at the hairdresser's. Ducasse sent him to work for Bocuse for two years, and to Michel Guérard for one week, before sending him to New York, where he opened the Essex House. Elena worked there for five years before going to Ducasse's Beige in Tokyo.

Didier took happily to the *terroir* of Champagne, turning out light and intense cuisine. Each dish worked well with the fine bubbles of the golden wine. Some dishes shocked, as when the region's traditional pork and cabbage hotpot—served as an accompaniment to sole with white sausage—was transformed, compressed, and given a rectangular shape. In the end,

Didier decided to return to the Côte d'Azur, to be closer to his roots. He left in 2009 and went to the Chèvre d'Or in the village of Eze.

To succeed him, a whiz kid of modern cuisine was needed. The Gardiniers and their manager Éric Fort found a diamond in the rough in the shape of Philippe Mille. This thirty-five-year-old from La Sarthe trained as a pastry chef with Gauthier in Gange, close to Le Mans, then at big Parisian houses (Ritz, Ledoyen, Lasserre, Le Pré Catelan, Drouant), and was Yannick Alléno's zealous and discreet right arm at Le Meurice for seven years, during which, together, they won the bronze at the prestigious Bocuse d'Or competition. He has the same seriousness and sense of grand bourgeois classicism that is generally attributed to the great Yannick. He fit into his new surroundings right away. Amid Les Crayères' gold, woodwork, and paneling, beneath the beautiful canvases by turn-of-the-twentieth-century minor masters, across from the grounds sparkling in the fall light, he managed to recreate a lighter, seemingly simpler style of cuisine following the "great French culinary tradition" and, moreover, perfectly suited to the spirit of the times.

So menus by Mille are entitled "Winter Notes," "Truffle Dance," "Of Love and Champagne," and are methodical in their execution and reliably full of distinct flavors. The grilled duck foie gras, still soft after being cooked with truffled white cabbage confit with juniper berries and potato cubes, has become one of his signature dishes; like the sole fillet cooked in meunière sauce and served with a potato and clam juice risotto and fabulous creamy leeks; or the zebra-striped Bresse chicken fillet and Rustici pasta with truffle juice. The marriage between rusticity and refinement, the "rabble chic" style, the grand bourgeois aspect first introduced here by Gérard Boyer when he baptized the kitchen—these all prevail, albeit with innovation and increased lightness.

There are also leeks braised with salted butter, served with walnut water zabaglione (sabayon), delicate artichoke and truffle ravioli with shards of foie gras and chopped hazelnuts, or a whole truffle in a sweet onion and beef-marrow ravioli consommé. These many masterpieces of precise flavor indicate that when the Gardiniers picked Philippe Mille for Les Crayères, they secured one of the greats. On top of this, the champagnes picked by eloquent, expert sommelier Philippe Jamesse are a marvel. The white from Sélosse in Avize (Heidsieck 2001) or the voluptuous red Ambonnay d'Egly-Ouriet, are just a few among a myriad of other rarities that seem to fill the wine list. The service is among the best in France. Bedrooms are charming as ever, with fine fabrics and antique furniture, and views over the extensive grounds and the St.-Rémi basilica in the distance. And, lest we forget, desserts offer a true moment of delight, still courtesy of Mille, the expert who was trained in pastry in his youth. The dessert called "Les Crayères" that combines Reims pink ladyfinger biscuits, grapefruit sorbet, and citrus gelled champagne, and the superb "iced caramel and passion fruit" with a crunchy bar of apple shards with fleur de sel, are to die for. Now that Reims is a mere forty minutes from Paris on the high-speed TGV train, and has regained a great menu, all the more reason for the entire world to feast there in elegant, refined, and discreet fashion. With the brand-new Philippe Mille, a star chef is born.

Les Crayères

64, boulevard Henry-Vasnier

51100 Reims

Tel: +33 (0)3 26 24 90 00

www.lescrayeres.com

For recipes, see pages 187–188

It is now Philippe Mille's turn to reign over the kitchens of the princely Crayères castle, with its high stucco and lambris ceilings, where the dessert of "Les Crayères" pink Reims lady fingers with grapefruit sorbet and sparkling gelled champagne is an elegant nod to the region of Champagne (pages 48–49). The kitchen is up to the task with zebra-striped Bresse chicken fillet with Rustici pasta and truffles jus (facing page).

A New Chapter at
the Crocodile

It is the mythical dining room in the heart of Strasbourg, taken to the heights by Émile Jung and constantly evolving ever since.

The restaurant, right by Place Kléber in the center of Strasbourg, has been there since the nineteenth century. It owes its name to the famous stuffed crocodile in the entry hall that was brought back from the Nile by Napoleon's officer and aide-de-camp to General Kléber, Captain Ackermann, after the Egyptian campaign. Mister Benz opened the place to the public in 1876, Louis Schmitt transformed it into a bar in 1894, and Georges Riedinger turned it into a reputable brasserie. Different owners followed, one after another: the widow Schmitt, A. Littel, André Reymond, Pierre Denu, Ernest Schenck, and the Hollaender brothers. The kitchen turned out good-quality brasserie dishes, such as the Holstein veal escalope. In 1960, it received one Michelin star, which it has held onto ever since.

The kitchen became renowned under the guidance of Émile Jung. From Masevaux in Alsace, he took over in 1971. He had been trained at the now defunct luxury hotel La Maison Rouge, then by Roucou at La Mère Guy in Lyon, and finally at Lasserre, La Marée, and Fouquet's in Paris. These experiences allowed him to blend the foundations of classical cuisine with the *terroir* of his region, giving him an added level of mastery. The good student became the teacher; between the moment when he obtained his first Michelin star in 1966 at the Hostellerie Alsacienne in Masevaux, and when he sold the Crocodile and retired inconspicuously in 2009, he inspired pupils throughout the world with a reverential devotion for his teachings.

His recipes instructed and his signature dishes were used as reference. Every year, with his wife Monique, who managed the front of the house like a ballet, he organized a celebration, the secret of which only he knew, which was dedicated either to Europe, the TGV (France's high-speed train), Jules Verne, Victor Hugo, or the Goncourt. They were stylish performances, with dishes related to the theme, and original decor. The "Croco" became a place of culture, literature, and art, as much as gastronomy.

Poet, peasant, and cook, Émile was also an inventor. Brillat-Savarin quail; pike perch braised with "Father Woelffle" sauerkraut; watercress flan with frogs' legs; "Princess" hop shoots served with a Hollandaise sauce; or pig's trotter stuffed with foie gras, re-formed, then garnished with truffles and topped with butter-braised cabbage; such were the hits of this seemingly grand bourgeois but classically minded cook, regaling countrymen who came for a night out on the town.

The "Croco's" decor resembled him, and Monique, too, his muse and guardian of the temple. The interior was plush and friendly, with its nooks, symbolic crocodile, and the great country fresco that decorated the back of the large dining room, comfortable chairs, and lovely table settings. Monique Jung was a steadfast mistress of ceremonies. The wine recommendations by the tenacious and competent Gilbert Mestrallet were a bonus.

Taken over by brilliant young chef Philippe Bohrer, who worked for Loiseau, Gaertner, and Lameloise at the Élysée, and

The dining room, with its grand countryside fresco is a show in itself and the perfect place to serve the Black Forest cake, revisited (pages 52–53).
Philippe Bohrer and his team pose beneath the stuffed crocodile brought back from Egypt by Napoleonic officer, Captain Ackermann. Classics like watercress flan with frogs' legs (facing page, top right) are always available and head sommelier Gilbert Mestrallet is here to choose the Alsatian Grands Crus (bottom right).
It's a grand moment when the sauces are served tableside.

Au Crocodile

10, rue de l'Outre

67000 Strasbourg

Tel: +33 (0)3 88 32 13 02

www.au-crocodile.com

For recipes, see pages 188–189

who helmed a dozen other places all over Alsace, from Colmar to Mulhouse by way of Rouffach, the Crocodile entered a new era complete with a spartan, modern decor, albeit with the stuffed crocodile and country frescoes remaining. Even if it is no longer Jung's version, the Crocodile is still there and is still a high-quality restaurant.

Émile and Monique are no longer there to compose the menu or welcome guests into what used to be "their" house, but Gilbert Mestrallet, who was with them for nearly forty years, went from being head sommelier to manager. He was named best French sommelier/maître d', and is still at the top of his profession. It is not surprising that he remains as guardian of the temple.

In the kitchen, Philippe Bohrer supervises with talent and rigor, while the young Ludovic Kientz creates modern cuisine that takes tradition into account. He rethinks local, regional, and grand bourgeois tradition—that is, grand old French cuisine—brilliantly. Watercress flan with frogs' legs, goose foie gras and bread with a "VT" gewürztraminer reduction, pan-fried duck liver poached in pinot noir, or Viennese-style cod with Alsatian mustard are hot, hip dishes that lack neither strength nor character.

Among the memorable yet still current dishes is a truffled pig's trotter wrapped "in crépinette," with heart of Savoy cabbage and potatoes, a light and delicate dish beneath its rustic appearance. In short, it's Jung without Jung. In the same way Karl Lagerfeld makes Chanel without Chanel, Philippe Bohrer and Ludovic Lientz maintain the establishment's ways almost as if nothing had changed, even if some of the magic vanished with Émile and Monique's departure.

Desserts, regional and imaginative, are a part of the well executed menu. The derivations on a theme of the "meeting" between rhubarb and Sarawak pepper, or the Black Forest cake, revisited, in which each element, like sour cherry or chocolate, is scientifically rethought on a theme of pastry and ice cream.

In terms of the cellar, with the punctilious Gilbert in the role of expert adviser, who can find otherwise unknown bottles such as fine white vintages (a grand cru Riesling from Schmitt in Bergbieten or a Roland Gassmann muscat), smooth pinot gris (from Paul Buecher), or first-class burgundy (from Denis Mortet), the house is still top-notch.

The new Crocodile is evolving and looking up. The demanding gourmet can now head to this great Strasbourg institution again as it turns a new page in its history book.

D is for
Ducasse

ALAIN DUCASSE'S PARISIAN ESTABLISHMENT IS THE CONTEMPORARY ARCHETYPE OF THE GRAND FRENCH RESTAURANT.

Everything has been said of Alain Ducasse. That he owned twenty-seven restaurants around the world, was the recipient of nineteen Michelin stars, was present in Tokyo (Beige) or Osaka (Benoit), London (The Dorchester) or New York (Adour), Las Vegas (Mix) or Hong Kong (Spoon at the Intercontinental), as well as in Tuscany (L'Andana), the Basque country (Ostapé), Monaco (Hôtel de Paris), and of course, Paris.

A globetrotter, jet-setter, man in a hurry, multifaceted chef full of ideas; there is all of that in this native of Orthez, who was born in 1956, raised on a farm in Castelsarrasin in the Landes, and is tied to his roots yet keen to share his passions. In Paris, he is everywhere, whether it's as a modernist at Spoon, bistro-owner at Benoit, at Aux Lyonnais, or at Rech, or all-encompassing restaurateur at Le Jules Verne, the Eiffel Tower brasserie. One might forget that he was also a publisher (he has published many works by his colleagues, including Paul Bocuse and Joël Robuchon), a teacher (of chefs as well as civilians), and of course the head of a chain (Châteaux & Hôtels Collection).

When one considers all of this, it is surprising that he still manages to constantly refine his empire, and without forgetting the icing on the cake: his presence at the Plaza Athénée. He consults for the brasserie (Le Relais Plaza), transforming the patio into an organic vegetable garden (La Cour Jardin), and keeping an eye on the gallery's snacks and pastries as well as on the bar's club sandwiches. The crowning glory of this whole operation is simply called "Alain Ducasse at the Plaza Athénée," located in the building's old Regency room, which was updated by designer Patrick Jouin to a style reflecting both its history and current trends.

There are the neo-Louis XV chairs turned into contemporary armchairs in beige tones, the muted gray background, and the light cast by the modern candelabra hanging from the ceiling like a celestial shower over the diners. The service, helmed by absolute specialist Denis Courtiade, who anticipates all wishes and has a solution for everything, is beyond perfection. Ducasse's cuisine proves, according to the adage cited so often by the master himself, that it is "better to have the turbot without the genius than the genius without the turbot."

Alain Chapel, who worked at the Pavillon Landais in Soustons (in the Landes), but also Michel Guérard, Gaston Lenôtre, and Roger Vergé, who are all an inspiration to Ducasse, all prized good ingredients above all else. Readily grand-bourgeois and always utterly respectful of the high tradition of French haute cuisine, from Marie-Antoine Carême to Auguste Escoffier, his manner is classical and his presentation gorgeously modern. Thus, creamed, truffled, semi-dried pasta with veal sweetbreads, cockscombs, and cocks' kidneys; Brittany lobster with spiced curry; hot-cold soft-shell crab; or Robert Blanc's magnificent green asparagus from the Luberon, served cooked and raw with a mimosa condiment and truffled vinaigrette.

This kind of cuisine, which comes from the *terroir* but also from tried and trusted know-how gleaned in a French kitchen, soon becomes an object lesson. Take the following dishes: pâté in a crust of chicken liver and foie gras, as was done by Lucien Tendret; the famed langoustines refreshed with osetra caviar with a reduction and a fragrant broth; sole with seashell marinière and a herbed sauce; and thick Brittany turbot with chowder, cultivated mushrooms, and a reduction of spiced red wine.

In the same vein of the classic dish rejuvenated, Bresse chicken with crayfish and an Albufera sauce (béchamel sauce with sweet peppers), cream, and foie gras, like the veal sweetbreads with green peas and truffled juice, are excellent staples of which one never tires. Ducasse, while reverent toward his predecessors, and concerned with not spoiling quality ingredients, is definitely very much in the present. Through his seasoned team, under the leadership of Christophe Saintagne—who at short notice replaced Christophe Morel, who has gone to Lasserre's, a sign that, at Ducasse's, chefs may go but the style remains—he sources the best of everything.

Amongst the virtuosos on Ducasse's team, pastry chef Christophe Michalak deserves a special mention. This pastry world champion is a master in creating rum babas; raw goat milk with caramel, pepper, and "strawberry tree" honey; variations on the Burlat cherry with pistachio ice cream; thin leaves of crispy yet melting chocolate; and an unforgettable contemporary meringue vacherin with mango, passionfruit, lemon, and vanilla, updating a classic, ceremonial dessert with finesse, freshness, and lightness.

After all of this, there is still the exceptional wine list put together by expert Gérard Margeon and suggested with precision by the clever Laurent Roucayrol. A grand restaurant, this "Alain Ducasse au Plaza Athénée" is like a kind of Franco-French translation of the "Riviera," very Franco-transalpine, Monegasque Louis XV. It is the modern archetype of the great French restaurant set in a Parisian luxury hotel.

Alain Ducasse au Plaza Athénée

25, avenue Montaigne

75008 Paris

Tel: +33 (0)1 53 67 66 65

www.alain-ducasse.com

For recipes, see pages 189–191

When he puts on his white apron or tastes the dishes to be sent out to the dining room of the Plaza Athénée, the multistarred Alain Ducasse becomes quite the seducer. Desserts like the "Hazelnut 2010" (page 57) are looked after by pastry chef Christophe Michalak. New dishes by Christophe Saintagne, like fruit and vegetables (below), or turbot, shellfish, and Swiss chard (facing page) carry the mark of the master. Led by Denis Courtiade, the dining room's better-than-perfect service is a joy to watch.

Pierre Gagnaire
Scientific Kitchen Maestro

HE IS A GENIUS OF FLAVORS WHO MAKES JADED GOURMETS PURR WITH PLEASURE.
IN A BEAUTIFUL BLUE SETTING, ADORNED WITH CONTEMPORARY PAINTINGS,
HE DEMONSTRATES THAT THERE IS ALWAYS MORE TO INVENT, TO CREATE, AND TO AMAZE.

How many Pierre Gagnaires are there? There is the jazz nut who builds syncopated menus; the one who practices wild rhythms with his pal Daniel Humair; the one who teams up with physicist-chemist Hervé This to construct a scientific menu that develops content and sensations; the contemporary art lover who has works by both Richard Serra and Simon de Voos at home; and finally the culinary Mondrian, delivering pure and aesthetic beauty from kitchen to plate.

All these Gagnaires are part and parcel of the same man, of course. There was, long ago, the man whose gamble to create an art-deco masterpiece in his hometown failed, and who was left alone to lick his wounds, surrounded by all the remnants, the beautiful, the good, the luxurious, and the sacrificed. There was the pots-and-pans adventurer who saw the cohort of supporters regroup around him when he was at the Balzac hotel in the heart of the Champs-Élysées in Paris. There was also the member of the "gang," for a while composed of the eight free electrons: Marc Veyrat, Alain Passard, Olivier Roellinger, Jean-Michel Lorain, Michel Troisgros, Jacques Chibois, and Michel Bras, fighting for the freedom to create in peace, to have a clean style, and to use spices as they wished.

But Gagnaire cannot be reduced to a formula, nor to a single adventure. He drifts as if in a Miles Davis solo, like "Solea", "Sketches of Spain", "It Never Entered My Mind", or as if in an obsessive, endlessly repeated phrase like a long, monotonous John Coltrane piece, "Body and Soul", "My Favorite Things", or "The Night Has a Thousand Eyes." Nothing is easy or transparent with Gagnaire. This manipulator of matter constantly searches for purity but also contrast, playing with hot and cold, soft and crispy, sweet and bitter. In a stroke of genius, he combines gnocchi and aged Cantal cheese; mango marmalade with herb juice and pine nuts; frothy milk and caramel.

Everything Gagnaire touches turns to gold. Was there a teacher? He was no one's pupil. He is aunt Alice's ex-commis chef, who stirred the salad bowls in Lyon; he was the cook's son, who, one summer in 1965, set off to Collonges to discover Bocuse's formidable energy, stronger than dynamite; he saw it all, retained it all, unlearned it all and retaught it to himself in his own way. This artist is a solitary soul. If he really belonged to a region, he would be an exile of the Rhône-Alpes. Or like Ferran Adrià at El Bulli in Catalonia, Dalí country, he would be the creator who managed to free himself of his roots.

The ingredients he loves are clear about their names and origins. They are Gauthier pigeon, crayfish from Lake Geneva, or blue fish from Lamparo, named after the traditional fishing boat of the Catalan coast. There's no point in kidding oneself,

though, this cuisine is complex: it shocks and disturbs the palate before seducing it. What can be said about the large langoustines generously brushed with walnut butter, braised and accompanied by foie gras? About the squid stuffed with hazelnut and lemon and topped with an emulsified artisanal cider juice? Or about the turbot fillet pan-fried on the bone accompanied by leek fondue? Or, finally, about the variations on lamb, with the shoulder breadcrumbed and fried, the cilantro rice, and the rack to which the chervil pesto gives an Italian slant? Gagnaire, our Pierre Soulages, our Nicolas de Staël, our Yves Klein, our Piet Mondrian, is first and foremost an eccentric creator.

His style is a benchmark. In their lyrical abstraction, his dishes can either be viewed as streamlined or baroque. His "*amuse-gueules*" tasters, like the most incredible tapas in the world, can constitute entire meals in and of themselves. His dessert symphonies prove that he leaves nothing to chance, to those who may doubt it; the souffléed chocolate biscuit with soft ganache and muscovado peanuts or the large plate of seasonal fruit are of high caliber; the walls, first lacquered then painted blue, have beautiful lines drawn by Michelle Halard; the young staff provide stylish service with humor; the cellar, though small, is daring in its selection; all of this is in sync. There is nothing surprising, then, in the fact that the restaurant is always full. Expert tasters, beginning with his colleagues from around the world, line up with notepads in hand to admire the feats of this craziest of contemporary chefs.

A genius of flavors? Indeed he is, enthralling gourmets the world over, by exciting their taste buds (something they thought was no longer possible) and amazing them with his creations and inventions. The pressed blue lobster with fresh seaweed and rice vinegar, the ideas brought back from Catalonia, mini squid, pesto, small mackerel, truffled salt cod galette, white tuna belly with Bellota ham, mackerel juice with churizeros pepper, leg of lamb macerated in goat's milk then roasted with silver thyme, with "beefsteak" cabbage and almond cream, are all dishes out of this world.

They will most likely be forgotten tomorrow, as he switches his attention to the red-legged crayfish in Champagne, served with Rennes Coucou Pascaline (poultry from Brittany), with a blend of green apples, fresh cilantro, and grated coconut; oysters with seaweed and Tarbais beans, or "Jodhpur" sea bass cooked *en papillote*, with Nora pepper paste and praline cream. This master of technical prowess, a bit like an acrobat of the genre, is constantly competing with his pal Alain Passard in the realm of virtuosos, but he deserves his own category in the guides. He is the mad inventor of our new emotions, the Einstein of our pleasures, and nothing escapes him.

As is too often forgotten, his ultimate area of strength is sweet, in which he explores new paths. His desserts are masterful compositions: jellied soft caramel with a touch of gingerbread and unctuous ice cream, mint tea, saffron dried fruit loukoum (memories of his recent journeys in the desert), Plougastel strawberries and crisp Andalusian wild strawberries, a red pepper galette with spicy artichoke and prunes in peppered liqueur, rum baba with fresh fruit, and variations on chocolate. All of this leaves one breathless with amazement. There is only one Pierre Gagnaire.

Pierre Gagnaire

6, rue Balzac

75008 Paris

Tel: +33 (0)1 58 36 12 50

www.pierre-gagnaire.com

For recipes, see pages 191–192

The intense gaze of Pierre Gagnaire, next to his Prat-Ar-Coum oysters from Brittany and simple scallops, grated pink radishes with horseradish, watercress disk, and smoked parsley water (pages 60–61).
And the chef again, on the facing page, in one of his favorite moments of concentration in the kitchen.
In the beautiful lacquered room, one is served rolled chocolate ginger cake and red beet confit with orange (above) or poached fattened hen in a pouch (facing page, top left).

Guérard
A Poet in the Countryside

THIS IS THE STORY OF HOW A GIFTED YOUNG PASTRY CHEF FROM THE ÎLE-DE-FRANCE AREA BECAME THE GASTRONOMICAL KING OF THE LANDES REGION.

A cook, also a charmer and a poet, he made the concept *"minceur active"* or "active lean cuisine" his banner, the Landes his territory, and, with his wife Christine, the concept of aesthetic hospitality his niche. In reality, though he may be multifaceted and have many tricks up his sleeve, there is only one Michel Guérard: the young boy from Vétheuil, long ago an apprentice pastry chef at Mantes-la-Jolie, artisan pastry chef and Meilleur Ouvrier de France (Best Craftsman in France) while at Paris's Crillon hotel, and a magnet for Paris's entire gourmet population while at Le Pot au Feu in the suburb of Asnières.

Before giving up on the follies of the capital, he was Régine's culinary consultant (during the time of Régin'skaya) thanks to Christine, daughter of thermal spa chain hotel magnate, Adrien Barthélemy. The clever Guérard, in whom Christine, a smart businesswoman and alumna of the HEC management school, saw much seductive potential, thereafter became the keenest "poet of the fields." Once in the Landes, he intelligently and passionately created the first "lean" village in the world, in the city of Eugénie-les-Bains, named for the wife of Napoleon III, Empress Eugénie.

There is La Maison Rose, the friendly guest house; La Ferme aux Grives, an ideal inn with its four heavenly, bucolic bedrooms; Le Couvent des Herbes, a luxury annex of the beautiful spa hotel Prés d'Eugénie; and La Ferme Thermale, a large, regional spa complex, later copied by the Marquèze eco-museum, dedicated to physical and mental health and to beauty. All together, they make up the Guérard empire, ruled over by the clever Michel and his good fairy Christine.

The first task they faced was to make those who were tired of eating all year round hungry again. "Lean cuisine" menus offer fish rillettes with horseradish sauce, oxtail salad, braised brill with shellfish in tomato sauce, rice and vegetable curry, veal blanquette with basil, banana, and piña colada jelly, and apple pudding. They make for peaceful evenings, and you then find yourself well rested and ready to have the best breakfast in the world, with cheese, brioche, ham, homemade yogurt, and freshly squeezed juices.

You can then choose between La Ferme aux Grives, with its oversize fireplace, in which pigs and ducks are roasted, and where a more roguish kind of cuisine is offered, or the "grand restaurant," where the boss Guérard's wise, disciplined pupil, Catalan Xavier Franquet Del Rey, along with his army of assistants, creates dishes like poached oyster with pancetta pastry, wild mushrooms and morels with asparagus tips, langoustines roasted with lemon blossom, grilled duck liver with muscat-soaked breadcrumbs, pastry stuffed with duckling and quail, vanilla mille-feuille, or iced berry gazpacho.

Is it cooking? It is, and it's pure poetry too. In fact, the menus have names like "Playing Hooky from School," "Gardens of the Sea," or "County Fair Day," as if he were a kind of

Page 65: Gillardeau
oysters with green
coffee.
*In his kitchen, Michel
Guérard checks the
quality of the pikes that
have just been delivered.
Amid the Napoleon III
setting, on superbly set
tables, he offers dishes
with poetic names,
like moonfishermen's
drunken lobster (facing
page, top right) or wild
mushrooms and morels
with asparagus tips
(bottom left).*

Les Prés d'Eugénie

40320 Eugénie-les-Bains

Tel: +33 (0)5 58 05 06 07

www.michelguerard.com

For recipes, see pages 192–193

Mr. Hulot of modern cuisine, directing our enjoyment in the manner of Jacques Tati. Guérard has an ingrained sense of simplicity, a freshness that stays intact, a vivaciousness on the tip of his brain. Everything he feeds you speaks to the heart and the mind as much as to the palate. His menu is divided between "Mythical Dishes" and "Cooking for Rustic Palates." On the one hand there are Gillardeau oysters with green coffee whipped cream, moon-fishermen's drunken lobster in a spring carpaccio, whiting in a vegetable papillote, "spiked" with a splash of orange Vermouth, or even sweet-and-sour grilled duck foie gras with sour cherry browned onions. These are all incredible dishes that enthrall the imagination as well as the palate.

On the other hand, there are the dishes of the moment that are often a return to the past: fresh Ouastous farm eggs scrambled with bacon and truffle, foie gras cooked in a Dutch oven buried in ash, "sublime" potatoes (which are named as such, and truly are) with truffle puree, Atlantic sea bass steamed with seaweed, and beef rib eye with potatoes and pancetta. Guérard's whole personality is there; the poet and peasant from Vétheuil, yet won over by the Landes and Chalosse. He is the charmer who distills the classic and the timeless.

But with him, the best is always yet to come. We mustn't forget what his first job was, and so, make sure to save room for the best desserts in the world. For example, the famous soft Marquis de Béchamel cake with melted rhubarb ice cream, a sensual compromise between a soufflé and crème caramel dessert, or the "Candide," a puff pastry tart with Eugénie strawberries and an unctuous (how could it not be?) whipped cream with grated lemon. There is also the "all chocolate" dessert with a soufflé cake, bitter ice cream and "pot de crème," and of course, the famous crêpes suzette, an homage to the original recipe created long ago at the Ritz for the Prince of Wales before he was Edward VII, named for his French friend; here it is served crispy with mandarin orange "snow."

By now, it should be clear that everything is enchanting at Guérard's, from sweet to savory, from the dining room to the lounges, so beautifully redone with their sanded furniture, their appropriately well-worn floor tiles, their gorgeous nineteenth- and early twentieth-century paintings which Christine so ingeniously collected. Their beautiful property, with large fields and wooded surroundings, resembling the set of a French remake of *Gone with the Wind*, is a stunning natural setting. And of all the gastronomical wizards of the twentieth century, Michel, expert innovator and organizational mastermind (he is the originator of serving dishes with bell-like covers) great chef that he is, is the one who will last with the greatest acuity.

With its large country-style kitchen open onto the dining room, the Ferme aux Grives is close to the gastronomic restaurant. Here while a whole pig roasts in the fireplace, Michel Guérard receives a delivery of cabbage freshly picked from the vegetable garden.

L'Auberge de l'Ill
A Fairy-Tale Setting

L'AUBERGE DE L'ILL IS A UNIQUE PLACE, A PASTORAL ENVIRONMENT ON THE WATER'S EDGE, WITH A NATURAL GENTLENESS AND TIMELESSNESS. THERE IS EVERYTHING HERE. AND ALSACE TOO....

To evoke L'Auberge de l'Ill is to evoke Alsace first, that wonderland in the heart of Europe. In 1881, it was known as L'Arbre Vert, "The Green Tree," and was the home of grandmother Frédérique and grandfather Fritz. Back then, the women were the cooks. Alsatian artist Jean-Jacques Waltz, better known as Hansi, went there to feast and once signed the paper tablecloth: "Long live France and the Illhaeusern matelote stew!"

The building was rebuilt after the war, looking elegant by the water's edge. The French army had destroyed the bridge in 1940 to prevent German invasion. The inn remained surrounded by beautiful trees. The Haeberlin's house became the Auberge de l'Ill. Paul, the cook, and Jean-Pierre, the artist, had set up shop there. The former had been trained at La Pépinière in Ribeauvillé by Edouard Weber, who had been the cook for the tsar, at the Greek court, and for the Rothschild family. Jean-Pierre had gone to the School of Fine Arts in Strasbourg.

Together, they built an innovative place. Paul, with culinary creativity, made Souvarov truffle, which inspired Paul Bocuse for his truffle soup V.G.E. (created for president Valéry Giscard d'Estaing), souffléed salmon, mousseline of frogs' legs, and Prince Vladimir lobster. Jean-Pierre was in charge of the gorgeous furniture, paintings, woodwork, and various pieces of porcelain that would adorn the most beautiful inn in the world. After all, that is what the Auberge de l'Ill became.

These days, it is in the same location, right on the water, with rows of willows, tables in the garden for drinks, and, on the eve of the twenty-first century, dining rooms redone in a modern fashion by decorator Patrick Jouin. In between then and now, the house has shed its skin several times, won the competition for Michelin stars (the first in 1953, the second in 1957, and the third in 1967) and the town, of which Jean-Pierre was the mayor, became a sister city of Collonges-au-Mont-d'Or to strengthen the ties with his friend, Bocuse.

The staff is loyal, friendly, and civilized. Michel Scheer, the manager for the last four decades, Serge Dubs, the world's best sommelier in 1989, and the rest of the team are like a big family. Marc Haeberlin, prodigal son, has been leading the brigade for the past twenty years, after training with Bocuse, Lasserre, Lenôtre, Troisgros, and at the Erprinz Hotel in Ettlingen, where Mr. Wanka played the same role toward him that Georges Weber did for his father—that of inspiring teacher.

While paying tribute to his father's specialties, even stating on the menu: "Dishes created by Paul Haeberlin that made the Auberge de l'Ill renowned," Marc also innovates and puts his own stamp on the food. Lobster is paired with veal head and pearled barley, tripe salad is made with goose liver and fava beans, and Nantua cream of crayfish soup is served like dim sum, with dumpling, soup, and shellfish. There are nods to tradition, but also to the *terroir* of Alsace, as if the pendulum swing

of the Auberge de l'Ill always stayed between the Rhine, the Ill river, and "the blue line of the Vosges."

European crowds, primarily local, all come to hold feasts in this establishment that is theirs in some way; the region of Colmar is a mere ten miles away, Switzerland close by, and Germans, as well as Belgians and Luxembourgers are neighbors. The Haeberlins' instinctive kindness and the modesty of this warm Lutheran tribe make for a very unique atmosphere here, and the cuisine they offer, full of memories and loyalty, is filled with emotion.

There is the famous foie-gras terrine with a splash of perfectly measured cognac, port, and sauternes, and a blend of spices that remains a secret. There is pike perch with frog tempura and pearled barley risotto with sorrel juice; deer nuggets with "bubbespitzle"—"everything in a pig is good"—where the piglet served as ribs, bacon, sausage or fillet, is lacquered in the Chinese manner; and lamb tenderloin dressed in green with sautéed potatoes, flavored with thyme and black olives, as is done in the Munster Valley. Everything here is measured and carefully distributed so that nothing feels heavy.

Desserts pay tribute to local traditions: grandmother's iced vacherin that manages a lovely balance between cream and ice cream, crunchy "Ill" barquette with caramelized cream puffs, and "Gaby Cherry" crêpes stuffed with sour cherries, flambéed and served with Tahitian vanilla ice cream, a nod to Gabriel Massenez, known for his liqueurs in the Villé Valley and a pal and associate of the house.

With all of these dishes, Serge Dubs proposes dry or sweet Alsatian wines from the famous grapes, suggestive of gold, but also grands crus of Burgundy, Bordeaux, or the Rhône Valley. One should have a glass of Metté's kirsch or Windholtz's marc in the lounge at the entrance, while looking at the paintings, which are worthy of an art collection, the old porcelain stove, and photos and memorabilia that recall the celebrities, singers, royalty, soccer players (Paul's great passion), presidents, gourmets, and chefs who have been through here.

This unique inn has an extension in the form of a magnificent hotel annex, located at the end of the garden. It is made to look like local tobacco drying sheds or fishermen's cabins, and houses beautiful wood-paneled rooms and suites. Antique and modern furniture are grouped together, playing traditional and contemporary decor off against each other. Marco Baumann, who is Danielle's husband and Marc's brother-in-law, and an ex-maitre d', runs the place with humor, good cheer, and an easy-going attitude.

Marc's daughter, Laetitia, flutters from the kitchen to the dining room. It looks as if the future is in good hands in this establishment where joy has always been the primary goal. Everyone is treated like a king here. Danielle and her uncle Jean-Pierre have a kind word for everyone, and many of the regulars leave with a signed menu, a book, or a tie with the inn's coat of arms on it. Above all else, this unique place clearly offers up a picture of happiness.

L'Auberge de l'Ill

2, rue de Collonges-au-Mont-d'Or

68970 Illhaeusern

Tel: +33 (0)3 89 71 89 00

www.auberge-de-l-ill.com

For recipes, see pages 193–194

Pages 70–71: Marc and Laetitia Haeberlin, followed by the whole team, walking on the lawn of the Auberge de l'Ill, and its traditional dessert, grandmother's iced vacherin. Standing behind a window of the dining room which looks out onto l'Ill, Marc Haeberlin welcomes guests with a permanent smile. Above, one of the house's signature dishes invented by Paul Haeberlin: mousseline of frogs' legs. Facing page, bottom right: venison medallions.

À l'Huîtrière

A Northern Institution

WITH AN EXCEPTIONAL SEAFOOD MENU, THE GASTRONOMICAL
TRADITION OF PICARDY IS ELEGANTLY AND RELIABLY MAINTAINED
UNDER THE GUIDANCE OF THE PROYE FAMILY.

Is this the best restaurant in northern France? We wonder how the *Michelin Guide* could have awarded only one star to a place of this caliber. The legend began in 1906 when Pierre Baillieul, an innkeeper at the Hôtel de la Plage in Sangatte, opened his restaurant at 6, rue Basse, serving oysters, shellfish, and snails. On September 1, 1928, the restaurant moved to 3, rue des Chats Bossus.

We are in the heart of old Lille. The window is decorated in the art-deco style, the mosaics and stained-glass windows by Mathurin Méheut of Brittany. The oysters come from Belon, the lobster from Loctudy, the salmon from Holland, Gdańsk, and Allier, the lamb from Pauillac, and the chicken from Bresse. A top restaurant now? It already was, through the extreme care paid to every detail. It won its first Michelin star in 1932, but Pierre Baillieul, perfectionist that he was, was surprised to receive only one.

"My establishment, shop, and restaurant were rewarded for the quality of the products available, which are far superior to anything of the kind Lille or northern France has ever seen," he wrote to the *Michelin Guide* just after the award. The restaurant won its second star between 1952 and 1961. There had indeed been a great effort to achieve that. Many years and four generations later, even if the setting has changed four times behind the unruffled art-deco façade, the effort is the same. After Pierre Baillieul's son, Charles, came his son-in-law, Jean Proye,

who has now been replaced by his son Antoine. In the meantime, the Proye family created a small empire for themselves. There is L'Ecume des Mers, an annex in the form of a chic pub, and L'Assiette du Marché, run by Antoine's younger brother, Thomas, in the old mint hall. In Lille, a city of work and leisure, L'Huîtrière, with its renovated Flemish-style moldings, touches of gold, and stucco, has been the reference point for local gastronomy for the past twenty-five years. People come for business meals, and later return with their families, even if that means breaking the bank to do so.

The mural woodwork, old-style candelabra, modern nooks, stylish furniture, and flawless service, in which every action looks like second nature, all reflect how smoothly the house runs. The wine list is one of the richest in France. There is not only Chablis from Raveneau, but Leflaive's Puligny, highly pedigreed Médocs, unbelievable Pomerol (ah, the series of vintages of Fleur Pétrus!), and rarities from all the wineries. What French restaurant, even counting Pic in Valence, can boast that it offers four vintages of the very rare Château-Grillet by the Neyret-Gachet family, which Curnonsky named as one of the five top white wines of France?

What the loyal Philippe Lor cooks in the kitchen, and has been doing so for a quarter of a century, is an exact reflection of one's expectations of eating there. It is a rational, perfect blend of regional tradition and classicism revisited in a modern way.

There is no doubt that between Antoine Proye and Philippe Lor, from dining room to kitchen, there is a constant dialogue, much like that which used to take place between Jean-Claude Vrinat and Claude Deligne at Taillevent.

The comparison is obvious: L'Huîtrière is clearly the Taillevent of northern France. The only difference is that the cellar is not down the road, as Taillevent's is in Paris, but on the premises. The fishmonger display, which marks the entrance of the restaurant, is the most beautiful in France, with its art-deco gold touches. It offers turbot, monkfish, eel from Boulogne or the region of Nantes, and Aberdeen haddock, as well as oysters and shrimp that can be eaten at the bar. Gin from Houlle and Wambrechies keep good company with the jars of herring. A visit here can replace one to the market.

The cooking? A demonstration of pure quality in the dining room: sea bass tartare with lemon confit and Aquitaine caviar; variations on langoustine, as tartare or ravioli with mushrooms, depending on the season; smoked eel with lukewarm vinaigrette; and warm Landes foie gras with radish confit. To that, one can add the slice of pan-fried turbot with Hollandaise sauce, monkfish in a spice crust with tangy sauce, and gray shrimp or red mullet in escabèche: all crafted with precision. The selection of meat dishes should not be overlooked: they include veal sweetbreads with rhubarb caramel, pigeon with sautéed cherries and pearled barley, lamb three ways (shoulder confit, roast rib, grilled leg), spiced duckling with its breast served pink, and confit leg and sauce made with gin in the local manner. This balancing act between the plentiful north and the grand French tradition is the binary code on which L'Huîtrière runs.

The desserts play this game as well, with the pairing of chicory, speculoos, and gin in a take on the tiramisù; the "cramique" brioche done like French toast and accompanied by beer ice cream; sweet and bitter lemon doughnuts; and of course the emblematic *crêpes suzette*, the real ones, served in the dining room like a ritual itself, with rubbed sugar, orange and lemon zest, and Grand Marnier.

The great chefs and high-end innkeepers, who come from other regions to Lille to spend a day or even more (we're thinking of Jean-Paul Arabian, then at Le Restaurant near the Sébastopol theater, or of Robert Bardot, who was king of the town of Le Flambard), speak of this exceptional place with barely contained emotion. A grand establishment with high-quality ingredients, intangible expertise, a huge cellar, attentive service, and a proper settting: such is L'Huîtrière, an exemplary house that is the gastronomical pride and joy of France's northern region.

À l'Huîtrière

3, rue des Chats-Bossus

59000 Lille

Tel: +33 (0)3 20 55 43 41

www.huîtriere.fr

For recipes, see page 195

Here in Lille, we are in the temple of fish. The ceramic, art-deco tile decor adds to the general impression of elegance and freshness. Warm oysters, and steaming lobsters like the one immortalized on one of the entrance walls are served in the restaurant. A young fishmonger shows off a turbot caught that morning. Monkfish, roasted (page 75) or poached (facing page, top right).

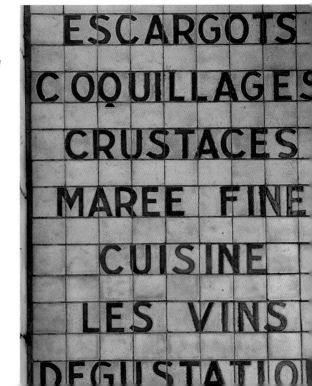

Lorain
The Little Prince of Joigny

TOO CLOSE TO PARIS, OR TOO FAR FROM IT TO BECOME REALLY FAMOUS,
YONNE IS HOME TO THIS DISCREET CHEF AND HIS FLAGSHIP RESTAURANT.

In 1945, Grandmother Marie Lorain started a family inn by the shore of the Yonne River. Her son Michel took over in 1957, and slowly transformed it into a luxury hotel and restaurant, with a tunnel under the highway, baroque and highly stylish apartments, and a covered pool facing the river. He dazzled diners with theatrical dishes: oysters in four flavors, truffle with cabbage, salmon cooked in a pig's bladder, and Saint-Jean-Cap-Ferrat veal sweetbreads.

Michel's son, Jean-Michel, was a pure product of the 1980s. Trained at Troisgros in Roanne, Girardet in Crissier, and at Taillevent in Paris, his inclination was toward restraint. This young man, measured yet full of ideas, (he writes a blog, meets many of his readers, and puts together thematic recipe books with his own pictures) won the coveted three stars in the *Michelin Guide* with his father, lost them, then won them again by himself through sheer persistence. "I was lucky," he admits today.

Through this experience, he found his independence, his personality, and his strength. While Michel turned into a passionate winemaker on the hills of Joigny, Jean-Michel carries on the family tradition. The modest roadside family hotel has become a luxury address facing the river. The Lorain domain is now comprised of new, modern bedrooms, airy dining rooms, a vast, practical kitchen open to diners, and a cellar that is continuously improving.

JML has made his mark all over the establishment, taking it to the peak of gastronomical glory without ever abandoning tradition. Frogs are served in kadaïf (thread-like pastry) with jellied gazpacho and dried tomato with a chlorophyll sauce; snails are pan-fried, accompanied by garlic cream and an emulsified mushroom sauce; veal kidney is breaded with gingerbread and served with a spicy onion puree, and Swiss chard dumplings come with citron confit chutney.

Is it new-wave Burgundy? There is a bit of that. And while Auxerre and Sens are just next door, Paris, the big city, is not even an hour and a half away by the A6 freeway and the Porte d'Orléans.

The region's wonderful climate, along with the most prestigious—though not necessarily famous—vintages (Adhémar Boudin's Chablis l'Homme Mort, Étienne Sauzet's Puligny-Montrachet, Charlopin-Parizot's Vosne-Romanée), lovingly cared for by Jean-Michel's mother Jacqueline, one of the best "noses" in the region, accompany these special moments.

La Côte Saint-Jacques

14, faubourg de Paris

89300 Joigny

Tel: +33 (0)3 86 62 09 70

www.cotesaintjacques.com

For recipes, see pages 195–196

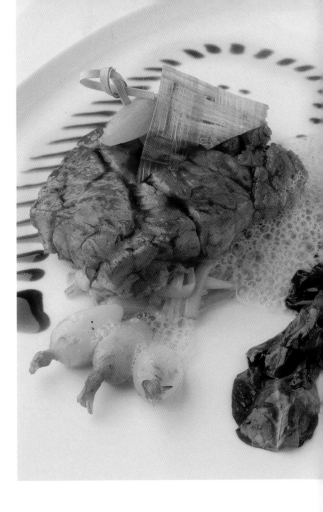

Demonstrating that tradition and innovation can go hand in hand, there are also "memorable dishes," those that had made the renown of La Côte Saint-Jacques and of father and son. There are oysters in an oceanic terrine, caviar-smoked sea bass, champagne-steamed chicken, and the famous truffle with cabbage, along with a fabulous blood sausage with mousseline potato puree, a splendid Hereford beef rib served with macaroni stuffed with foie gras and truffles, and small confit turnips.

Finally, desserts are always an unforgettable experience. An extremely delicate three-cream mille-feuille, thin fig tart, vanilla-poached rhubarb, or lime soufflé are some of the well-tempered notes of a symphony that is delivered in a flurry of small, pleasurable portions.

The tone here is that of a luxurious establishment that has managed to stay rooted and wise. Rural and urban, refined and rustic, Jean-Michel Lorain's Burgundy has the precise acidity of a Chablis and the mellow roundness of a Chambertin at its best. His rigor and discretion contribute to this, his new legend.

Jean-Michel Lorain, who managed to build up his restaurant without ever abandoning traditions, and "variations on an oyster theme" (pages 78–79). The Côte Saint-Jacques, its cellar rich in great Burgundies, its dining room with a view of the Yonne, and its historic dishes like medallions of ginger-scented sweetbreads with pearl onions, rhubarb and pink radishes (above) or smoked sea bass with caviar (facing page, bottom right).

What's New, Lasserre?

LASSERRE—OLD, BUT STILL GORGEOUS;
IT IS IMPOSSIBLE TO GROW TIRED OF THIS PARISIAN INSTITUTION,
WHICH EVOKES THE MAGIC OF THE 1950S.

A legendary restaurant? Lasserre! René Lasserre, an innkeeper's son born in Bayonne in 1912, learned on the job: on the cruise ship Île-de-France, at the Normandy in Deauville, at the Lido, the Pavilion d'Armenonville, Drouant, at the Pré Catelan, and Prunier in Paris. In 1942, he bought a modest, wood-planked bistro at 17 Avenue Victor-Emmanuel-III. It had been built for the 1937 World Expo in the gardens of a dilapidated private mansion. The avenue was renamed for Franklin Roosevelt after the war, and the place soon became famous.

With the help of his mother Irma, the Bayonne native installed Venetian glass lanterns, hidden under multicolored parasols. They rebuilt and enlarged the space, with a modest façade lit by lanterns, entrance hallways and lounges, and an upstairs room with a mechanical roof, painted by Louis Touchagues, which could be accessed by a stylish staircase. All was furnished with period furniture that went seamlessly with the pure Cocteau/Bérard style that was all the rage in the 1950s.

The waitstaff, wearing coattails, serves traditional cuisine with a focused, serious attitude. The first Michelin star was obtained in 1949, the second in 1951, and the third a decade later in 1962. The *Michelin Guide* rewarded the flawless cuisine as much as the very chic Parisian ambience, a "Lasserre style" unlike any other. René Lasserre created the "Club de la Casserole," which brought together his regular customers, including Charlton Heston, French actor Fernandel, Salvador Dalí, and André Malraux, to whom Lasserre dedicated a stuffed pigeon.

Chefs followed, one after another, but the kitchen's tone was always set by the master of the house, while his deputies and heirs, Mr. Henry or Mr. Louis, managed the front. "I am as much the chef as I am the maître d'," Lasserre liked to say. Many of the great chefs of the time were trained in his kitchen, like Guy Savoy, Jacques Lameloise, Michel Rostang, Jean-Paul Lacombe, Gérard Boyer, and Marc Haeberlin. All of them learned the craft "the hard way," cooking the Landes Mesclagne that was inspired by his mother Irma (chicken mousse stuffed with foie gras), the timeless duck à l'orange with its caramelized skin, carved and served tableside, asparagus with Maltese sauce, Lobster Newburg, or the Élysée timbale with fruit in a sugar cage.

The current chef, Christophe Moret, is a worthy heir to this kitchen, lauded for its visual as well as gustatory efforts. This former protégé of Alain Ducasse, trained in his style, under his direct supervision at the Plaza Athénée, has helped update the house style—as Jean-Louis Nomicos did before him—making it lighter, without watering it down. The service feels younger, but hasn't lost its flawlessness, and the decor has kept its 1950s theatrical style, though it is admittedly more restrained now, in tones of beige.

The Lasserre of today? Faithful to its heritage. Every year, the lounges on the first floor host the Interallié literary prize committee during their deliberations. The antique furniture has kept its sheen. The ceiling with the mechanical roof by Touchagues has been restored by Corbassière. The fabric on the walls is now in yellow tones, to fit with the sense of sobriety. However, the colorful lift, which René Lasserre used to call his "little box of secrets," remains unchanged. Is that enough to show that the establishment has stayed faithful to its reputation and that Lasserre still really is Lasserre, surviving changes of era, style, and fashion?

When it comes to food, Moret's cuisine is complex and exquisite. He has cleverly retained the great classics. Not necessarily the duck à l'orange, which is only available in season, and has been replaced by duckling with roasted figs in a salmis sauce, nor the Landes Mesclagne (chicken mousse stuffed with foie gras). But certainly the André Malraux pigeon and the fillet of beef "Rossini," accompanied by the customary potato puff.

In addition to the classics, he offers a contemporary repertoire, just like his predecessor, Jean-Louis Nomicos. The famous macaroni with black truffles and duck liver, the fine royale of lettuce with caviar and light cream seasoned with lemon, the medley of raw and cooked cep mushrooms with tomato confit, and the brill with apples and vin jaune, are all delightful, without going against tradition. Of course, there's a Russian diner just behind you whose telephone goes off unexpectedly, but you don't even notice. Because you're too busy concentrating on the wonderful mechanical roof and the very civilized service of the wait-staff who carve at your table as if it were second nature to them.

The best thing? A very reasonable lunch menu with excitingly bourgeois dishes such as spit-roasted shoulder of lamb with crispy skin and juicy flesh, served with vegetables in a navarin-style jus: absolutely delicious! What's new? Some very pretty desserts by Claire Heitzler, formerly of the Ritz, who is updating the repertoire. Along with "Elysée Lasserre" timbale and crêpes suzette, you can now sample soft Guanaja chocolate soufflé and the gorgeous crisp chocolate with raspberries and soft Manjari ganache. Two seductive compositions that show that Lasserre is evolving without straying from the path of sense and good taste.

Lasserre

17, avenue Franklin D. Roosevelt

75008 Paris

Tel: +33 (0)1 43 59 02 13

www.restaurant-lasserre.com

For recipes, see pages 197–198

Lasserre, where refined and visually appealing cuisine is always served, such as citrus-scented sea bass (right) or these two desserts by pastry chef Claire Heitzler: crisp chocolate with raspberries and soft Manjari ganache (page 83) or figs roasted with olive oil (facing page, top right).
The only great Parisian restaurant where a man in a red uniform awaits you for the elevator ride up, this is Lasserre, with its mechanized roof on which chef Christophe Moret poses.

Ledoyen
A Parisian Legend

In the heart of the carré des Champs-Élysées
can be found a restaurant that is out of the ordinary,
with a turbulent past but now with a well-behaved,
technically solid chef whose service is better than perfect.

Perhaps you have heard of the movie *Le Grand Restaurant*. Famous French comedic actor Louis de Funès played the role of Septime, who was willing to sacrifice anything for the greater glory of his gorgeous restaurant. The restaurant in the film was Ledoyen. In the beginning, it was a modest inn measuring forty by twelve feet, with white walls and green shutters. This was in 1779, when it was the property of Mr. Desmazure, located close to the Place Louis XV (now Paris's Place de la Concorde) in the Carré des Ambassadeurs of the Champs-Élysées. On August 4, 1791, the building was rented to Antoine-Nicolas Doyen, former cook of the president of the Bordeaux tribunal, and inventor of the Strasbourg foie-gras pâté with Périgord truffles. He had come up with such a luxurious creation to entice convention members to his restaurant (the convention was located close by at the Jeu de Paume in the Tuileries).

In 1848, the architect Jacques Hirtoff, who created the Saint-Vincent-de-Paul church on Place Franz-Liszt and who reconfigured the Champs-Élysées, moved the restaurant to the other side of the avenue, where it is presently located, and installed a noble neo-Greek façade with statues, interior colonnades, and large bay windows. In the middle of the twentieth century, Ledoyen, which now belonged to the city of Paris but was managed by the Lajeune family, experienced real popularity and success, with two Michelin stars. Many great chefs, such as Guy Legay, who was the chef at the Ritz, or Christian Constant,

who would later know glory at the Crillon hotel, were trained at Ledoyen under Francis Trocellier.

The house was transformed under the new ownership of the Générale des Eaux (the Veolia Water company) and Jean-Marie Messier. The big dining room on the ground floor, which opened onto the gardens of the Champs-Élysées, became a sitting room, and in the second-floor dining room, with its stucco ceiling dedicated to gastronomical cuisine, Ghislaine Arabian took the helm and became Paris's grand lady from the north. Next came Christian Le Squer and the Épicure Group.

Born in Lorient in 1962, the son of a carpenter, Le Squer embarked on a trawler at the age of 14; hard work is instinctive to him. If there are kitchen-horses, as one might say there are workhorses, Christian Le Squer is definitely one of them. This native of the Morbihan in Brittany became the talk of the town at the Ritz, and then at the Restaurant de l'Opéra at the Grand Hotel Intercontinental, where the *Michelin Guide* gave him two stars. At Ledoyen, he molds himself perfectly to a setting created for others, while showing evident technical mastery.

The earth and the sea inspire him to superb feats of skill. The *amuse-gueules* tasters, which sometimes borrow tricks from molecular cuisine, but without being as provocative, like the exquisite mozzarella marbles, tell the story of modern cuisine without losing themselves in long-winded presentations. This passionate Breton shows that he can do anything. He can create a "small" lunch menu (on the Champs-Élysées no less!), which offers up an elegant summary of his style. His "Melba" grilled toast of foie gras with jellied sour cherries, peppered tuna belly with watermelon, and smoked caramel Norwegian omelet, embody masterful moments that take tradition into account while revisiting it in a light and refreshing way.

But everything he cooks in the classic manner, brilliantly reimagined, is truly fabulous. His turbot fillet with fork-mashed ratte potatoes beaten with truffle butter is a masterpiece of the surf and turf genre, at which he excels. His soft-shelled crab with pressed juice in an iced shell is in the same vein, evoking his Breton roots, a clear and pure homage to his origins. As are his Belon oyster concentrate, slices of fried sole with Jura "yellow wine," and smoked eel on burnt toasts with wine dregs. The sublime veal sweetbreads with lemongrass stalks and herb juice make a royal dish on the theme of variety meats, which are treated here with care and finesse.

Discreet, in the way they know how to be in Lorient, Christian Le Squer stays out of the limelight. But his appearance as a tall, slender, enthusiastic, congenial fellow makes him eminently likable and, in truth, this modest Breton deserves to be a Parisian star. The excellent service that supports him, an imposing wine list (which has always been a strong point here), the serious decor with stylized ceiling, and the bay windows beneath the trees, sets Ledoyen apart from the others. It tops the capital's offerings.

For good measure, we'll add that the service, led by Patrick Simiand, is one of the most astounding in Paris. The sommelier, Géraud Tournier, from Aveyron, who trained at Saint-Chély-d'Apcher before Tain-l'Hermitage, then worked for Ducasse and Troisgros, gives the best, most practical, and concise advice for such precise differences (the unknown Domaine de l'A from the Derenoncourt family and the surprising Château Bellevue-Tayac Margaux signed Thunevin are both stunning discoveries). This is a bonus for an establishment already at the top. Nevertheless, Ledoyen is probably the least star-like of the capital's great restaurants.

Ledoyen

Carré des Champs-Élysées

1, avenue Dutuit

75008 Paris

Tel: +33 (0)1 53 05 10 01

www.ledoyen.com

For recipes, see pages 198–199

The grand staircase (page 86) is a throwback to the period of the Revolution. Whether standing between the caryatids of this Republican temple or in his kitchen, this is Christian Le Squer, a discreet and serious Breton.

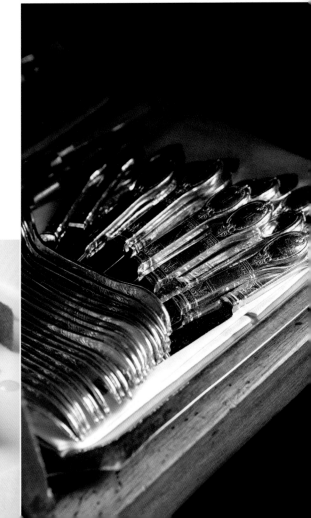

His coffee-infused foie gras squares are marvelous pre-meal tasters, and the peppered tuna belly cooked with watermelon (page 87) won't cause the CEO's of big French corporations to gain too much weight. The small private room with an angled view over the gardens has been privy to the secrets of power.

Louis XV
The Man of the Riviera

KING DUCASSE, GLOBE-TROTTER AND GLOBAL GASTRONOME,
CAN BE REDISCOVERED AT HOME IN MONACO.

He is the man with twenty-seven establishments, nineteen Michelin stars, and restaurants on every continent. Spoon on Île Maurice, Beige in Tokyo, Mix in Las Vegas, Adour in New York, and, of course, L'Andana in Tuscan Maremma and Reine Didon in Carthage. However, Alain Ducasse, originally from Orthez, raised on a farm in Castelsarrasin in the Landes region of France, is first and foremost a lover of the Mediterranean and his primary domain is in Monaco, the bastion upon which he built his glory.

He has become fully Monegasque, crowning twenty years of service to the Grimaldi family and their Société des Bains de Mer by taking on the nationality of the Principality. The Bar et Boeuf, the Grill de l'Hôtel de Paris, but above all, the Louis XV, which is where one must come to discover him, in a very *"grand siècle"* setting, sum up his story perfectly. *Riviera* is the title of one of his books. It is under this label that his two chefs, Franck Cerutti and Pascal Bardet, create their masterpieces. One, a native of Nice, worked for a very long time for Pinchiorri in Florence, elegantly practicing the tradition of grand transalpine cuisine. The other, from Figeac in the Lot, managed through experience (most notably at 59 Poincaré) to fit himself into the mold created by the master.

Everything they propose, dictated by the Ducasse spirit, demonstrates sheer virtuosity and flawless technical skill. Raw spring vegetables served with a fabulous anchovy tapenade and barbagiuans (typically Monegasque crispy ravioli), sieved green pea soup with quail egg ricotta gnocchi, or green asparagus risotto are very "peasant with leather boots" in their sincerity and forthrightness, with a real look of honesty. In fact, his range of seemingly simple pasta, breads, and risotto is truly exceptional.

"Better to have the turbot without the genius, than the genius without the turbot," Alain Ducasse has a habit of saying. It is his way of underlining the fact that—more than anything—great cuisine is about the "royally simple" treatment of marvelous ingredients. Shellfish, shrimp, small squid, and borlotti beans in a warm salad; morels braised in Arbois wine with Mona Lisa potato gnocchi and borage leaves; denti fish cooked with bouillabaisse broth with braised sucrine salad; Larzac pig caramelized with sage and served with vegetables and eggplant condiment; and the mustardy pig's ear—all these dishes will have you on your knees.

Served in an ornate and charming room, with its gold, stucco, and bust of the beautiful marquise so dear to Louis XV, these creations represent moments of pure grace. There are also the lovely desserts (wild strawberries with warm juice and sorbet, full-cream milk ice cream, and a sublime baba). The large cellar is in harmony with it all, with the wines of Provence dominating, but also housing the best of Burgundy and the Bordeaux grand crus.

It would be remiss not to mention the service, the very best in its field, which smiles, advises, tells stories, and becomes familiar without being too personal. In short, it is a summary of the Ducasse spirit in its most intricate and composed detail. According to Saint Ducasse, the globe-trotter and global gastronome, can it be that the truth of all things lies in Monaco?

Le Louis XV
Alain Ducasse

Place du Casino

9800 Monte-Carlo, Monaco

Tel: +37 (0)7 98 06 88 64

www.alain-ducasse.com

For recipes, see pages 199–200

One enters the restaurant through the majestic hall of the Hôtel de Paris (page 90). The tables are impeccably set and the gold vermeil cutlery is polished every morning. Showing absolute virtuosity in the Ducasse spirit: full-cream milk ice cream with fleur de sel, caramel crunch, and ewe's milk curd cheese (page 91) and mesclun and black truffles, seasoned with new olive oil, with a tuber melanosporum sandwich (below). Beneath the gold and stuccos of Louis XV's charming dining room, the maitres d'hotel supervise the last preparations before service begins.

Bernard Loiseau's
Spirit Endures

RETURN TO SAULIEU AND LA CÔTE D'OR,
IN THE SHADOW OF THE GREAT DEPARTED CHEF.

We imagine him watching over his dwelling from a cook's paradise. For him, we would believe in heaven. His classics still reign over the menu: frogs' legs with garlic puree and parsley jus, pike perch with shallots in a red wine sauce, chicken breast and foie gras with truffled mashed potatoes. It's as if the shadow of Bernard Loiseau, departed much too soon, still hovered over the shoulder of his former assistant.

Patrick Bertron now wears the title of chef. This hardworking native of Rennes, as serious as can be, who never raises his voice for any reason, may not have the charisma of the master with whom he worked for two decades. But he has understood everything in Loiseau's manner, learning his style to perfection, taking up his flavorful, iodized juices, his short cooking times, his strongly rooted, definite ideas.

Dominique, the active widow, leaves him room to maneuver. In truth, nothing seems to have moved in the gastronomical temple of Saulieu. The beautiful neo-rustic dining room, the garden with its blanket of flowers where once was a garage, and the Zen-like peace of the spa, all have made us forget the old Côte d'Or of Alexandre Dumaine. In the dining room, Éric Rousseau smiles as Bernard Loiseau did, describing dishes through mime with the same convincing gestures. And the meals are still grand feasts.

The *Michelin Guide* has understandably, and despite rumors to the contrary, not budged one iota about the place and left three stars to what appears now to be an institution of the Morvan mountains. Here, the best seasonal and regional ingredients of Burgundy are treated with a mix of science, respect, simplicity, and naturalness. Top ingredients, the right flavors, and colorful dishes await you here. That, and the very best wines of Côtes de Nuits or Beaune, Chablis, and the Mâconnais.

You will feast on crayfish with asparagus and mushrooms, snails in lettuce cream and almond oil, or arctic char with iced turnips. A dish fit for a king? That would be the fabulous spit-roasted veal's kidney with Madeira sauce, gingerbread mustard, and its delicate fat, masterfully cut at the table in a stylish exercise befitting a grand restaurant. But the Charolais beef fillet cooked in a bed of hay in a clay crust represents another great carnivorous moment.

As Bernard would say, and in an expression often repeated after him, the ingredient is the star. Offal, sea or freshwater fish, beautiful poultry, and vegetables from nearby markets are treated with respect here. The local artisans are also passionately sought out: the admirable wild blackcurrant or bitter orange jams by Jacky Sulem in Saint-Léger-sous-Beuvray or the Haut-Folin ham in Arleuf, which amateurs of delicious breakfasts use as if it were honey on some of the best country breads in the world.

But do not, whatever you do, skip the desserts! They have always been essential to the experience here and continue to be so, especially the hazelnut "cazette" with grapefruit sorbet and soft salted butter caramel. Or that Burgundian masterpiece of blackcurrant sorbet stuffed with violet granita served with Genoa bread. It is a marvel of taste and digestion, just as Bernard loved, which even on its own would make the trip to Saulieu worthwhile. There is also the famous sand rose with chocolate ice cream and coulis of orange confit, another pure marvel, this time of delectable acidity and freshness.

The wines are suited to the setting, from Chablis to the big Côtes, and the rooms and suites worthy of an exemplary Relais & Châteaux. Yes, of course Bernard, you can come back: your house hasn't changed....

Le Relais
Bernard Loiseau

2, rue d'Argentine

21210 Saulieu

Tel: +33 (0)3 80 90 53 53

www.bernard-loiseau.com

For recipe, see page 201

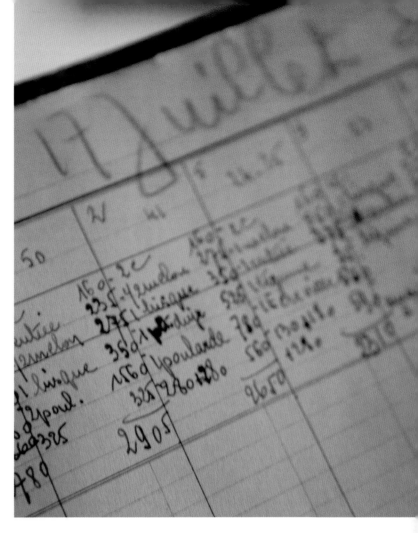

In the historic dining room, the accounts ledger has been left open to Bernard Loiseau's date of birth, July 17, 1951. The classics are still served, including frogs' legs with garlic puree and parsley jus (page 94), but also Patrick Berton's more recent creations, such as this John Dory roasted in a potato crust (facing page, top right). The garden hasn't lost any of its charm nor has the kitchen lost its old luster, with its copper pots hanging on the walls.

While one of the sommeliers pours a fine cru into a glass in the sitting room, another pulls out a bottle of Romanée-Conti in the cellar. The dish right: free-range roasted Quercy rack and saddle of lamb, Lautrec garlic clove, braised lima beans, and fennel.

On Monday evening, February 24, 2003, the world of cookery was plunged into mourning for Bernard Loiseau, who had killed himself with a shotgun.

In 1975, when Bernard Loiseau arrived at La Côte d'Or, he came in through the back door. He was twenty-four years old, just an employee of Claude Vergé, the man from the "Barrières" in Paris (he had worked at the one in Clichy). Loiseau lived in a room at La Rubempré, which was in Alexandre Dumaine's old house. On top of his dresser, he had a pile of *Paris-Match* magazines with pictures of the Troisgros' third Michelin star. In one of them, he was recognizable as a young, awestruck apprentice. He decided then that, one day, he too would have three stars.

But in Saulieu, the game wasn't easy. La Côte d'Or was often empty. In the kitchens, Loiseau found cans of shrimp bisque, which the *Michelin Guide* had declared was one of the specialties of his predecessor François Minot! He had an image to rebuild. The press made the trip from Paris to Loiseau: 157 miles on the A6 and then the N6

highways. They recognized an innate talent, sang the praises of "cooking with water," as it really was water that was used to deglaze the cooking juices.

The revolutionary was mocked (Bocuse, in front of his bridge in Collonges, exclaimed ironically: "Ah, all that good sauce that Bernard lets get away.") But Loiseau refined his style and managed to convince them all. Henri G. and Christophe M. of Gault-Millau gave him four chef hats, and the *Michelin Guide* followed with three stars. It was the approval he had been waiting for, and he became the subject of unending press articles.

The road to glory continued. It took ten years to build a hotel worthy of Relais & Châteaux, with superb suites and hallways dedicated to the Bocuse model and the Troisgros professors. It took fifteen years to restructure the restaurant, demolish the old garage and the outdated kitchens, set up a vast and functional laboratory and new rooms with views of the English-style garden. And it took sixteen years to finally obtain the third and most coveted star.

Originally from Chamalières in Auvergne, and Burgundian by adoption, the great Bernard grew new roots by starting over from the beginning. No more wild inventions; this was not that type of era, but a slow rediscovery of the real flavors of things: caramelized

cauliflower soup, crayfish cooked in a spicy bouillon, pike perch with red wine sauce and sautéed shallots, suckling veal rib and its sauce, steamed hen with truffles in an homage to Dumaine.

The gourmet's palate is no longer overwhelmed; it is cajoled and it is comforted. Like Chapel in Mionnay long ago, Bernard Loiseau fussed over his clientele, providing constant care to soothe the stress away. He offered desserts that were bareley sweet: iced caramel parfait and crispy puff pastry, or chocolate-coffee puff pastry.

A blissfully peaceful spa was created in the old Côte d'Or, and a swimming pool was added in the garden. The customer was pampered in rooms where wood and stone worked together in harmony. In the morning, breakfasts were warm and cozy, and the staff was always attentive. Dominique, the mistress of the house, straightened bow ties and orchestrated every little change, without forgetting to prepare the master's succession: his children, Bérangère, Bastien, and Blanche all have the same initials.

Bernard Loiseau had just celebrated his twenty-eighth year at Saulieu. He was in his twenty-first year when Dumaine's centenary was celebrated—Dumaine was born in 1895 and present in Saulieu for thirty-two years. Loiseau's debut on the stock exchange, the first for a

chef, which had been in the works for a long time and finally took place at the end of 1998, gave an image of the conquering chef unafraid of anything, as comfortable on television as in his Côte d'Or, provincial, and solidly grounded.

Was the pressure too much? Loiseau, king of the media, had gone beyond the confines of the food pages. He was then in the celebrity pages of the magazines. He had a dazzling smile, but was his mental state just like the façade? Those close to him knew that the giant from Auvergne hid a tender, fragile heart. The pressure increased. He called friends: "Am I still the best?"

He was cajoled and he was reassured. French newspaper *Le Figaro* suggested that he was in line for star demotions in the 2003 *Michelin Guide*, and that Michelin had called him in for reprimands. It emerged that the new *Gault Millau* had suddenly removed two points from his score.

No one thought he cared. He was in talks about new improvements and fittings at La Côte d'Or. He made appointments for the spring. His death came completely unexpectedly to those around him. His story, of against-the-odds success, was full of hope an inspiration; it is hard to accept that it should end in tragedy.

A Visit to Mount
Marcon

A MAGICAL PLACE SITS HIGH UP IN THE VILLAGE OF
SAINT-BONNET-LE-FROID IN THE VELAY REGION,
WHERE EXCITING THINGS ARE HAPPENING ALL THE TIME.

It is a gem deep in the countryside, almost completely isolated from the rest of the world. Yet Saint-Étienne is less than an hour away, and Lyon and Valence are not far. This is a way of saying that the Marcons' restaurant is situated at the intersection of all roads and the confluence of all worlds. Cévennes, Forez, or Ardèche are its reference points, but here it is Auvergne, Haute-Loire, and Velay. The establishment never empties. People come from all over to discover it: its location, its innovative chef, its natural cuisine, and its hotel with the eco-label.

At the end of the 1970s, Régis and his wife Michèle took over the inn created in 1948 by his mother, Marie-Louise Marcon. After enlarging, modernizing, and improving it in a number of other ways, it became their annex to which they added a bistro. They waited until 2005 to be able to build a restaurant, and then until 2008 to add the hotel, which looks as if it just landed in the wilderness, up on the village heights. Perched at a height of more than 3,600 feet, it looks like something from outer space, with its wood, glass, and stone, its incredible view over the Ardèche mountains, the neighboring pasturelands, and the forest, attracting amazed gourmands and the curious alike.

The hotel and restaurant are full during the three "good" seasons; fall here is radiant, summer is flamboyant and luminous, and spring is restorative. But they are closed from Christmas to Easter. It is true that winters are tough, snowy, windy, and cold, as the name of the village accurately indicates ("froid" in French means cold). One must just be patient for three months, to reserve and find a room in this unique place. A large and enthusiastic staff is here to serve happy guests, and innumerable walks are possible, during which one can dream, digest, stroll around, or just take a breather.

While long ago people came to the Velay region to visit Mount Gerbierde-Jonc, they now come to visit Mount Marcon, and for a more gastronomical pilgrimage of sorts. Self-taught and trained by his mother in her inn-café in Saint-Bonnet-le-Froid, he then went to Sussex to learn English. He came back to settle down, created an inexpensive menu, and eventually won the race for the Michelin stars. Régis Marcon became the king of the Haute-Loire, spreading quantities of good students and delicious tables around him. The artist from the heart of Auvergne, and the conqueror of the Bocuse d'Or competition and the Taittinger Prize, remained stubbornly loyal to his village.

In October 2005, seven months after obtaining the ultimate reward of three long-awaited Michelin stars, he moved to the perched site called Larsiallas, and a new life began. He moved his team (about twenty cooks in the kitchen, almost as many staff in the dining room) into a peaceful and solitary retreat, with a central stone tower that was a reproduction of his mother's house, and an ultra-panoramic, bright dining room, opening out onto the landscape and its natural beauty.

Restaurant Régis et Jacques Marcon

Larsiallas

43290 Saint-Bonnet-le-Froid

Tel: +33 (0)4 71 59 93 72

www.regismarcon.fr

For recipes, see pages 201–202

In their Zen-like retreat on the heights of Saint-Bonnet, Régis and Jacques Marcon, father and son, await you (page 100). The large dining room overlooks the plateau. The mushroom is king, with jelled garden peas with mousserons (page 101) or porcini mushrooms picked and cleaned by Régis Marcon, in chestnut leaves with a grill-scented zabaglione. The verbena jelly with confit lentils recreates the austere freshness of the flavors of Auvergne (right).

He is the master of his own house, working alongside his son Jacques, who was most notably trained by guru Philippe Rochat at Crissier in Switzerland. He continues to blend inspiration from old recipes with the ingredients of today. Mushrooms are his treasure, as are chestnuts and green Puy lentils. But the lukewarm lobster, served like pho, the soup from Saigon that is so easily digestible, with verbena, spaghetti squash, and enoki mushrooms, or in a stew with a lemon thyme crust served with a ragout of green Puy lentils, is a pure delight.

Also marvelous are the ragout of vegetables with Grazac snails and young chanterelle shoots; porcini in chestnut leaves with a delicate, grill-scented zabaglione (sabayon); tomato jelly compote with cream of young zucchini and green peas; and vegetable tempura fritters. Or the famous Margaridou skewers, inspired by the recipe notebook of a famous cook of Cévennes, who breathed fresh life into her local *terroir*, combining veal sweetbreads, morel mushroom fritters, and ham. At Jacques and Régis's restaurant, the dishes have history, tell stories of travels, and evoke their roots.

Fannie Romezin's arctic char, which comes from a fish farm in nearby Vercors, is as delicate and fresh as if it were wild, with such tender flesh, crispy skin, and a "natural" accompaniment of almond and artichoke, chanterelles, and cilantro. Like the hedgehog and milk-cap mushrooms picked not far from there, or the beautiful, thick scallop served with Burgundy truffles (depending on the season), or the cabbage stuffed with porcini, chanterelle, and black trumpet mushrooms served with a fabulous grilled mushroom zabaglione (sabayon), it shows that the father and son duo can do anything and everything.

The saddle and thin fillet of free-range rabbit with chanterelles and Mirabelle plums shows the same talent, as does the Saugues lamb in a hay crust with porcini mushroom praline. Cheeses from Auvergne (Saint-Nectaire, Fourme de Montbrison, Fourme d'Ambert, Salers, Cantal, Gaperon with garlic, farm goat cheese) are slathered with mouthwatering jams. His hot and cold desserts are precise and delicate, and all amazing. Banana skewers with morel caramel; chocolate mousse and sorbet with puff pastry biscuit and praline; peach Melba revisited, with an Eyrieux Valley nectarine and meadowsweet ice cream; or variations on Mara des Bois wild strawberries as mille-feuille or sorbet.

The wine list is complementary to both shores of the great Rhône, which flows at the foot of the mountain, with Condrieu, Crozes-Hermitage, Saint-Joseph, or Côte-Rôtie. And the two locations, Clos des Cimes in the heart of the village and the grand panoramic table at Larsiallas, make one want to split oneself between the bottom and the top of the village. Especially since this great man, modest as he is, is wise enough not to sell his talents at unreasonable prices in the heart of Auvergne.

Both the village house with its cozy rooms in a closed formation, and the one up above with its bright, designer rooms and panoramic bay windows giving the mountain a large role as backdrop, play on the region's natural resources: stone, shale, basalt, and wood. We are on a windy plateau; during the summer nights, the cool air is guaranteed. Spring makes nature bounce back mischievously. If the cuisine of Jacques and Régis Marcon is natural, it is because the land around them still is too.

Meneau

The Zealot

A CONCISE PORTRAIT OF AN INSPIRED
AND INDOMITABLE CHEF.

High-level French gastronomy has no lack of disturbed and disturbing restaurants. There are the trail-inspired, the mountain-pasture-crazy, and the herb-friendly, such as Michel Bras, Régis Marcon, Jean-Paul Jeunet, or Marc Veyrat. Then there are the crazy guys of Brittany, such as Olivier Roellinger, capable of looking for seaweed and shellfish growing on the water poles of the bay to renew his region's palette. There was also Bernard Loiseau, the prophet of cooking with water, and Alain Ducasse of three-starred multi-menus.

Insane or innovative, they cannot leave their creative impulses alone. The craziest of the lot? Without a doubt, Marc Meneau, prophet, herald below the hill of Vézelay, who philosophized with the last hermit and writer of the place, Jules Roy, who now resides alongside illustrious men in the cemetery. Meneau says he is inspired by his neighbor on the hill, the basilica dedicated to Sainte-Madeleine. His grand-bourgeois, baroque style is that of an acrobat of flavors.

Long ago, he labored to dazzle his clientele with breaded sole bones, cinnamon soup, asparagus floating in hazelnut oil, poultry "ambroisie," presented as a foie gras and truffle tart, eggs soft-boiled as if they were tripe, a trilogy of lamb (which he now calls a "piece of art") with zested lemon and foie gras fritters, from which the warm filling flowed out after the explosion of this breaded "candy" in the mouth. Meneau was self-taught and trained at the Strasbourg school of hotel management, while his mother ran the café-grocery in Saint-Père. He built his vision alone, and his kingdom with the help of his wife Françoise (née Plaisir), who is one of the few hostesses of a grand restaurant to ask: "Would you like some more?"

Meneau's imagination never sleeps, nor does his heart rest. This passionate man, who was the disciple of André Guillot, the retired master of the Vieux Marly, and who read Menon's recipes of domestic and princely cuisine, can hardly be compared to his contemporaries, except perhaps the late lamented Alain Chapel of Mionnay. Their taste for old styles of finishing dishes is similar. "He is an artist, a grand poet of the kitchen, destined to feed the princes of this world and offer his cooking only to those who love it," observed neighbor Jules Roy in the second tome of his journal (*Les Années Cavalières*, published by Albin Michel, 1998). Roy had also visited and appreciated the charms of his neighbors in Joigny, Saulieu, and Vonnas.

The dishes that Meneau creates can hardly be compared to anything else: toast with bacon; amazing truffle cream with olives, in which the olive intensifies the taste of the truffle without masking it; toast with scallop and bone marrow, seasoned with sea urchin that tastes of iodine; or different preparations of venison—as a cutlet with Armagnac-soaked raisins, as round cuts of fillet on a skewer, or as an expertly prepared sausage.

To complete the picture are desserts to make one swoon (unmolded cream with cherry compote, curdled milk crisp with warm apples, and molten chocolate tart with outrageous vanilla ice cream) and some of the best Burgundies at the moment (Chablis de Raveneau, Vosne Romanée Cros Parentoux). Clearly a meal in his manor, with the glass-walled room facing the garden at the foot of the basilica, is truly an exceptional experience.

Inspired by God? Yes, especially if it's a question of making one sin without having a guilty conscience. After a feast here, one can make penitence by revisiting the Vézelay cemetery and paying tribute to the famous hosts buried there: Yse, the heroine of Claudel's *Partage de Midi*, Georges Bataille, Maurice Clavel, Max-Pol Fouchet, Jules Roy, of course, already invoked here, and the Zervos family, whose home in the village was transformed into a museum. This is a place where not only the spirit is alive, but where the palate stays alert.

Marc Meneau is indestructible, like the phoenix. He was thought to be ridden with debts, buried even, since he was overlooked by the *Michelin Guide* for a year. He was even more spectacularly reborn. He sold the golf course of Aillant-sur-Tholon, which weighed heavily on his overheads, and focused on his holdings in the beautiful village of Saint-Père, at the foot of the hill at Vézelay, where one finds his restaurant, the delightfully named Espérance (meaning hope), his Moulin des Marguerites, and his bistro Entre les Vignes.

His poetic, baroque, grand-bourgeois, but also light and streamlined cuisine has never been so good, so right, and so full of life. Partly self-taught and a collector of books of magic spells, and imitator of Édouard Nignon (one of the most famous French chefs of the twentieth century), he endlessly recreates the taste of his time from ingredients and flavors of a past era.

His pig's head in a breaded roulade is a marvel of the rustic-refined type, his lobster with arugula jus is a miracle of freshness, and his lamb shoulder with peppered watercress an object lesson. He is a lover of vegetables and salads, and makes us rediscover them with renewed vigor. And he is also a slightly anarchic ecologist, a fan of iodine, and is as comfortable making jellied oysters with Camembert cream as he is making lukewarm oysters with a shallot broth.

Moreover, there are eggs Florentine (with spinach and Parmesan in a paper-thin dough) that are a modern homage to Escoffier, the (ever so light) raw, marinated, and grilled porcini mushroom tart, and the langoustines with radishes and turnips cooked in a Dutch oven. The fabulous Miéral Bresse chicken, called "La Campine," is stuffed with herbs, roasted in paper, and served with "beaten" potatoes. These are all odes to grand classicism, but rejuvenated, lightened, and modernized.

Lukewarm artichokes with soft roe and crayfish, like the marvelously delectable desserts, make one want to take up residence here. There are the Marie-Antoinette strawberries, a sundae with mousse, fruit and hibiscus flower granita, created for Sofia Coppola on the occasion of her movie *Marie Antoinette*, as well as a crispy vanilla mille-feuille, buttered apple tart, or apple tartar with praline.

Spending a weekend at the foot of the inspiring hill, not far from Saint-Léger-Vauban, is like a respite in the life of a modern gourmet, a tranquil space in time, free of modern distractions. An air of spirituality permeates the property.

Service is organized by the lovely Françoise, the best Burgundies are skillfully suggested by a sommelier at the top of his game, and rooms are smart, cozy, and tastefully done. These are the offerings at Meneau's L'Espérance. What a joy to be able to treat oneself in this extraordinary establishment!

L'Espérance

89450 Saint-Père-Sous-Vézelay

Tel: +33 (0)3 86 33 39 10

www.marc-meneau-esperance.com

For recipes, see pages 202–203

Whether holding a flower between his lips or walking on his grounds, Marc Meneau is a poet-cook in search of the absolute. Lobster with arugula jus (page 104), veal rumpsteak (facing page, top left), or Marie-Antoinette strawberries (top right) are splendors.

The New
Mère Brazier
Has Arrived

THIS IS THE STORY OF MATHIEU VIANNAY, A BRILLIANT CHEF IN HIS 40S,
WHO HAS REJUVENATED A MONUMENT THAT IS HISTORICAL,
GASTRONOMICAL, AND PURELY LYONNAIS.

He was the young wolf of Lyonnais cooking, Meilleur Ouvrier de France 2004 (Best Craftsman in France), born in Versailles into a family originally from Angers. He became the herald of grand Lyonnais values. His challenge? To make La Mère Brazier one of today's top restaurants again. This dashing, extremely slender cook, with his air of a conquering rock star, looks nothing like a cook from the past.

Trained in Paris by Jean-Pierre Vigato and Henri Faugeron, he has been in Lyon for ten years now. He redid the decor of the saintly Mère Brazier, given three Michelin stars long ago, as well as that of the restaurant at Col de la Luère (see boxed text), with the help of his friend Vavro, a designer. He removed the 1950s wood paneling, recovered the original ceramic from 1923, showed off the wood flooring and stained-glass windows, dusted off the bar that was used to feed the chauffeurs back in the day, and redecorated the rooms in a cozy style, with lightness and cheerfulness. The place is unmistakably chic. The kitchen, entirely redone, is visible from the big hallway.

One passes the kitchen when going to the restrooms upstairs. Mathieu, as efficient a technician as he is a clever practitioner, has returned to basics with a great rebellious spirit. Herring with potatoes is served with oysters, condiments, Aquitaine caviar, and a light cream of celery leaf. The pâté in a shortcrust dough, as done by Lucien Tendret, encases Bresse poultry, delicate jelly, and foie gras, and is accompanied by black cherry jam. The ultra-classic artichoke hearts with foie gras (which used to be from a can!) are deconstructed, with sliced artichokes, pan-fried foie gras cooled down with balsamic vinegar, and foie gras terrine placed on a whole artichoke heart.

There is also roasted lobster with oysters and apple puree; sole in brown butter with young leeks, shellfish sauce, and scallions; and roasted pigeon with confit legs, offal toast, and barberry juice. Or the "Bresse chicken in half mourning" (made with so many truffles inserted under the skin that it appears to be wearing black) for two or four people, served with lobster as a nod to the traditional Dauphinoise dish of chicken with crayfish.

The desserts do not escape Mathieu the magician. Paris-Brest with caramelized hazelnut ice cream, delicate chicory tart with arabica coffee ice cream, or a legendary Chabraninof (apples flambéed in Calvados with salted butter caramel and vanilla ice cream) speak of gold. The wine list is gorgeous, and the public always delighted.

In Lyon, it is neither a revolt, nor a revolution, but rather a happy reunion.

We have certainly not forgotten that Eugénie Brazier, known as "La Mère Brazier" (Mother Brazier), who was born in Bourg-en-Bresse in 1895 and died at Mas-Rillier in 1977, was the first woman to receive three Michelin stars in two places, on Rue Royale in Lyon and at Col de la Luère in Pollionnay. The daughter of Bresse peasants, she did her apprenticeship at La Mère Filloux in Lyon, where she learned the art of simple cooking with high-quality ingredients. She set up modestly on her own in 1921, offering langoustines with mayonnaise, as well as pigeon with green peas and flambéed apples. When her doctor advised her to get some fresh mountain air, she decided to cook in an open-air café at 2,230 feet and 12 miles from Lyon, where she would become renowned. Her son Gaston, trained by her, took over for her in town. The café became a beautiful wooden

establishment attracting gourmets from around the world. Numerous chefs, from Paul Bocuse to Bernard Pacaud, learned the trade there. She may have lost her stars at Col de la Luère in 1961, but Eugénie gained one back in 1962, then all three straightaway—a rare phenomenon—in 1963. Her classic menu, which was then followed through by her granddaughter, Jacotte, had artichoke hearts with foie gras, quenelle of pike in a gratin, chicken in half mourning, Saint-Marcellin with a salad, and finally, the Chabraninof, whose tradition is still carried on today. The mayor of Lyon, Édouard Herriot, had a well-known saying about Eugénie: "She has done more for the good reputation of this city than I have." One day, when Herriot was ordering his usual from the menu, his secretary reminded him that he had to be careful about his diet. "Get rid of the salad then!" he cried.

This is the porcelain, art-deco world of historic restaurants: La Mère Brazier has now been taken over by the young Mathieu Viannay. This dynamic star has breathed new life into the famous apple Chabraninof (page 108). Bresse chicken in "halfmourning" is offered as a nod to the past (above right). The chef's hand adds a touch of emulsion to the plate before it goes out to the dining room.

La Mère Brazier

12, rue Royale

69001 Lyon

Tel: +33 (0)4 78 23 17 20

www.lamerebrazier.fr

For recipes, see page 204

The Alléno
Magic

HE IS THE NEW PARISIAN ROBUCHON, WITH THE SAME SMALL-TOWN ORIGINS,
THE SAME TECHNICAL RIGOR, AND THE SAME DISCRETION,
TREADING THE SAME PATH.

Yannick Alléno has created an event, or rather a succession of events. He has been revolutionizing Parisian gastronomy ever since taking occupation of the extremely chic ground floor of the Meurice. Born to parents from the Lozère, this suburbanite, who was a Silver Bocuse winner while working as Louis Grondard's sous-chef at Drouant, after having worked at the Royal Monceau Garden, and before that at the Scribe, is now "exploding" under the arches and columns of Rue de Rivoli.

In this fancy setting, he seems to have found the perfect style of great contemporary cuisine with traditional roots. He uses tableside service, precise and visual preparations, shows off the dining room, and makes the ingredient the star. As the head of a brigade of seventy cooks, the great Yannick creates, invents, recreates, tests himself, and mixes pleasures, but always lands on his feet. In the sumptuous classical dining room that evokes a room in the Château of Versailles, albeit on a smaller scale, the luxury hotel cuisine suits the time period. Alléno's rapid ascension is reminiscent of Robuchon's, long ago, when he worked his way up from L'Étoile d'Or at the Concorde-Lafayette Hotel to the Célébrités at the Nikko Hotel and, finally, to Jamin.

This alumnus of the Martinez, the Lutétia, the Royal Monceau, and the Sofitel Sèvres, knew how to best use his training in luxury hotels and conjure with the new flavors of our time. He pays meticulous attention to cooking methods and times, changes the menu at breakneck speed, and matches it to the season. Some of his convincing successes? Abalone with salted butter and bean stew, or shelled crab claw with avocado and caviar Bavarian cream. There is also the very classical-seeming, but almost light Bresse chicken in cream sauce braised with a cake of fresh chicken liver; it is lively, precise, simple, and visually appealing.

Each preparation seems to awaken the taste buds. The marinated and barely seared tuna belly with eggplant puree is to die for. And one could say the same of the herb-braised fillet of sea bass with a sweet pepper fondue and sardine cream, of the exceptional plate of sole with shelled cockles and baked new potatoes with lemon thyme, of the delicious veal sweetbreads with Jura vin jaune served with salsify, lard, and truffle sauce.

In his artful reinterpretations of classical themes, Alléno seems to improvise and show new things to see, taste, and smell, the same way Coltrane would replay Gershwin but create his own touchstones. His menu is evolving constantly, but then artists must be able to express themselves, and this one is in his creative phase. Everything will probably have changed by the time you arrive here. Will there be celtuce (a type of root, cousin of asparagus hearts, cultivated just for him) with caviar, smoked salmon and scallop coulibiac, Souvarov hen with celery and horseradish ravioli, or suckling lamb fillet and ribs on a skewer?

Desserts likewise reach perfection. Warm pineapple and coconut cream tart, mille-feuille to order "as you like it" (vanilla, chocolate, or coffee), transparent red berry ravioli, or a cube of chocolate enlivened with mint and confit sour cherries, are all irresistible. The selection of wines in the cellar, under the direction of the vivacious Estelle Touzet, who always has the right accompaniment for each dish, remains one of most spectacular in the capital.

We almost forgot to mention that Yannick Alléno, henceforth king of Paris, celebrates the *terroir* of Paris or Île-de-France at lunch every day. With his dexterous and grand bourgeois manner, asparagus from Argenteuil, watercress from Méréville, cabbage from Pontoise, dandelion from Montmagny, saffron from the Gâtinais, chicken from Houdan, and mint from Milly find new reasons for being. Respectful of tradition, Alléno revisits recipes in a light, honest, and flavorful manner. His versions of white wine mackerel, egg and mayonnaise, onion soup, or "Père Lathuille" chicken, while all sublime, are also extremely different from bistro fare.

The other day, his *"coque en pâte au vin"* served cold, was possibly the most delicious pâté in a crust ever, prepared using the famous recipe by Lucien Tendret, with red wine jelly, foie gras, chicken, and rooster (the pastry shell being cooked separately is and remains totally crisp). The braised sole Île-de-France, like a fish royale, finely blended with lobster juice, spinach pillows, ham, and beurre blanc sauce, called to mind the most delicate quenelle. Clamart veal, cooked until pink in the center, with peas and artichokes, was as tender and juicy as could be imagined. Add to that the regional cheeses (Gris de Lille, Seine Marne goat cheese) from Marie Quatrehomme, or the macaroons polished with apple fondue, served with a milk jam ice cream made with milk from the Viltain farm, which all brought their sweet, delightfully feminine, and creamy touch to this otherwise virile and sharp meal.

Overall, we have a Parisian cook who knows how to tantalize the taste buds of the greats of this world in Courchevel (the Cheval Blanc) or in Marrakech (the Royal Mansour), but who is really himself at the Meurice, *the* Parisian luxury hotel.

Le Meurice

228, rue de Rivoli

75001 Paris

Tel: +33 (0)1 44 58 10 55

www.lemeurice.com/

For recipes, see pages 204–206

Handsome Yannick Alléno, who reigns over this grand classical decor, will be the guide to your heart's desire (page 112). The dining room is worthy of receiving the curry lobster (page 113), the tarte fine of scallops with caviar, or the cristalline with unctuous coffee-chocolate cream and soft meringue (below). Checking the alignment of the glasses a few moments before the dining room opens (facing page, top left). Beneath the chandeliers and gold of this Versailles-style dining room, everything is double-checked to the finest detail.

Marc Meurin
The North Star

THE GREAT CHEF FROM NORTHERN FRANCE, SELF-TAUGHT AND GIFTED,
CAN BE DISCOVERED IN HIS MODERN CASTLE.
WHEN WILL FASHION DECIDE IT IS TIME TO MAKE AN ICON OUT OF HIM?

He did not train under Troisgros, Bocuse, or Guérard. He hardly knows who Marc Veyrat or Marc Meneau is, nor Alain Ducasse or Guy Savoy. He never did an internship in another chef's kitchen. He saw the light, not with Frédy Girardet in Switzerland, as was the trend in the 1980s, or with Alain Chapel, who was the wise man of the Rhône-Alpes region but, more recently, in New York, with Daniel Boulud and Jean-Georges Vongerichten.

Almost entirely self-taught, he did pass through the Lille school of hotel management. He set up shop, first close to Armentières, then on the Grand Place de Béthune, in an old notary's house. He is finally at home, sumptuously set up in a brick castle with a modern wing, contemporary bedrooms, veranda-style dining rooms, cozy nineteenth-century sitting rooms with chimneys and stucco, and a hip bistro (Le Jardin d'Alice) sought out by the whole Nord-Pas-de-Calais region, who make reservations there three weeks in advance.

Still Meurin doesn't blow his own trumpet. He smiles at everyone, and not just the media. Clearly this Marc Meurin is a special case. He's a funny character for such a star, with his modest appearance, naive look, the air that suggests he might be both stubborn and clever. More than anything else, this regular guy from northern France has managed to mark out his territory in a relatively unknown area. A native of Lens, without résumé or label, he is like an alien in the small world of haute cuisine. Who can he be compared to, if not himself?

Marc Meurin works the vegetables of the Hortillonages (the floating gardens of Amiens) and the swamps: sweet onion, beet, and capers (his sablé with these last two ingredients is part of an anthology), and the fish of the Channel or of the North Sea. He does not disregard emulsions. He has visited the great chefs of Spain, paired up with his New York counterparts, occasionally dabbles with hydrogen and molecular cuisine, but stays true to his own style: that of a Ch'ti—a Picardian—who can start with Gillardeau oysters in a leek jelly, and finish, as if at a Flemish county fair, with berlingot candies, marshmallow, speculoos ice cream, and a ton of caramel.

His foie-gras mousse with port and asparagus cream is a masterpiece. His truffle three ways, including an irresistible croque-monsieur, is a treasure.

But his Boulonnais scallops with mushroom jam and porcini dust, his asparagus in Comté aspic with Jura vin jaune and baby morels are no less extraordinary. This modest technician, who thinks carefully about his profession, knows how to surround himself with the right people. The vast kitchen with numerous cooks, guys wearing caps in the bistro, and passionate staff, as well as dynamic service with expert sommeliers, are all impressive.

Meurin remains unfazed. This self-made man talks about the cuisine of his time in his own lively way. Coastal turbot with asparagus and burnt onion cream, and lamb shank with Flemish goat and squab, with confit tomatoes and zucchini aïoli served

One falls back into childhood at the sight of the Pierrot Gourmand trolley with marshmallows and coconut balls, but is completely floored by the lima bean granita balls and milk-fed veal with seasonal vegetables (facing page, top right). Page 116: Crisp of monkfish.

with a crispy cigarette of ratte potato with Merlot salt, are clean and precise in tone, pure in spirit, and grounded.

His desserts are all mouth-watering: rhubarb bouquet, orange caramel puff pastry, and Bordier's thick cream have a play of acidic and sweet, and a plethora of contrasts. The wine list, representing all vineyards, from the well-known Médoc to lesser known Cabardès, is one of the most thorough in France. His series of menus, straightforwardly called "Market," "Curiosity," "Discovery," or "Prestige," are demonstrations of good sense. In this self-assured Ch'ti, regionalism is like second nature.

The fish of the North Sea meet short cooking times and spicy sauces. The rich accompaniments of vegetables from Artois and Picardy are hymns to the clean air here. The *amuse-bouches* tasters, including onion and smoked bacon puff pastry, waffle with herring cream, sea bass tartare with marjoram, Maroilles cheese puffs, cauliflower cream with shrimp, and tellin shellfish cassolettes, all sing of reconciliation between the North and the South.

Other examples of his classics include pheasant mousse with foie gras, fruit chutney, and quince confit; frog in pastry with Locon smoked garlic (a cousin of Arleux garlic), parsley juice consommé, fresh white beans, and mustard greens; sole cooked firmly in segments with delicate oyster hash; or coastal turbot with a pig's trotter chip, garlic nougat, and braised endives. Add to that the Bresse chicken with Jura vin jaune, and a galette of breaded Jerusalem artichokes and mushrooms.

As for the desserts, they are better than perfect: licorice entremets, brown sugar crème brûlée, iced parfait of chicory and Persyn family Houlle gin, mango cannelloni, and coconut ice cream. It becomes clear that northern France holds its own, just before L'Huîtrière in Lille, which is the region's Taillevent, with its restrained, modest, charming, and creative offerings, and its great chef who is both innovative and grounded, as well as incredibly serene.

The British definitely get it; just out of the Channel Tunnel, they are here to peacefully "invade" his restaurant. Much like the Belgians who, as rightful neighbors, often occupy the seven bedrooms. While small, the rooms are well appointed and perfect for a night's stay. It's about time to discover Marc Meurin, the mischievous wizard of the North.

Le Château de Beaulieu

Rue de Lillers

62350 Busnes

Tel: +33 (0)3 21 68 88 88

www.lechateaudebeaulieu.fr

For recipes, see pages 206–207

Bernard Pacaud
The Art of Precision on the Place des Vosges

Unrivaled, in the very heart of Paris,
is perhaps the city's best classical French cook.

He is the most discreet of our great chefs, and the least prone to effusiveness. He is the least open to the media, even if a television movie by Frédéric Laffont for Arte introduced this unusual character to the general audience. A Rennes native, orphaned at an early age, Pacaud was raised by his grandparents. He was placed at La Mère Brazier at Col de la Luère, close to Lyon, at the age of fifteen, where he was instilled with a strong work ethic, a taste for quality ingredients, and the art of doing things both simply and skillfully. He was then an apprentice at Tante Alice before going to Paris, becoming a line cook at La Méditerranée, and then sous-chef at La Coquille on Rue du Débarcadère.

He had his revelation about creativity and technical finesse at Claude Peyrot's restaurant in Vivarois. Peyrot, a chronic worrier, psychoanalyzed by Jacques Lacan and confessing to Marc Oraison, made him rediscover, among other things, "the gift of sharing." The fresh truffle puff pastry, bell pepper Bavarian cream, duck and foie gras tart: these are some of the marvelous "reinvented classics" ("but does one really invent a dish?" he asks himself) that he learned with Peyrot, the mad genius, poet, and inspirer.

In 1981, when Bernard and his wife Danièle finally set up shop on the corner of Rue de Bièvre on the banks of the Seine in Paris, they had François Mitterrand for a neighbor. Mitterand graced the Pacaud's small, discreet, even austere restaurant with his presence. The *Michelin Guide* quickly became aware of this artisan chef who was content with tending to twenty covers, no more, with exceptional ingredients and precise preparations, and gave him two stars. On the Place des Vosges since 1986, Bernard now sees the high society that refused to visit him in the fifth arrondissement.

The magnificent neo-eighteenth-century setting by decorator François-Joseph Graf, who resuscitated the ambience of this aristocratic dining room, is a crowd-pleaser. If Bernard's discretion and taciturn side were proverbial, the gift of the gab of his smiling and affable Corsican wife, Danièle, were equally famous, as was sommelier Pierre Le Moullac's mischievous scientific gift of pairing wines with the anthological dishes that came out of Bernard's kitchen. The third star came quickly in 1988, and the restaurant was unanimously liked.

What does one come here for? Classic fare lightened to the point of perfection. This is what characterizes langoustines in sesame puff pastry, truffled foie-gras aspic with a celery apple remoulade, lightly breaded soft-boiled egg with watercress, seared sea bass served with miraculous asparagus from Robert Blanc in the Luberon, fresh truffle puff pastry, and oxtail in caul fat with red wine: so many object lessons in the art of doing just what is needed without overdoing it.

In his tiny, narrow, drawer-filled laboratory, both labyrinthine and functional, he is backed by a motivated, carefully selected team. Bernard Pacaud tells the story of his seasonal and market-fresh cuisine as if he were working out his own concept of the world.

There is no showing off, no foams or emulsions, nothing but the real flavor. Truffle coulis, mushroom mince, and a coral or Genevoise sauce will season whatever indisputably fresh ingredient is at hand, trimmed to its best form and rendered as purely as possible. Let us dare to state the facts: one will not like L'Ambroisie if one does not like cooking to begin with. The decor—with tapestries, moldings, and comfortable chairs that all revive the ambience of a bourgeois dining room from another time—is important. Just as important is the service, under the direction of Pascal Vetaux, who follows the rules of etiquette of a bygone era.

The house's legendary sommelier, Pierre Le Moullac, has retired. He was replaced by Christophe Sponga, who has been there for more than twenty years. But when it comes time, during a meal, for Paris's most passionate clientele to taste a wine, Pierre's subtle politeness, affable discretion, and understated humor while presenting a Côte-Rôtie, a Cornas, a Nuits-Saint-Georges, perhaps a Tuscan Caberlot or a high-class Médoc, will be long remembered. The pairing of food and wine has always been a perfect union here. An example of an exceptional match would be the good lineage whiskey that accompanies the legendary dark chocolate tart with Bourbon vanilla ice cream, or the Venezuelan rum that enhances the caramelized puff pastry served with fromage blanc and lemon confit.

It is clear that this is a joyful place where everything is done with wisdom and care. There are no raised eyebrows at L'Ambroisie, nor unnecessary outbursts, simply multiple murmurs from both sides of the dining room, everyone sharing the same moment of bliss. Here is an establishment touched by grace.

Pages 120–121: In the reinvented seventeenth-century decor, with its chandeliers, medieval tapestries, silverware, and purple velvet chairs, one experiences the history of the Place des Vosges, while enjoying the legendary chocolate tart.
Facing page: Tuna pastilla with apricots (top left) and braised medallions of veal sweetbreads (bottom right) are a few examples of the lightened classical style pushed to perfection by Bernard Pacaud.

L'Ambroisie

9, place des Vosges

75004 Paris

Tel: +33 (0)1 42 78 51 45

www.ambroisie-placedesvosges.com

For recipes, see pages 207–208

Alain Passard
The Artist

THE FORMER MAD DOG OF PARISIAN CUISINE
HAS BECOME A REFERENCE AND AUTHORITY ON COOKING.

He is the most peculiar of our great chefs, the most technical, the best communicator of ideas, a new-style teacher, an apostle of rigor, a maestro of ingredients, and master of the plate. This, of course, is Alain Passard, who maintains seemingly eternal youth as a wire-thin, parachuting champion, a slightly Gavroche-style mischievous fellow, a bit of a "lord of the manor" type from the Sarthes, and a solitary artist.

This native of La Guerche-de-Bretagne (in the Ille-et-Vilaine department of Brittany), who was trained by Michel Kéréver at the Lion d'Or in Liffré, Gérard Boyer in Reims, and Alain Senderens at the Archestrate—which means right here at 84 Rue de la Varenne, across from the Rodin Museum, and now redone with an austere sort of elegance—has quietly passed the fifty-year mark. He doesn't care about trends and he hardly ever travels. While he used to have two Michelin stars at the Carlton in Brussels, he refuses to set foot anywhere else anymore, or to create annexes or even publish cookbooks.

This virtuoso of beautiful ingredients is a gardener on Sundays at his home in the Sarthe, not far from the bay of Mont-Saint-Michel, but also the Stradivarius of Chausey lobster (sliced thinly, brushed with honey, paired with turnip), the Paganini of celeriac (with Orléans mustard), and the Picasso of boar (the juicy rib is a moment of pure delight). In short, like a graceful soccer player, he feints, evades, tricks, shoots, and scores with artistic passion, and is a kind of consecrated expert of all exceptional ingredients.

Not simply content with signing his dishes like others sign their paintings, this true creator has invented a thousand dishes that are imitated by his peers. Thus, the chocolate mille-feuille, to which the Troisgros paid tribute in their first cookbook, or the "bouquet of roses" tart, on which copyright has been registered and in which each piece of fruit, resting on delicate puff pastry, has the shape of a flower, resulting in something soft and crunchy at the same time. Or the caviar-marinated langoustines, one of the most copied appetizers in the world, including by three-starred restaurants in Belgium and Germany (it has been spotted at Restaurant Bruneau in Brussels and at the Sonnora Hotel in Wittlich), and the confit tomato with twelve flavors. All him and nobody else!

Alain, meticulous as he is, carefully labels the origin of all the marvels he uses, like a painter with his palette. There are so many carefully composed masterpieces, quietly offered to the curious gourmet, like finely sliced Léon abalone with lemon, "simple" potatoes in their jackets, smoked with oat straw and served with a horseradish mousseline, "Crimean Black" tomato gazpacho, "Seville" mauve runner beans with purple basil, and whole John Dory cooked at low temperature, still pink at the bone. In particular, there is the "vegetable collection," which is his trademark, his uniqueness, and his signature. He offers vegetables from his own soil, including his "Monarch" celeriac carpaccio with hyssop and hazelnuts; delicate garden raviolini in a bouillon of spicy tomato water; hummus made from mojhette beans of Pont-l'Abbé with chervil pesto; "celerisotto" with sorrel; yellow "Gold Ball" turnip with tangerine and almonds (a fabulous dessert!); and small caviar tomatoes (an absolute rarity). Each one is worthy of royalty.

Transformed into a paragon of natural cuisine, Alain Passard became our Rabindranath Tagore, our Sri Aurobindo, our watchman of virtues. In his minuscule laboratory, as in his subdued and slightly austere dining room lit by Lalique-encrusted pear-wood panels, he is assuredly the least boastful of the great chefs of his time. His thing? Pure ingredients. His trademark? Freshness. A handful of vegetables from his "ephemeral crop" (fava beans combined with pea pods and fresh almonds) draws tears of emotion from the overjoyed diner.

Before those more recent creations, there was the soft-boiled egg with allspice, sweet onion gratin with Parmigiano Reggiano, yellow zucchini soup with Black Forest ham, and a delicate soufflé cream. Thin slices of sole with Savagnin wine are already considered a classic. Hibiscus-lacquered Challandais duck with turnips, onions, and leeks from the garden, resembles the free-range chicken, both being juicy, and firm yet tender.

This artist who puts together spring and winter collections trusts no one but locals from Mayenne for his vegetables, from Finistère, Côtes-d'Armor, Ille-et-Vilaine, or Manche for crustaceans, fish, and shellfish, and goes to the Vienne department in the Poitou-Charentes region for his free-range poultry, the same way he demands of brother Marie-Pâques, the cellar-keeper of the Saint-Honorat Abbey in the Lérins Islands, his best red and white vintages. In this way he is an Yves Saint Laurent of flavor.

We should also mention Bernard Antony's cheese plate, which offers the essentials with some seasonal variety, centered around two huge pieces, such as crumbly Salers or marvelous vintage Comté. And the nimble service and the loquacious but not pedantic staff, presenting this instructive cuisine and its lovely explanations given by Hélène Cousin, the sweet front-of-house manager.

L'Arpège, which goes above and beyond, with commensurate prices, is the exception to all the rules. The decor, with its paneling and opalescent crystal details, tables devoid of embellishments, and simply comfortable chairs, is an example of restrained, even slightly austere elegance. It is an ideal environment, where friendly diners give the impression of belonging to an enthusiastic fan club.

Alain does the rounds of the dining room beneath the watchful eye of his grandmother Louise, who was the cook in a bourgeois restaurant in Rennes and whose framed portrait sits in front of the entrance to the kitchens. And he still has the same mischievous smile he had as a rebellious child. An outstanding pastry chef as well (his mille-feuille with "seasonal colors" is still a masterpiece of the genre), he is the lone crafter of his own glory, and could be considered the Vatel of our most discreet celebrations. The god of gourmets, who seems to have gifted Alain with eternal youth, may transform him into an immortal wizard yet.

L'Arpège

84, rue de Varenne

75007 Paris

Tel: +33 (0)1 45 51 47 33

www.alain-passard.com

For recipes, see page 208

Impishly, the chef sticks his head out of the kitchen to peek into the dining room. His apple mille-feuille and its chocolate version have been copied worldwide (pages 124–125). The vegetables used in the ravioles consommé or in the "harlequin jardinière" (vegetable plate) were picked that morning in Alain Passard's vegetable garden in Mans, and arrived by high-speed train to be served in this understated dining room, decorated with Lalique-encrusted pear-wood panels.

Passédat
The King of Marseille

THE BEST MODERN BOUILLABAISSE CAN BE FOUND IN A TRANQUIL
SETTING IN THE RESTAURANT OF THE DIVINE PASSÉDAT.

His name is Gérald Passédat, and he has reigned over Marseille's gastronomic scene for two decades. He turned his back on the Old Port, made Maldormé's cove his kingdom, the Kennedy Boulevard his border, and the mountain ledge his paradise. He surveys his city and country from this vantage point. Passédat is a solitary man, who skillfully plays at seduction. He transformed the Greco-Italian eponymous restaurant of Mamy Louise, singer and courtesan, into an ultramodern hotel. He made it into a delightful solitary retreat, dedicated to contemporary Mediterranean cuisine, to Marseille, and to all lovers of Provence and of the sea.

Trained under Troisgros and Guérard, then at the Bristol and the Crillon hotels in Paris, Gérald took over his father's kitchen without renouncing his legacy. The bass fillet and "bouille-abaisse" with Oriental spices were already dishes fit for kings in their day. But he has raised the bar and continues to build on these foundations. He is one of the most recent three-star restaurants in the *Michelin Guide*. He deserves this top ranking, has the approval of his peers, and is enthusiastically applauded by a public dazzled by his work with seafood.

In the former residence of his grandmother (the opera singer), now tastefully updated, with a Zen-like, panoramic,

and sky-blue setting, Passédat wines and dines his clientele with divine dishes that are as modern and trendy as they are rooted in tradition. Vegetable mousses (pumpkin with mango vinegar, parsley and bottarga, apple and celery), delicate purees accompanying an oyster (cauliflower, zucchini, purple carrot), a succession of mini puff pastries (layered Swiss chard and Parmesan, brandade with mushroom juice, savory sablé with onion and Jabugo ham), totenes (tiny crabs) with parsley, and crawfish with laurel, may tend toward gimmickry.

But when he tends toward the more pure, concrete, and traditional, and "finds his roots" so to speak, the magnificent Gérald touches the sublime. Denti fish with shellfish sauce, sole with leeks, "beautiful-eyed" sea bream with a smoky flavor, or young turbot with fennel; all deliver the true taste of the sea with majesty and a real sense of diversity.

His masterpiece? The three-dimensional bouillabaisse, offered in a layered menu, touches the heart of Marseille lovers: plain shellfish with rainbow wrasse fish both fried and in its juices, presented in a paper cone; fish and shellfish (sting fish, gurnard marine fish, John Dory, lobster) in a marvelous saffron broth; and gurnard and red porgy with a spicy soup. But there is also another famous, classic dish of his, the sea bass as Lucie

Passédat liked it, a lovely and eternal tribute to his grandmother who founded the restaurant.

Desserts focus on fruit, freshness, and lightness, and are full of depth (like the green apple with its pulp and beautiful, cloud-like pink pralines). When it comes to the wines of Provence (Bandol Blanc Sainte-Anne, Coteaux d'Aix Hauvette), they act as grand escorts to a cuisine rich in iodine. This is an important Marseille restaurant that makes its public rediscover the beauty of the city itself with fresh eyes.

Le Petit Nice

Anse de Maldormé

Corniche J. F. Kennedy

13007 Marseille

Tel: +33 (0)4 91 59 25 92

www.passedat.fr

For recipes, see pages 209–210

Pages 128–129: Gérald Passédat catches the last rays of sunlight and offers up a taste of the famous sea bass, as Lucie Passédat liked it, in homage to his grandmother.
Facing page, top, left to right: the Mediterranean langouste with bay leaf souplesse, pear, and cucumber and the "immaculately white vacherin" are like a breath of fresh air after a summer day. The cheeses of Provence and elsewhere are carefully lined up on the tray. Overlooking the inlets of Marseille, Le Petit Nice has a totally unique and gorgeous view, such as this one from the dining room at sunset.

Pic
The Next Generation

A HISTORIC HOME ON THE ROAD TO THE FRENCH MIDI,
CLOSE TO THE RHÔNE, HAS BEEN COMPLETELY
RENOVATED BY ITS DYNAMIC HEIRESS.

The story began in 1889, on the other side of the Rhône in Ardèche, when Sophie Pic, the current owner's great-grandmother, opened her Auberge du Pin on a sinuous mountain road right above the Saint-Péray vineyards. The country restaurant quickly became popular with gourmets who came to taste the gratins, blood sausages, sautéed rabbit, and chicken fricassee, all simple and hearty fare.

Her son, André, who learned the trade in Lyon and Paris, took over the inn's kitchen in 1924. He cooked much like his mother, whom he used to watch for hours, but followed the principles of Auguste Escoffier. He became renowned for his lobster with cream, spit-roasted hare, Duzon crayfish, bladder-cooked chicken, and Richelieu blood sausage. He obtained his third Michelin star in 1934, after which he crossed the Rhône in 1936, and set up shop on the mythical Nationale 7 road in Valence. His son Jacques kept the restaurant going.

Jacques was trained in classic restaurants of the 1950s, including La Réserve de Beaulieu, the Buffet Cornavin in the Geneva train station, Dorin in Paris, and then Mahu in Villerville, Normandy. When he returned home in 1956, he made a serious effort to follow in his father's footsteps. The style he intended to carry on had Escoffier as foundation, but in lighter versions, with high-quality ingredients and attention to detail. He created a "Rabelais" menu that was of course rich, but surprisingly light,

and which gave pride of place to the luxury ingredients of French cuisine. Under his guidance, the family restaurant proved its role as ambassador of French haute cuisine for curious gourmet tourists who came to learn, taste, and be surprised. To the crayfish gratin, truffle turnover, and bladder-cooked fatted chicken, he added sea bass with caviar, duck liver with Hermitage grapes, and rock lobster with olive oil and truffles.

Maison Pic, which lost its three stars after the war, got its second star back in 1960 and the third one back in 1973. Jacques passed away in 1992. His son, Alain, who was his sous-chef until then, filled the gap. But the restaurant lost its third star in 1995. It was then Anne-Sophie's turn to step up to the stoves. Her talent was completely unforeseen; she surprises, seduces, lightens, and innovates. She blends fruit from the Rhône Valley with ingredients of grand tradition; innovates with startling combinations; and applies sweet touches where they are least expected. Red berries accompany lobster, a stalk of rhubarb lends acidity to Drôme pigeon, and tuna is paired with foie gras. Why not?

But Anne-Sophie's skill is to weave her web by modernizing and enriching traditions without abandoning them. To wit, her menu says "Pic Generations," in which she picks up the old thread and creates blue lobster with various tomatoes (Black Crimean, striped Green Zebra, yellow Saint-Vincent), her grandfather and great-grandmother Sophie's admirable crayfish gratin with truffles, line-caught sea bass, steamed and served with Aquitaine caviar with a light sauce, beef and foie-gras mille-feuille with leek and nutmeg cream, or the timeless warm Grand Marnier soufflé served with an iced Grand Marnier soufflé; these are all dishes to marvel at.

Anne-Sophie trained in management at the Institut Supérieur de Gestion d'Île-de-France, one of Europe's leading business schools, and there met her husband and fellow native of Valence, David Sinapian. Having traveled to the US and Japan, fragile-looking Anne-Sophie proved herself to be a remarkable leader. She created a modern bistro, dedicated to Nationale 7, with classic, creative dishes put together by her disciple, Stéphane Rossillon. She also updated the old hotel that used to have only four bedrooms, which became, under her and David's direction, first a charming Provençal rest stop, then a stylish contemporary luxury hotel.

Students of Philippe Starck favor luxurious materials and soft or neutral tones, which is exactly what designer Bruno Borrione used in the modern and calming rooms, creating a contemporary hideaway with white vaulted ceilings and colorful, high-tech furniture. The dining room is somber, yet chic. The staff is in sync. The exceptional sommelier, Denis Bertrand, looks after the best wines from the Rhône Valley, Saint-Péray, and Châtillon-en-Diois, without forgetting of course Hermitage, Côte-Rôtie, and Saint-Joseph, all with the best names. The Pics

actually have their own vineyard in Saint-Péray, which they co-manage with their winemaker pal Michel Chapoutier.

A cooking school, named Scook, is the final part of their domain. All of this doesn't prevent Anne-Sophie, now the mother of little Nathan, from creating new dishes. Hermit crab with a creamy texture enhanced by lime, large langoustines both as tartare and plank-roasted with a Korean mint broth, Drôme pigeon with foie gras and rhubarb, veal sweetbreads with sautéed apples, transparent Créances carrot, and lavender fondant are all fine examples of her amazing palette.

Impossible to forget the incredibly gifted Philippe Rigollot and his extraordinary desserts! This Pastry World Champion and Meilleur Ouvrier de France (Best Craftsman in France) conceived compositions during the Bocuse d'Or competition that shocked, disturbed, and seduced. On the theme of "sweet but not too sweet," he created the 2008 Collection: Opera with Blue Mountain coffee cream, wild Mara des Bois strawberries and rosemary. And for fruits paired with grand cru chocolate (with a spicy note), he created raspberry and green aniseed chocolate profiteroles.

All in all, the Pic restaurant will skillfully delight, transport, and charm you. Grandfather André's old establishment has changed considerably; the memory of great-grandmother Sophie endures, and Papa Jacques's dishes are now relics that have been cleverly updated. Never a dull moment! Thanks to Anne-Sophie, Valence remains in the ranks of the great French culinary stops.

Maison Pic

285, avenue Victor Hugo

26000 Valence

Tel: +33 (0)4 75 44 15 32

www.pic-valence.com

For recipes, see pages 210–211

Anne-Sophie Pic is resplendent on page 132. Next to her, the timeless warm Grand Marnier soufflé (page 133). The dining room is bathed in light and upon entering the restaurant, one finds a unique collection of old Michelin Guides. Facing page, top, left to right: Dishes of the day: veal sweetbreads with carrot and lavender, and lobster with red berries.

Above, and on facing page: the restaurant's dining room and breakfast room. Above, right: marbled tuna with foie gras. Below, another dish of memories: on a plate honoring her father, "sea bass fillet with caviar by Jacques Pic."

Le Pré Catelan
The Magic of the Bois de Boulogne

A HISTORIC SETTING, THE GRAND SERVICE OF JEAN-JACQUES CHAUVEAU,
AND THE AESTHETICALLY GORGEOUS CUISINE OF FRÉDÉRIC ANTON ALL
CONTRIBUTE TO THE CHARM OF THIS GREAT COUNTRYSIDE RESTAURANT.

There is the magic of the Bois de Boulogne, its greenery and park dedicated to Théophile Catelan, hunting captain of Louis XIV. The site of country strolls at the end of the eighteenth century, it was ravaged by the Prussians when they set up camp there in 1815, and left to decay for years. It was then renovated by Napoleon III who, as an admirer of English parks, commissioned Baron Haussmann to make it into a landscaped park for the public. Haussmann called upon architect Gabriel Davioud and engineer Jean-Charles Alphand to design alleys, lakes, waterfalls, benches, street lamps, fountains, and chalets.

In 1855–6, Nestor Roqueplan, administrator of the Opéra-Comique and Variety shows, installed a restaurant, an open-air theater called the Theater of Flowers, a glass fountain, and an aquarium. But the story of our modern restaurant only began in 1905. The city of Paris commissioned architect Guillaume Tronchet to build a luxury casino-restaurant inspired by the Folies shows of the eighteenth century. The rotundas were organized following classical symmetry. Pilasters, colonnades, and balusters adorned the white façades; basins and groups of sculpted angels lined the flowered terraces on the upper floor.

Léopold Mourier, owner of Fouquet's, the Cafés de Paris, and the Pavillon d'Armenonville, took it over in 1908 and turned it into one Paris's most popular places. The round hall, decorated with allegorical stucco motifs, looks onto the current main lounge, which runs the length of the whole building. Across

from the large bay windows, gem-studded mirrors reflect the gardens. In the dining room, which houses the current restaurant, Caran d'Ache drew and Badin sculpted the moldings on the ceilings and the bas-reliefs above the doors, including children's games, cherubs, and hunting scenes.

When Mourier passed away in 1923, Charles Drouant, owner of the eponymous restaurant on Place Gaillon, bought all of his establishments, raising the Pré Catelan's food and service to the highest level of Parisian tradition. In 1976, his grand nephew and heir sold it to Gaston Lenôtre, who then took over the concession and made renovations. The original large dining room became a reception hall, with the covered terrace having a capacity of up to a thousand guests. The reception rooms on the upper floor were converted into rooms for private events and business meetings, while the restaurant finally settled into its spot amongst the best Parisian tables.

A lineup of talented chefs went through the kitchen, such as Patrick Lenôtre, Gaston's nephew, and Roland Durand, who received two Michelin stars. Frédéric Anton has brought the restaurant into a new era over the last decade. This native of Épinal in the Vosges, a former student at the hotel management high school of Gérardmer, worked for Gérard Vessière at Capucin Gourmand in Nancy, learned creativity with Robert Bardot at the Flambard in Lille, and grand bourgeois cuisine with Gérard Boyer at Les Crayères in Reims, before becoming the last sous-chef Joël Robuchon had on Avenue Raymond-Poincaré in Paris. "It's very simple: I owe him everything," he says, gratefully, of Robuchon.

At the Pré Catelan, Anton received a second Michelin star in 1999 and a third in 2007. Pierre-Yves Rochon's subdued redesign of the charmingly historic setting, into a contemporary modern one, lends itself well to the grand service orchestrated by the ever-present Jean-Jacques Chauveau, with more than twenty loyal years there. There is also the fabulous cellar and the expertly crafted desserts by Christelle Brua, also a native of Lorraine, from Sarrebourg, who worked most notably at L'Arnsbourg. But it is really the cuisine of Frédéric, Meilleur Ouvrier de France (Best Craftsman in France) in 2000, that takes center stage with its aestheticism, as he knows how to prepare very high-quality ingredients scientifically and conscientiously. His particular skill lies in presenting a recipe in three parts, giving a fish, a vegetable, and a meat the proper setting, spirit, and flavor, somewhere between purity and fastidiousness. Such is the story told by his brilliant and seductive menu, which reads like a poem.

Combining simplicity and refinement, sardines in oil with shards of butter and olive bread, then in a salad with curried fennel, and finally in a bouillabaisse jelly with rouille sauce and its lovely "Robuchonian" dots, all forming a royal portrait, is a masterpiece of contemporary haute cuisine. In a similar vein, there is the pan-fried artichoke with herbs, capers, and acidic juice; chanterelle mushrooms marinated in the Greek manner; and finally purple artichokes stuffed with mushrooms: an amazing dish for a lovely garden vegetable.

Tomato salad with vanilla-flavored olive oil and lime zest, served with mozzarella in jelly or in the Provençal manner, plays a similar tune: fresh, light, and abundant. Beautiful to look at and lovely to eat, his dishes are a treat for the eye as well as the palate. There is also the dish that will henceforth be a classic, bone marrow grilled in a shell with black pepper or stuffed with a ragout of chanterelles and green peas, both of which have stewed in gravy. And there is the complexity of portioned sole, cooked plain, glazed with spiced soy juice, pan-fried with soy beans, and accompanied by a slightly tart mango, shellfish marinière, and salted butter.

This stylish and artistic cuisine is deliberately unnerving, meant to strike every sense, and goes perfectly with the theatrical decor highlighted by the Caran d'Ache frescoes. High praise goes to the lamb cooked *a la plancha* with its lovely offal (brain, sweetbreads, kidney), served with delicate herbed cheese ravioli seasoned with licorice grain mustard. As well as to the grand cheese platter by Bernard Anton, another fellow from eastern France and cheesemonger in Vieux-Ferrette, on the border of Franche-Comté in the south of Alsace, whose delightful, lengthily aged dry cheeses combine well with vintage Bordeaux.

Lastly, a mention for the desserts that are on the rich and dazzling side. Paris-Brest with fig compote, crispy choux pastry and light chicory cream, espresso zabaglione (sabayon), whipped ganache, crème-brûlée ice cream with crushed almonds, and of course the spectacular crisp souffléed apple filled with caramel ice cream, hard cider, and sparkling sugar, which is simply astounding! Parisian in every way, its clientele is as much "family" as it is "show-off." Pré Catelan lends itself to any and all parties; here, the radiance is permanent and the legend is still alive.

Le Pré Catelan

Bois de Boulogne

Route de Suresnes

75016 Paris

Tel: +33 (0)1 44 14 41 14

www.precatelanparis.com

For recipes, see pages 211–212

This is the work of Frédéric Anton, the captain of this elegant vessel, who awaits us behind the copper-studded leather door (page 138). A table looking out onto the Bois de Boulogne, two of the attentive waiting staff, and two stone cherubs in the garden: the stage is set to appreciate the crab prepared in its shell with fennel cream and an aromatic herb jelly (facing page, top right).

Iced and almost translucent soy glazed prawns with avocado seem made for the elegant setting of the Pré Catelan (right).

Guy Savoy
Everyone's Pal

HE IS THE CHEF EVERYONE LOVES, THE COUNTRY BOY WHO MADE PARIS HIS PLAYGROUND,
AND THE RESTAURANT ON RUE TROYON A CLUB FOR LOVERS OF GASTRONOMY.

There is a "Savoy fraternity." This modest man, confident of his artistry, obtained three Michelin stars twenty years later than he should have. It got to the point where everyone was surprised that—as prodigy of the Troisgros sons and friend of Loiseau—he was still in the background. He was discreet, consistent, and better than perfect, all that without the fanfare. He waited patiently for his Legion of Honor medal, receiving it with utter delight.

He has been at the forefront of the culinary scene for the last five years—but always quietly. This little pastry chef from Bourgoin-Jallieu, son of a "Swiss worker," apprenticed at Troisgrois in Roanne, then with Louis Outhier in the time of L'Oasis at La Napoule, before becoming a virtuoso chef himself, working under Claude Verger at La Barrière de Clichy in Paris. He revealed himself to be a solitary artist on Rue Duret, then at the old Bernardin of the Le Coze brothers on Rue Troyon, which Jean-Michel Wilmotte transformed into a contemporary and chic club.

It really is the same Guy Savoy who has been delighting us for more than a quarter of a century with lentil cream with langoustines, foie gras with gray salt, scallops *a la plancha* with a surf-turf sauce and stuffed cabbage, sea bass grilled with sweet spices, duckling roasted the old-fashioned way, or delicate vanilla mille-feuille.

The purity of the ingredients, the tried and tested pairings, and the artfully combined textures (like the thin slices of duck breast and foie gras, firm yet melting, which he created in 1979 on Rue Duret); these are the "tricks" that he mixes with unparalleled technique.

Guy Savoy, who had replicated his talent at several fashionable bistros, reduced his empire by half (he still owns La Butte Chaillot, L'Atelier Maître Albert, Le Chiberta, and Les Bouquinistes, but sold his three Bistrots de l'Étoile, his Version Sud, and his collaboration at Cap Vernet), tightening his grip on his talent to better control the output. These days, we could even imagine aficionados talking among themselves of a fourth star for Rue Troyon.

Textures, flavors, and colors dictate the seasonal pleasures in this great chef's extremely popular restaurant, with its precious wood-paneled dining room and overall modern club setting designed by Wilmotte. Red mullet in consommé in a white truffle jelly, tuna with caviar and walnuts, and grouse with mushrooms are all high-flying dishes. But also of equally high stature is the truffle royale with turnips and truffle juice; red mullet pan-fried in liver sauce, accompanied by eggplant fritters and Maxim's apples; and artichoke black truffle soup, served with a puff pastry brioche made with mushrooms and truffle butter, now a classic Savoy dish.

Turbot with a scaled garnish, John Dory with mushrooms and its superimposed plates, or even poached and grilled pigeon with small salads, are totally self-assured and reliable, just like the offal in a beetroot and mushroom mille-feuille. The same can be said of the hot-cold dish of blood orange and the composition "Around Milk," which are both to die for; fine dishes, but also object lessons.

If there is a heaven for cooks and gourmets, the great Guy, with his kitchen and dining room team as tight-knit as a rugby team, together with sommelier Éric Mancio's divine wines, might well hold its key. He cooks without preaching, tells a story, and presents it to us on his beautiful, shiny plates.

Of all the chefs present across the globe through their students and disciples, his teachings are some of the most ubiquitous. The obvious example that comes to mind is his former Scottish intern, Gordon Ramsay, who was awarded three Michelin stars on London's Royal Hospital Road before Guy received his, and who reproduces faithfully one of his signature desserts: the crisp and tender green apple that is a sort of unmolded Granny Smith apple crème brûlée, and a miracle of fruit and freshness.

His lieutenants of all stripes labor everywhere with the same will to make the ingredient the star. No chemical flights of fancy, no inappropriate emulsion in Savoy's manner. Instead, it is a demonstration: good cuisine is first and foremost about exceptional ingredients handled at the peak of their freshness, true nature, and purity. Truth be told, this maestro of flavors is a wizard.

Page 144, and on the facing page: the well-known and always charming Guy Savoy, offering crispy and tender lamb with vegetables, sea bass grilled with its skin in mild spices, and "Coco" coconut dessert. His debonair smile makes him one of the most endearing of the great chefs.
Page 145: Jellied summer tomatoes with seaweed and lemon granita.

Guy Savoy

18, rue Troyon

75017 Paris

Tel: +33 (0)1 43 80 40 61

www.guysavoy.com

For recipes, see pages 212–213

Taillevent
Paris's Most Impeccable Club

MORE THAN JUST A TRADITIONAL RESTAURANT,
TAILLEVENT IS A CLUB FOR ELITIST GOURMETS.

Is it a restaurant? It's a funny question. And yet, it seems to be more of an institution of fine French manners. So it is indeed a restaurant, but more a club, where nothing special is required to gain entry. Is it a role model? Undoubtedly, and especially an ambassador of good food and civility. Taillevent is certainly the most well mannered of the great Parisian restaurants.

Imagine, just a couple of steps away from the Arc de Triomphe and the bustling Champs-Élysées, a sort of temple of taste, where one speaks in hushed tones. It is the site of some of the great discussions of our time (there is the tale of the scallops served in their own stock, shared between Jacques Chirac and journalist Maurice Siegel, narrated by the latter in his memoir, *Vingt ans, ça suffit!*—"Twenty years, that's enough!"). An oasis of calm and diplomacy, where it is possible to quarrel happily, and to divorce while drinking the best possible wines.

Taillevent is the perfect example of a restaurant for contemporary gourmets; honest, well-behaved people, who are never outrageous, spread the word to meet up there. It is a paradigm of modesty itself: less expensive than Ducasse, not as loud as the Laurent Restaurant, not as media-crazed as Arpège, the Meurice, the Bristol, Guy Savoy, or Carré des Feuillants, and less ostentatious than Lasserre. In all honesty, it is not far from being worth all of them put together, in terms of its luxury and prestige.

It has a legendary sense of modesty, a proverbial sense of discretion; in short, a certain way of being. It began as a hotel from the Second Empire, built in 1853, and carefully ushered into the limelight by Jean-Claude Vrinat. This cunning boss, with the look of a monk, who composed his wine list as Ravel did his Bolero, played with his dining room, hallways, and reception rooms like an orchestra conductor. The restaurant was his thing, Taillevent was his creation. He launched Claude Deligne, Philippe Legendre, Michel Del Burgo, and Alain Solivérès—all experts in southern flavors—in an effort to change things a bit.

Did it really need change? That is not the question. Jean-Claude Vrinat succeeded in showing that his nineteenth-century establishment had taken a clever turn into the twenty-first century. And in truth, a whiff of air from a more civil time wouldn't hurt the most refined clientele in the world. After Vrinat passed away, his second in command, Jean-Marie Ancher, took over as house manager and continued to uphold the work of Alain Solivérès. A native of Béziers, Solivérès first trained with Ducasse and then Cirino at the Élysées du Vernet, and instilled a touch of modernity into an unchanging and always fashionable neoclassical menu.

Taillevent, the "club," became hip in a way, with its neutral-toned banquettes, wood paneling, double dining room, beautiful lights, contemporary artworks, and grand service, including tableside service that seemed like second nature. Civility is like a fine art here, displayed through shellfish sausage and Bresse chicken with foie gras, or dill-scented crab rémoulade with light lemon cream, red mullet with an exquisite accompaniment of artichoke puree and Argan oil, escalope of warm foie gras with Banyuls, fillet of sea bass cooked on the skin, or scallops pan-fried in aïoli.

Dishes that must be mentioned are the current classic spelt risotto with chanterelles and truffles, as close to perfection as can be, or the "translucent" lobster ravioli with mango and vanilla pod, even if the latter is not really in the style of the restaurant. But after all, to each his own, and they must have dishes to appeal to all tastes. And, if what we love first and foremost about Taillevent is a certain classical style, a perpetual sense of tradition, it would be easy to find fault with a slightly gimmicky appetizer of asparagus cream with almond "espuma," or a pairing of foie gras and smoked eel mousse with green apple.

Even if the herb-braised shoulder of lamb plays the role of an anthological dish modernized with fantasy and sensitivity, it doesn't mean that the old classics have been abandoned (or not so old). What remains are the warm oysters, shellfish sausage, andouillette with foie gras, truffle-roasted guinea fowl, and whole kidney in its own fat. Desserts were always a strong point, and remain so today, with spur-of-the-moment ideas in the same elegant vein as the other parts of the meal.

Some of the pure delights that can be sampled at the end of a faultless meal include salted butter caramel mille-feuille, variation on raspberries, Fougerolles sour cherries with freshly churned pistachio ice cream, and of course that medieval dessert called blanc-manger (an almond milk bavarian cream dessert), which originally comes from the medieval recipe collection *Le Viandier de Taillevent.*

Moreover, the service is strictly up to snuff, the wine list is one of the most beautiful in the world, and its grand white Burgundies, venerable Médoc crus, pure malt whiskies by Michel Couvreur, or admirable François Ier vintage Pineau des Charentes complete the arsenal of Paris's most refined establishment. If a criticism had to be found, it wouldn't even be of the check.

Here, care is taken never to abuse the diner, and on Rue Lamennais the check is always less than one might expect from a restaurant of this caliber. Oh, how irritating to find a restaurant that is practically perfect!

Taillevent

15, rue Lamennais

75008 Paris

Tel: +33 (0)1 44 95 15 01

www.taillevent.com

For recipes, see pages 214–215

Taillevent has had only five chefs in a period of sixty years: Lucien Leheu, Claude Deligne, Philippe Legendre, Michel Del Burgo, and now Alain Solivérès.

The first Taillevent was not on Rue Lamennais, but on Rue Saint-Georges, where it was created in 1946 by Jean-Claude's father, André Vrinat, in the area known as Nouvelle Athènes in the heart of the ninth arrondissement.

What is the origin of the name? It comes from the first author of a famous gastronomical work, Guillaume Tirel, alias Taillevent, who wrote the *Le Viandier de Taillevent* in the fourteenth century, and was the cook of kings Charles V and Charles VI.

There is another Taillevent in Tokyo, which Jean-Claude Vrinat created along with his friend and partner Joël Robuchon, called the Château-Taillevent-Robuchon (Yebisu Garden pl. 1-13-1 Mita, Meguro-Ku, Tokyo 153-0062 JN. Tel: +81 03 54 24 13 38). You'll find a wood-paneled dining room in the style of Château de Cheverny, which accurately captures the ambience of Rue Lammenais.

Here we are in the ambiance of a club, with its aged woodpaneling, that seems both spacious and cozy. The staircase (page 148) leads to the private rooms. Two new classics of the house are the dill-scented crab rémoulade with light lemon cream (page 149) and the upside-down chocolate and coffee cake (facing page). In the basement, the sommelier stands on a ladder as he picks a bottle of wine.

The Bézards'
Kingdom

In the heart of the forest, on a mythical stop off the Nationale 7 road, one can find grand meals of wild game, traditions upheld, and unparalleled service.

On an isolated strip of the road that runs from Paris to the Italian border, right by Montargis, known as "the Venice of the Gâtinais," and on the edge of the big Orléans forest, there is a large inn. It has wide wooden beams and medieval architecture, a cobblestone courtyard and, in the back, a hotel property, set out in lovely little houses. It is genteel luxury, ideal to rest both body and mind, just a few steps away from the traffic of the freeway.

Long ago, it was medieval military and religious headquarters, built by Évrard des Barres, third Grand Knight Templar from 1147 to 1152, which was then destroyed under King Philippe Le Bel. The edifice was rebuilt by postmaster Louis Gennois around 1690. Damaged in a massive fire, it was rebuilt as a postal relay point in 1799, and remained one until the middle of the nineteenth century, after which, as postal relays disappeared with the arrival of the railroads, it became a farm.

In 1939, the Dépées bought the property from Mr. Foucray, the owner of the Moulin Rouge at that time, and converted it into a hotel in 1946. They were tired of Parisian life; he was a lawyer, passionate about wine and good food, and she was a remarkable cook. They received guests with lavish hospitality, offered a classic and seasonal menu, started to envision the hotel of their dreams and, along with a few friends, created the Route du Bonheur (Road to Happiness), which became the chain Relais de Campagne, precursor to Relais & Châteaux.

The restaurant received two Michelin stars. Mrs. Dépée left the kitchen, and a lineup of talented cooks followed, always leaving the same stylistic imprint: classical, delicate, plentiful, giving "dishes the flavor of what they are" according to Curnonsky's wish, adding a touch of genius here and there, and tying the traditions of Sologne, the Gâtinais, and the Loire Valley to those of the Puisaye side of Burgundy. The wine list is tremendous and rather rich in Burgundies. Philippe Dépée, their son and passionate oenophile, gives it his signature by printing his own choices on the back of the menu, just like at Paris's Taillevent. His wife, Françoise, a former Chanel model and qualified cook, occasionally replaces the chef when needed.

The list of chefs who left their mark on L'Auberge des Templiers is long; there is Jean-Claude Rigolet, who later opened his own place in Chinon; Christian Willer, who became the maestro of the Palme d'Or at Cannes's Martinez Hotel twenty years later; Grégoire Sein, the energetic Basque who became the star of the Palais in Biarritz; Bernard Marillier, later a recipient of Michelin stars in Lyon; and Jacques Rolancy, who would go on to be the chef at the Laurent in Paris under Joël Robuchon. These are merely the ones that immediately come to mind, and there are obviously many more. In half a century, the Bézards saw a parade of talented chefs richly contribute to the house style.

Though chefs may come and go at the Templiers, this style endures. In the maze of rooms, under the wooden beams and painted ceilings, behind the large bay windows that open out onto the ten-acre park, the balletic service is run by Philippe and Guillaume Dépée, father and son. The table setting is important. Meals here are served in Gien porcelain that is crafted just a few miles away. The most beautiful crystal glassware makes the gold and red tones of the wines shimmer.

And the cuisine? Always sumptuous, delicate, proud, and scientifically developed, even if the guides have given it differing assessments. The restaurant, after a long flirt with three Michelin stars, has only one now, which makes hardly any sense at all. The diner gets lessons in updated tradition from chef Hervé Daumy. Calf's trotter carpaccio with condiments; Burgundy snails in sweet garlic and parsley sauce; soft-shelled crab and raw sea bass in an artichoke marinade; and a fricassee of deboned frogs in a creamy sorrel broth—joyful and mischievous flavors are played with through light and refreshing appetizers.

The sea is treated with subtle and honest touches: cod fillet in a spicy broth of aïoli-seasoned vegetables, red mullet fillet in a Gâtinais saffron and crab aroma, scallops served in their shell with truffled shredded leeks, or wild sea bass served with pork belly, fennel, and star anise sauce. Here, rustic is tied to refined, and regional traditions go hand in hand with the flavors of the Brittany coast and the Mediterranean. The Auberge des Templiers, which welcomes the whole world and especially the Belgians, Germans, and British who transit here on their way to the South of France via the Nationale 7 road, clearly shows that it is an ambassador of fine French taste.

But the restaurant's best season is definitely fall, the time of undergrowth, shrubbery, and hunting. Thus, while the foliage close to the auberge takes on golden-reddish tones, gourmets arrive in anticipation of the wild mushroom ravioli served in a delicate and creamy soup of truffles; duck with mild spices and seasonal fruit and vegetables with summer savory herb; young boar with peppercorn, sucrine endive crisps, and onion confit with mace; as well as hunter's venison, hare royale, or venison medallions *en poivrade*. Hunting season is a permanent celebration here.

Much anticipated as well are the desserts that honor grand traditions: Rothschild soufflé (made with fruit confit) with vanilla ice cream, a superb *tarte Tatin* (invented nearby in Lamotte-Beuvron by sisters Caroline and Stéphanie, who had mistakenly cooked their apple tart upside down), which is incomparably soft here, or poached and caramelized pear with a Guanaja chocolate shell and Earl Grey tea sorbet.

These fabulous dishes are accompanied by equally outstanding wines: Lucien Crochet's white Sancerre Chêne Marchand, Raveneau's Chablis Valmur, Savigny-les-Beaune from Domain Pavelot, Echezeaux by Jayer-Gilles, or Clos de Vougeot by Méo-Camuzet. Naturally, there's no lack of high-class Bordeaux in such a huge wine list, but Sancerre, Chablis, and the great hills of Burgundy are so close that it seems obvious that the best vintages of the best wines are carefully chosen by the Dépées.

A big cellar, an excellent table, a beautiful inn with opulent Relais & Châteaux suites, breakfasts to die for, attentive service, and a discreet bar where one comes to drink a Jerez or Manzanilla before a meal, or the best clear brandies or aged cognacs after it. This is what one can look forward to in this inn from another era, one that miraculously does not suffer the passage of time.

Auberge des Templiers

45290 Boismorand

Tel: +33 (0)2 38 31 80 01

www.lestempliers.com

For recipes, see page 215

In the archetype of the traditional hunting lodge, the maitre d'hotel presents Philippe Dépée with the pheasants that have just been shot. Venison medallions en poivrade with juniper-scented Brussels sprouts will taste wild (pages 152–153). Facing page, clockwise from top left: Golden scallops and Tanariva chocolate cannelloni with whole raspberry sorbet, and one of the lodges on the Templiers' grounds.

Eternal
Tour d'Argent

UNIQUE AND IMPERVIOUS TO TRENDS,
THIS IS AN ADMIRABLE PARISIAN RESTAURANT.

Though it is the subject of numerous criticisms, nothing shakes the foundations of the Tour d'Argent. Across from the spectacle of an illuminated Notre Dame cathedral, the Île Saint Louis and the Seine, this monument never flinches. It was built in 1582 with silver-flecked stones from the region of Champagne; hence its name meaning "the Silver Tower." It sheltered lords who were tired of dining in rougher Parisian haunts; while out for a fun outing, Henri III learned to use a fork there.

It endured through centuries and endless trends. Henri IV would send out for its thick slices of heron pâté from there. The owner, Rourteau, called himself a "cook, listener, and caterer." In the seventeenth century, Cardinal Richelieu had a whole cow served there for thirty people. Exiled in Vitré, the Marquise of Sévigné dreamed of its "exquisite chocolate." Duke Philippe of Orléans feasted in good company there during the early eighteenth century, just as the Duke of Morny would later treat his "girlfriends" in the mid-nineteenth century.

But it was not until the late nineteenth century that it received proper recognition under the direction of the new proprietor, Frédéric Delair, who numbered his ducks (in the famous blood sauce) and made them the grand specialty of the house. In 1910, he sold the restaurant to André Terrail, the grandfather of the current owner, who was a businessman and promoter, and who created and purchased hotels (the Roblin, the San Régis, the George V, the Saint Christophe in Miramar d'Estérel, the

Picardy in Touquet). His particular contribution was to move the restaurant up to the sixth floor, elevating it to great heights.

André's son, Claude, who wanted to be a comedian, presided over the restaurant and gave it its luster. He enlarged the cellar (which holds 400,000 bottles) and received Parisian high society, crowned heads, and the beautiful people of the world. He benefited from a few large loans. And we know he was quite close to Ava Gardner. Cuisine, for him, was "a feast of the five senses." Hearing, smell, touch, and taste are celebrated here like nowhere else, of course, but above all, vision first, with the unforgettable view.

Under his direction, the ducks continued to be numbered but their forms were varied and they were dedicated to famous gourmets. The Challans duck (bred in Vendée and sold by Burgaud) is the star of the house: with blood sauce, of course, but also grilled with a Béarnaise sauce, in a peppered broth, in its own juice, with green pepper, *à l'orange* or with cherries, and sliced in the dining room by an army of skilled servers. But English-style poached asparagus, pike quenelles in the style of André Terrail, lobster Thermidor, seven-hour lamb, kidney flambéed in aged cognac, and crêpes "Belle Époque" also partake in the festivities.

After a half-century of service to the republic of food lovers, Claude Terrail, with his stentorian voice and ever-present flower in his lapel, took his final bow in June of 2006. Just as

his tall and elegant silhouette wandered the panoramic decor of the Tour d'Argent back then, his son, André, named for his grandfather, now holds the mantle. He has the same grandness, the same elegance and distinction about him, but with a touch of discretion and shyness; this from a young man who pursued his studies on the east coast of the USA.

The cuisine, too, remains proud and elegant. In the same way that management of the establishment passed quietly from father to son, so did the chef, Jean-François Sicallac, leave his position to his sous-chef upon leaving for the port of Concarneau in Brittany. The young Stéphane Haissant had formerly worked for Michel Guérard and Alain Senderens; in turn, he passed the reins to Laurent Delarbre, Meilleur Ouvrier de France (Best Craftsman in France), who was trained here, then worked at Café de Paris, and who now revisits the house's classics in a measured, classical manner.

Naturally, one doesn't come to the restaurant—which became forever fashionable in the sixteenth century—for flighty cuisine, which will be out of date as soon as trends have changed, but to be schooled in the classical grand tradition. So, the *amuse-gueules* tasters (including mustardy croquettes), dynamic appetizers like foie-gras royale seasoned with sea urchin cream, brilliant pike quenelles in the style of André Terrail, so unctuous, with mushroom stuffing and lobster claws, are all simply marvelous here. Just as the lobster tail, its claws pressed with anchovy, is a wonder of freshness, so the turbot with chanterelles is very precise and clean. The "Marco Polo" roasted duckling with green pepper, grain mustard, and melty and superbly souffléd potatoes is juicy and effusive; yet another lesson in grand classicism.

There is also the unchangeable duck *à l'orange* with souffléd potatoes, its thigh in a spinach shepherd's pie; whole veal kidney cooked in blood sauce, served with crayfish and a delicate Jura vin jaune sauce; passion fruit and guava ice cream parfait; and, for well-behaved children, the "Parisian Life," a pear dessert composed of pieces of pear poached in a vanilla cream flavored with Williams pear brandy and served under a hard caramel top. This is one of the most delicious desserts there is! It has recently been reinvented as a mille-feuille, but this is simply a way of modernizing the classics without destroying them.

We should add that there is an admirable lunch menu, which is an opportunity to enthusiastically discover the Tour d'Argent without breaking the bank. The service in coattails and square collar, like the panoramic setting across from Notre Dame, maintains an ineffable charm. The wine list as devised by David Ridgway, Paris's most British sommelier, remains one of the most spectacular in the world. Wonderful Tour d'Argent!

La Tour d'Argent

15, quai de la Tournelle

75005 Paris

Tel: +33 (0)1 43 54 23 31

www.latourdargent.com

For recipes, see pages 216–217

One goes to the Tour d'Argent for its timeless dishes like duck Tour d'Argent (in blood sauce, seen on page 157), the "Parisian Life" pear dessert (above), and pike quenelles (facing page, bottom left).
One goes for its cellar too, one of the most beautiful in the world, with bottles like this Petrus 1983. And one goes, of course, for the view of the River Seine, especially when seated at "the Queen's table," named for Queen Elizabeth II who lunched there (page 156).

Trama
The Self-Taught Chef

CUISINE AS A GAME: THIS IS WHAT IS ON OFFER AT THE AUBERGADE, A FABULOUS SMALL LUXURY HOTEL THAT HAS BEEN REDECORATED FOR DREAMLIKE GOURMET FEASTS.

He is the lone man of the Lot-et-Garonne, a passionate, sharp, self-taught kitchen acrobat. His biography is unusual in the world of great chefs. Born in Constantine, Algeria, in 1947, he was set to study psychosociology but didn't finish the course, and so became a kitchen busboy at Club Med, then held a series of junior positions. He owned a restaurant called Sur le Pouce in Paris on Rue Mouffetard, then had an epiphany while reading Michel Guérard's *La Cuisine Gourmande*. He left the capital on a whim in 1978, and while in the heart of the Lot-et-Garonne, discovered an old stone house from the eighteenth century with a restaurant that needed to be taken over.

It was the village of Puymirol and the Aubergade that received a Michelin star in 1981, a second star in 1983, and finally the third star in 2004. In between, Trama was an intern for Bernard Loiseau at La Côte d'Or in Saulieu and for Jacques Maximin at the Negresco in Nice, and dazzled the small world of gourmets with his truffle dishes and his nods to trends (hamburger, lamb club sandwich, and pepper steak). With the assistance of his wife Maryse, his spokesperson, his publicity rep, and his defender, he creates dishes, has fun, and tells stories with food.

Under the direction of this acrobat, a truffle is served finely sliced with truffle juice ("the truffle with truffle"), or in a papillote with truffled potatoes baked in chard leaves (chard being a vegetable he adores) with very black truffle juice. Foie gras is presented as a lollipop with amaranth popcorn, or as a warm hamburger with porcini mushrooms, as well as in a lemongrass scented pot-au-feu. At Michel Trama's restaurant, traditions are sent packing and haute cuisine is pushed aside.

So wrapped up are we in the cuisine that we might forget to describe the location, which was turned upside down and inside out by Jacques Garcia in 2000. The zany interior designer for the Costes brothers and the Barrière Group in Paris redid the entire building in the manner of a mini luxury hotel for bigwigs who had come to visit their country cousin in the Lot-et-Garonne. It is funny, beautiful, playful, and opulent. There are scalloped curtains, pillars, paneling, canopied beds, mid-nineteenth-century furniture, and wooden beams that have been painted off-white to match the vintage-glazed floor tiles—and do match superbly, it must be said.

Over here, a medieval staircase leads to heaven; over there, a hideaway emerges; a pool is unveiled; a baroque dining room shows off its finery with sofa or boudoir-style armchairs. Garcia, who usually goes over the top, managed to stay reasonable here, just capturing the "madness of Trama." There is something of the singing madman, the playful spirit, the constant verve with the unpredictable Michel. Maryse assists him beautifully, happily playing the country version of Tintin's Castafiore, and helps him to fight his anxieties by occasionally mocking him. Just like Peyrot at the Vivarois in Paris long ago, Trama isn't afraid of revealing his doubts.

He is one of the few great chefs who will ask a random guest who, having lost his or her way in Puymirol and ended up eating at the Aubergade: "Did you enjoy the meal?" Michel Trama may also worry a critic with an improvised and roughly sketched dish, but seduce him with a new flavor; or intrigue him, especially with the fish ball with fennel (wild fennel from his own organic garden) to be dipped in fennel juice, or with tomato croquettes, both juicy and crispy at the same time. In short, there is not a dull moment to be had with Trama.

Breads are as varied as they are delightful, and breakfasts as delicious as they are clever, with small almond creams, fruit, compotes, and pastries, all making it one of the gems in the Relais & Châteaux hotel and restaurant chain. We haven't mentioned that Trama, who is almost entirely self-taught, is a specialist when it comes to sweets, both simple and complex. Such legendary desserts as the chocolate teardrop with sour cherries, the double Corona with a tobacco leaf and pepper, iced nougatine mille-feuille with praline, or floating island with vanilla, infused drop by drop, have made their rounds among all the great chefs.

Self-taught, yet an inventor of great originality, Trama is undoubtedly one of the most copied chefs in the world. His green apple or pineapple "cristalline," like his aforementioned chocolate teardrop and mille-feuille, have been taken, adapted, stolen, pastiched, and basically imitated with more or less success. "A copy is a tribute paid by mediocrity to talent," said Coco Chanel. With Trama, one finds the original and authentic piece that he, as a constant improviser, has managed to preserve, refine, and artfully rework.

A meal at his place? Both an enchantment and a rediscovery, with dishes such as langoustines sautéed with coconut and citrus vinaigrette, or the extremely subtle Thai-style soup of coconut and lemongrass with chopped soft shell crab, or crab ravioli with Argan oil. Though he no longer makes his amusing (purposely dated) "Y2K" pepper steak, in which the gray pepper cream was encased in an exquisitely tender fillet of beef, he delights the palate with his lightly roasted squab with spices and carrots that melt in the mouth, or his funny and delectable lamb club sandwich in which potato replaces the bread and mustard is made with arugula.

As you might have guessed, with Trama cuisine is like a game, a permanent form of recreation, a school playground where one plays by passing around secret recipes. Nothing is ever permanent here; the seasons and the markets lead the way; foreign lands inspire; spices, reminiscent of southwest France, enhance and enliven. This is a festive house where all sorts of culinary and gourmet surprises are still possible.

Pages 160–161:
Pineapple millefeuille with pineapple ice cream. Illuminated by a candlestick, Michel Trama watches over the playful and plush dining room decorated by Jacques Garcia. In this mysterious setting lit by narrow medieval windows, and with a museum-worthy kitchen, modern and provocative dishes are served, such as the gondola of entrees including foie gras lollipops, shrimp with asparagus, and kaffir lime lobster roll or the lamb club sandwich.

L'Aubergade

52, rue Royale

47270 Puymirol

Tel: +33 (0)5 53 95 31 46

www.aubergade.com

For recipes, see pages 217–218

Troisgros

IN THE CITY OF ROANNE, THERE IS A BUILDING ACROSS FROM THE TRAIN STATION THAT IS KNOWN WORLDWIDE. ITS TRADITION IS PERPETUALLY BEING RENEWED UNDER THE DIRECTION OF ITS ENERGETIC HEIR.

"Thank you for calling La Maison Troisgros," says the voice in English. "Please hold the line." If one were to question the permanence of this place across from Roanne's train station, the hold message on the phone would quickly reassure you: this heart of France really is in the heart of the world. The train station is still there, unchanged except for the orange paint that replaced the color of the restaurant's famous salmon dish. Since the rail network added a regional train to Lyon, a trip here is similar to a gourmet adventure. Your mouth waters before arriving, just thinking about the veal tripe with tomato and two truffles (white and black) or the Châteaubriand (beef tenderloin) steak with Fleurie wine and bone marrow. Your mind hesitates between old and modern, knowing that both genres are represented with utmost care behind the façade of Maison Troisgros.

The place has been completely redone from top to bottom. So much so that the original Hôtel des Platanes, in which Jean-Baptiste and Marie Troisgros, originally café owners in Chalon-sur-Saône, became restaurateurs, is difficult to remember; at one point the hotel was renamed Hôtel Moderne. The name gave warning: Roanne had been a travel stop since antiquity because of its famous hosiery tradition; it would now be one for pleasures of the palate.

Jean-Baptiste's two sons, Pierre (born in 1928 in Chalon-sur-Saône) and Jean (the elder by two years, who died in 1983) apprenticed at Lucas Carton in Paris, and then with Fernand Point in Vienne (near Lyon). The restaurant obtained its first Michelin star in 1955, the second in 1965, and the third in 1968, while never losing any, which is a rare feat. Pierre and Jean complemented each other. The former specialized in meats, the latter was an expert in wines. But it was working together that they created their famous dishes, such as salmon fillet with sorrel sauce or the aforementioned beef tenderloin with Fleurie wine and bone marrow.

As rightful heir, a hard worker, and someone who questions authority, Pierre's son, Michel, is not satisfied with simply accepting his inheritance. Born in Roanne in 1958, he trained under the tough leadership of Frédy Girardet in Switzerland, as well as with Roger Vergé in Mougins, Alain Chapel in Mionnay, at Taillevent in Paris, with Michel Guérard in Eugénie-les-Bains, at Comme Chez Soi in Brussels, at Chez Panisse in Berkeley, and at the Connaught in London. He is not afraid of ruffling feathers by turning accepted ideas on their heads. Part of the new gourmand club, along with Olivier Roellinger and Pierre Gagnaire, Michel uses ideas from his travels with an unbridled creativity. But first, he reinvented the family establishment in a contemporary way: dining rooms and lounges filled with modern furnishings, and clean, tranquil, brightly lit bedrooms.

Every year, he is the spokesperson for the Rhône-Alps region at the conference that takes place at the Hyatt Hotel in Tokyo. This is where he gained a spirit of sobriety, a love of pure, clean lines, and a taste for innovation that is only slowed down by technical rigor. The modernity of the setting marries well with that of a cuisine that, though firmly rooted in tradition, has espoused progress without reservation. His creations often seem to be pure feats. There was gray shrimp jelly with a sesame poached egg that made for a very edgy pre-meal taster, and "steam" of fennel and sea urchin that gracefully imitated Japanese tofu.

Pan-fried frog satay with coriander and crushed peanuts is a somewhat exotic reminder that the Troisgros family, originally from Burgundy, is inclined to travel. But the style is constantly being renewed. Thus, there is yellow corn paired with Bleu d'Auvergne cheese in a fine jelly, John Dory "lace" with crispy capers and cucumbers, and warm oysters with sorrel and green pepper. The dominant flavors are acidic and spicy. Michel's manner wakes the palate and never lets it fall back asleep.

A section in the menu dedicated to family tradition is reminiscent of the one started by Marc Haeberlin in Illhaeusern, with his "specialties that made the Auberge de l'Ill renowned," and which is also found as "Pic Generations" in Valence. Here it is simply "Cuisine in the Family Tradition." The "Atlantide" crab rolls, created by Michel in 1986, are served before the ritual salmon fillet with sorrel sauce, created in 1965. Blue lobster grilled with Cancale butter, created in 1970, still precedes the Charolais Châteaubriand with Fleurie wine and bone marrow, created in 1960.

Here, everything is in flux and nothing stands still, much like the master of the house, who might be at the Hyatt in Tokyo or at the Lancaster in Paris, and who was at the Koumir in Moscow, long ago. His mother, Olympe, left him with an Italian influence that can still be seen in the exquisite truffle and parmesan mezzaluna, Venetian-style tart and bitter-sour shellfish, iced eggplant in jelly, Treviso-style langoustine with vinegar, or crayfish with purple olives wrapped in Zibello bacon. But Japan is definitely present too, spicing up local ingredients such as kidney with ichi-mi powder or veal rib with yuzu.

Wines remain a highlight of the meal, mostly dedicated to Burgundy, either from the three Côtes (Nuits, Rhône, Beaune) or the Mâcon, as are the cheeses made by their neighbors, the Mons, in Saint-Haon-le-Châtel. The "sweet fantasies" by expert Benoît Céréda are more evanescent, playing with mists, lightness, and freshness; pairing wild strawberries with slightly bitter grapefruit zabaglione (sabayon), or figs and tomatoes in an escabèche. But he never forgets the classics, revisiting and updating them, such as the Trois-Rivières rum-spiked pear Ali Baba, or the Oriental-style orange soufflé.

The modern mischievousness of Michel Troisgros also results in sometimes exotic but always generous dishes at the pretty Café Central next door to the main restaurant. In a chic bistro/deli setting with a nineteenth-century (circa 1880) dining room with Corinthian pillars, gray fabrics, brown chairs, and wooden tables, a recent menu of the day proposed a ham bruschetta with tomato and basil, a tagine of lamb shoulder with artichokes and lemons, and a chocolate and banana galette with passion fruit—to die for. These are little gems of culinary artistry sold at unbeatable prices.

And to show that his roots are still a primary preoccupation for him, as crazy for Asia as he might be, Michel, along with architect Patrick Bouchain, designed a modern yet rustic property in Iguerande, in the heart of Charolais. An old barn was redone as a modern space, and unusual cabins were updated from the dry stone winemaker's cabins of yore, all up on a hill. It is a place to rest, but more so to enjoy rustic treats (crêpe-cake with basil cream, trout with butter that sings in the mouth, rich buckwheat tart), which bring one back to the family tradition. It will make you remember that grandfather Jean-Baptiste was a café owner long ago in Chalon-sur-Saône.

La Maison Troisgros

Place de la Gare

42300 Roanne

Tel: +33 (0)4 77 71 66 97

www.troisgros.fr

For recipes, see pages 218–219

Always with a spoon in hand, Michel Troisgros continues to taste everything that comes out of his kitchen (page 164). Oysters in smoked beet jelly (page 165). This is the famous Maison Troisgros, the exterior and interior at night.
Among the latest creations are the truffle and parmesan mezzaluna and the piquant red mullet and tart red Belgian endives (facing page, top right and bottom left).

The Glory of the
Véfour

Guy Martin has returned the luster
to this antique restaurant at the Palais Royal.

It is the only restaurant in Paris that has a link to the Directory (1795–9) government: a charming house that is both ancient and intact, and which is an integral part of the capital's history. The Comédie Française was only a few steps away from where Mr. Aubertot, a lemonade-maker by trade, opened a café in 1784, making it the canteen of high society after shows. It became the Café de Chartres during the Revolution, harboring meetings of the Ultra-royalists after Thermidor in 1794. The painted ceilings, glass wall paintings, and banquettes gave it a style that would endure.

During the early nineteenth century, Jean Véfour gave it his name and transformed it into a restaurant of great renown. Grimod de la Reynière praised the "Marengo fricassee of chicken with poultry mayonnaise." On February 25, 1830, the night of the "theater" battle of Hernani (between the classicists and the new school of Romantics), Victor Hugo dined there with his friends. On the menu were vermicelli, breast of mutton, and white beans. The Grand Véfour would be glorious during the mid-nineteenth-century Second Empire, thanks to Lamartine, Sainte-Beuve, Mac Mahon, and the Duke d'Aumale, who all had their election table there. It became the meeting place of minor society during the Belle Époque at turn of the twentieth century, starting with actress La Belle Otéro, who brought her lovers there.

It would have to wait until after the world wars to experience a purely culinary kind of glory. The owner of Maxim's, Louis Vaudable, who had purchased it after the Liberation, sold it to Raymond Oliver, who had come from Langon in the Aquitaine in 1948. The latter made it the headquarters of the entire Parisian gourmet crowd. Berl, Cocteau, Colette, all neighbors on Rue de Beaujolais, had their tables and now have plaques there. Guitry, Sartre, Aragon, Jouvet, and Malraux ran into each other there too. Raymond Oliver, with his famous beard, who became the first culinary star of French television, reigned there for thirty-six years, championing eggs "sunny side up" with foie gras (named "Louis Oliver" for his father, who was the head chef of the Savoy in London) and "Véfour" pigeon stuffed with variety meats. He welcomed the greats of this world in his restaurant and obtained three Michelin stars.

Those who followed after him would be numerous, though not always lucky. Of note would be André Signoret, who was Jean-Paul Bonin's sous-chef at the Crillon Hotel, and the Lhonneur brothers. But for the last two decades, it has been Guy Martin, the good-looking mountain kid from Savoie, who has restored its reputation. His cooking is classic, playful, light, and modern, but with a very attractive regionalism about it (chopped artichoke with Beaufort cheese, salmon terrine with smoked milk). Under his guidance, the place has not only stayed beautiful, with gold trim and glass wall paintings, and maintained its atmosphere, both historic and intimate, but has actually become prettier and cozier. The impeccable service, led firmly but kindly by Christian David, is one of the most precise in the capital. As for the great wines, selected by expert Patrick Tamisier, the experience always tends to the sublime.

In short, the aura of this mythical restaurant remains the same, no matter the changes or the number of Michelin stars. Foie-gras raviolini with truffle-rich cream, frogs' legs "meunières" with parsley and melting sweet garlic spheres, roasted langoustines with tender celeriac and cardamom-scented chestnuts, like the herb-steamed fillets of sole accompanied by a frothy juice of cockles and razor clams, all demonstrate a classicism both timeless and renewed.

Truffle and game season adds a definite plus here: ratte potato salad with truffles or wood pigeon cooked in a woodcock. Beautiful desserts (hazelnut and milk chocolate wafer with dark caramel ice cream; or a daring artichoke crème brûlée with almond milk ice cream) are also a very strong part of the experience. Guy Martin, the charming, svelte chef, author of many cookbooks (*La Cuisine des Blondes*, *Sensing*) and culinary encyclopedias, has given a new and trendier facelift to this establishment rich with history. Long live the Véfour, which has rightfully deserved its place in Paris.

Le Grand Véfour

17, rue de Beaujolais

75001 Paris

Tel: +33 (0)1 42 96 56 27

www.grand-vefour.com

For recipes, see pages 219–221

In a moment of infinite reflections in the multiple mirrors, Guy Martin seems amused by the idea of traveling through time (page 168). From the vantage point of its two hundred years, this setting now sees modern dishes quite different from those that were served during the Revolution: lamb fillet and salsify au jus and au vinaigre with delicately pureed Hubbard squash, preserved lemon, and chervil (page 169); roasted langoustines, melting celeriac and cardamom chestnuts (facing page, top left); and Manjari chocolate cubes, spiced pineapple, shiso foam, and tonka bean sorbet (bottom, right).
The main dining room of the Grand Véfour has perfectly preserved paintings behind glass and its entrance on the garden of the Palais Royal.

Recipes

L'Arnsbourg p. 8–11

Blue Lobster, Garden Pea Bonbons, Yuzu, and Verbena (see photo p. 8)

Serves 10

4 ¼ pt. (2 liters) lobster court bouillon
2 lobsters, each weighing
1lb. 2 oz.–1 lb. 5 oz. (500–600 g)
1 pinch Maldon salt
Lobster butter as needed

Garden Pea Bonbons
4 tablespoons (60 g) butter
½ onion chopped into 3 pieces
1 lb. 5 oz. (600 g) peas
4 cups (1 liter) cream
1 teaspoon (3 g) tapioca powder (Kappa)

Yuzu Jelly
2 teaspoons (10 ml) yuzu juice
2 teaspoons (10 ml) water
1 generous tablespoon (15 g) sugar
¾ teaspoon (2 g) tapioca powder (Kappa)
Scant teaspoon (4 g) agar-agar
1 teaspoon (4 g) gellan gum

Coconut-Rice Sauce
2 teaspoons (10 ml) olive oil
3 ½ oz. (100 g) julienned onions
¾ cup (5 oz./150 g) Thai rice

¾ cup (200 ml) milk
2 cups (500 ml) crustacean court bouillon
Fish sauce, to taste
½ cup (120 ml) coconut milk
Verbena leaves, to taste

Special equipment:
Ten 2-in. (5-cm) diameter rings

Plunge the lobsters in the hot court bouillon, add the salt, and cook the body for 3 minutes and the claws for 5 minutes.
Shell and cut the lobster and arrange the slices in the rings en chartreuse, in layers. Each 2.2 lb. (1 kg) will yield 5 portions.

For the Garden Pea Bonbons
Sauté the chopped onion in the butter. Add the cream, and when it starts boiling, place the peas in the pot. Remove from the heat and set aside for 20 minutes.
Process in a food processor and strain through a sieve. Bring to the boil and add the tapioca powder.

When it has cooled and the tapioca has set the mixture, form it into balls, allowing 2 per person. You may use special spherical molds.

For the Yuzu Jelly
Heat the yuzu juice, water, and sugar, and then add the tapioca powder, agar-agar, and gellan gum. Leave to cool and then process. Chill until set.

For the Coconut-Rice Sauce
Cook the onions in the olive oil and add the rice. Leave to cook until it is translucent. Pour the milk and court bouillon into a saucepan with the fish sauce. Allow to simmer gently and then add the coconut milk. Strain through a chinois and infuse with the verbena leaf or leaves.
To serve, place the lobster chartreuse in the center of a large, deep plate. To the left place 2 pea bonbons and a small scoop of yuzu jelly. Spoon a little of the coconut-rice sauce into the plate and finish with a little lobster butter.

Pigeon Breast and Corn Puree (see photo p. 11)

Serves 10

10 pigeons
Crushed Maldon salt and mignonette
pepper as needed

Reduced Jus
1 generous tablespoon (15 g) sugar
⅓ cup (80 ml) balsamic vinegar
5 cups (1.2 liters) pigeon stock
7 tablespoons (100 g) butter
1 pinch salt

Textured Beets
2 lb. (1 kg) cooked beets (beetroot)
10 oz. (300 g) beet trimmings
¼ cup (60 ml) beet juice
⅛ teaspoon (½ g) tapioca powder (Kappa)
Scant ½ teaspoon (1.6 g) agar-agar
¼ teaspoon (1 g) gellan gum
1 pinch salt

Gelled Balsamic Vinegar
Scant ½ cup (100 ml) water

Scant ½ cup (100 ml) balsamic vinegar
⅛ teaspoon (0.5 g) gellan gum
Scant ½ teaspoon (1.6 g) agar-agar

Corn Puree
⅔ oz. (20 g) onion
2 teaspoons (10 g) butter
1.5 lb. (600 g) corn
¾ cup (200 ml) cream
1 pinch salt

Sear the whole pigeons for 3 minutes on each side. Leave to rest, then cook at 400°F (200°C). Remove the breasts. Prepare a gastrique sauce: put the sugar and the balsamic vinegar in a saucepan. Pour in the pigeon stock and reduce. Incorporate the butter and season with salt.

For the Textured Beets
Cut the cooked beets into disks using a cutter.
Combine the beet trimmings with the beet juice. Bring to the boil and add the tapioca, agar-agar, and gellan gum and season. Leave to cool and then cut into cork shapes.

For the Gelled Balsamic Vinegar
Bring the water to the boil with the balsamic vinegar. Add the agar-agar and gellan gum. Allow to cool, process, and transfer to a pipette.

For the Corn Puree
Sweat the onion in the butter. Add the corn and cream and leave to cook. Process and push through a sieve. Season with salt.

Draw out 2 lines of corn puree on a 12-in. (31 cm) diameter plate. Arrange 2 beet candies in jelly and 1 plain beet candy on the plate, with 2 beet disks in between. Place the 2 pigeon breasts next to them. Drizzle over the reduced jus. Sprinkle with Maldon salt and mignonette pepper.

L'Oustau de Baumanière p. 12–15

Hen's Egg
Green Asparagus with Black Truffle Fumet *en chaud-froid* (see photo p. 15)

Serves 4

13 green asparagus
7 oz. (200 g) sandwich loaf
Scant ¼ cup (50 g) clarified butter
A few yellow celery leaves
A few flat parsley leaves
A little olive oil
Scant ½ cup (100 ml) whipped cream (medium firm peaks)
4 eggs
⅓ oz. (10 g) snipped chives
⅓ oz. (10 g) chopped truffle
½ oz. (15 g) truffle puree
Fleur de sel and freshly ground pepper to taste

Asparagus Puree
¼ lb (250 g) baby spinach leaves
2 scallions
14 oz. (400 g) asparagus trimmings
2 cups (500 ml) white chicken stock
A little olive oil
Fleur de sel and freshly ground pepper to taste

Wine Sauce
2 lb. (1 kg) veal trimmings
Scant ½ cup (100 ml) olive oil
7 tablespoons (3 ½ oz./100 g) unsalted butter
3 ½ oz. (100 g) shallots
20 garlic cloves, unpeeled
1 bouquet garni

3 cups (750 ml) red wine, half for the sauce and half for the miroir
4 ¼ pints (2 liters) white chicken stock
1 oz. (25 g) mignonette black pepper

Trim the asparagus and cut 6 of them into three parts: use the base for the purée, cut the middle section into a brunoise, and reserve the tips for finishing.

Take 4 asparagus and use them to make shavings. Set aside in the refrigerator. Finely slice the sandwich loaf and, using a pastry cutter, cut out large rectangles. Brush the bread with the clarified butter. Place the slices between 2 sheets of parchment paper and bake at 250°F (120°C) until they are crisp and golden.

Dice the remaining bread and sauté the cubes in clarified butter.

Fry the celery and parsley leaves and set them aside.

For the Asparagus Puree

Remove the stalks from the baby spinach leaves, wash and dry them. Prepare an asparagus puree using the scallions, asparagus bases, baby spinach leaves, and white chicken stock. Season it with fleur de sel and freshly ground pepper and lightly whisk in a little olive oil.

Divide the puree into two: half to glaze the eggs and half to make an asparagus marmalade.

For the Wine Sauce

In a cast-iron pot, caramelize the pieces of veal in olive oil. Add the butter and aromatic garnish. Sweat the ingredients together for a few minutes.

Remove the fat and pour in half the red wine.

Reduce by half and pour in the white chicken stock.

Simmer for 2 hours until the sauce has thickened nicely.

Meanwhile, prepare a red wine miroir. Reduce the other half of the red wine slowly and without boiling until all the alcohol has evaporated.

Strain the veal jus through cheesecloth (muslin) over the wine miroir, add the black pepper mignonette, and thicken the sauce with some butter.

Leave to infuse for 30 minutes and strain again through cheesecloth. Set aside.

To make the glaze, thin half of the asparagus puree slightly with the white stock, olive oil, and whipped cream. Season with fleur de sel and freshly ground pepper and keep in a warm place. To make the marmalade, add the remaining asparagus puree to the asparagus brunoise and combine with oil. Check the seasoning and keep in a warm place.

Separate the eggs, keeping the yolks in small oiled ramekins.

Whisk the whites to stiff peaks.

Season with fleur de sel, freshly ground pepper, and snipped chives, and add the chopped truffle.

Coat the molds with the egg-white mixture and arrange a yolk in the middle. Season with fleur de sel and freshly ground pepper. Cover with beaten egg white and bake in a steam oven at 170°F (75°C) for 6 minutes.

Arrange the asparagus marmalade on each plate. Arrange the croutons around it, placing a fried parsley leaf and a fried celery leaf between each one.

Draw out rings around each plate with the truffle puree and the asparagus puree. Take the eggs out of the oven and glaze them with the rest of the green asparagus puree.

Halve the remaining asparagus, heat them in the asparagus cooking liquid and place them on the marmalade. Top each egg with a slice of toast and place one in the center of each plate.

Season the reserved asparagus shavings with olive oil, fleur de sel, and freshly ground pepper. Place the asparagus shavings and tips attractively on the plates and serve immediately. Accompany with the wine sauce.

Souffléed Crêpes Baumanière (see photo p. 14)

Serves 4

Crêpe Batter
2 cups (7 oz./200 g) flour
4 eggs
2 egg yolks
½ teaspoon (3 g) salt
4 cups (1 liter) milk
Scant ½ cup (100 g) browned butter

Soufflé Batter
4 cups (1 liter) pastry cream
Scant ½ cup (100 ml) Grand Marnier liqueur
2 candied (crystallized) oranges, roughly chopped
6 egg whites

2 cups (500 ml) custard
1 cup (250 ml) 30° syrup
1 cup (250 ml) orange extract
Butter, for greasing

For the Crêpe Batter

Whisk together all the ingredients with the cold milk until the batter is smooth. Stir in the scant ½ cup (100 g) browned butter—using this means you will not have to butter the pan. Make 8 crêpes.

For the Soufflé Batter

In a round-bottomed mixing bowl, combine the pastry cream, Grand Marnier, and roughly chopped candied

oranges. Whisk the egg whites to firm peaks and fold them carefully into the mixture.

Butter an ovenproof dish. Place a crêpe in the dish and some of the soufflé mixture on one half. Fold over to form a half-circle. Repeat the procedure with the remaining crêpes.

Prepare a custard and a 30° syrup and incorporate the orange extract into the mixture. Bake the crêpes at 400°F (200°C) for about 5 minutes, until they rise. When they are done, pour the custard mixture over the souffléed crêpes.

Georges Blanc p. 16–19

Pigeon Supremes and Lobster on a Bed of Eggplant Lasagne with "Ochre Velvet" of Sweet Bell Peppers and Coral Oil (see photo p. 16)

Serves 4

2 lobsters (preferably Breton), each weighing 1 lb. to 1 lb. 5 oz. (500–600 g)
2 pigeons (preferably Bresse)
2 tablespoons (30 g) butter
2 pinches each fleur de sel and freshly ground pepper
Thyme flowers
3 garlic cloves
1 eggplant (aubergine)
Grape-seed oil for cooking
4 small flowers for garnish, such as pansies or borrage
8 sprigs chives

Ginger and Cilantro Marinade
Scant ½ cup (100 ml) virgin olive oil
A few sprigs cilantro (coriander), chopped
1 tablespoon (15 ml) soy sauce
1 tablespoon minced fresh ginger
1 teaspoon grated lime zest
1 pinch cumin seeds

Coral Sauce
2 tablespoons (30 ml) olive oil
2 lobster heads
1 carrot
½ celery stalk
A few sprigs tarragon
1 teaspoon minced fresh ginger
1 tomato
Scant ¼ cup (50 ml) vegetable stock
1 tablespoon (15 ml) cognac
1 star anise
1 small pinch ground paprika
Salt and freshly ground pepper

Ochre Velvet of Sweet Bell Peppers
2 red bell peppers
1 tablespoon (15 ml) acacia honey
¼ oz. (5 g) lemongrass (1 ½ in., 4 cm)
¼ oz. (5 g) fresh ginger (¾ in., 2 cm)
Pinch of turmeric

1 teaspoon (5 ml) sherry vinegar
1 tablespoon (15 ml) orange juice
⅔ cup (150 ml) shellfish liquid, or mussel liquid
2 heaped tablespoons mayonnaise

Cook the lobsters in salted boiling water for 8 minutes. Remove the coral and set it aside for the coral jus. Remove the shells and cut the tails into slightly angled medallions. Cut the claws in two lengthways and set them aside to use as the head of a butterfly when you plate the dish.

Place the pigeons in an ovenproof dish with the butter. Season them with salt and freshly ground pepper, thyme, flowers and garlic cloves. Cook at 350°F (180°C) for 10 to 12 minutes. They should be barely pink. Remove from the oven and leave to rest for 10 minutes. Remove the breasts and cut them into thin, slightly angled slices under ⅛ in. (2 mm) thick. Set aside. You can use the thighs for an taster or even as an accompaniment to a simple salad.

For the Marinade
In a bowl, combine the scant ½ cup (100 ml) virgin olive oil, chopped cilantro leaves, soy sauce, minced ginger, 1 teaspoon finely grated lime zest, fleur de sel, freshly ground pepper, and a pinch of cumin seeds. Set aside.

Cut the eggplant lengthways into slices ¼ in. (5 mm) thick. Season with salt and freshly ground pepper. Slow cook them in a pan with seasoned grape-seed oil. Remove 4 eggplant slices and trim them into rectangles. (Keep the others for another recipe.) Brush them with the marinade ingredients. Set aside.

Coral Sauce
Pour the olive oil into a pot and place the lobster shells and remaining pieces in it. Cut the carrot and celery into fine dice (brunoise). Add the carrots, celery, tarragon, ginger, and the quartered tomato to the pot. Leave to simmer until well reduced and flambé with cognac. Pour in the vegetable stock, add a star anise and paprika, and bring to the boil. Leave to simmer for about 20 minutes. Strain through a fine chinois and reduce to the desired consistency. Add the reserved lobster coral and blend together. Set aside.

For the Ochre Velvet of Sweet Bell Peppers
Wash the bell peppers and liquidize them in a blender. Take 7 oz. (200 g) of the liquidized pepper and pour it into a saucepan, adding the acacia honey, lemongrass, ginger, turmeric, orange juice, sherry vinegar, and shellfish juice. Cook until reduced to a syrupy consistency. Strain through a fine chinois and thicken with 2 heaped tablespoons of mayonnaise. Blend to combine and check the consistency, which should coat the back of a spoon. Set aside.

Plate the dish: make an attractive zigzag with the ochre velvet of peppers using a pipette or a spoon. Set out the gingered eggplant slice and on it place the lobster claw and medallions, the pigeon supremes, the coral sauce, a small flower for garnish, and 2 tips of chives to represent the butterfly's antennae. Season with fleur de sel and freshly ground pepper.

Light Tempura of Frogs' Legs *en chaud-froid*
A "Surf and Turf" Tartare (see photo p. 19)

Serves 4

4 oysters, Isigny, marennes d'Oléron,
or other fine oysters
1 sheet (2 g) gelatin per scant ¼ cup
(50 ml) water, the seawater that about
4 oysters will render
4 large porcini (ceps)
Butter
1 tablespoon of mayonnaise
Dash of yellow wine vinegar (optional)
1 teaspoon pureed ginger
Squeeze of lime juice

20 frogs' legs
Kosher salt to arrange the oysters

Tempura Batter

1 cup plus 1 teaspoon (3 ¾ oz./105 g)
flour
2 level tablespoons plus 1 teaspoon
(22 g) corn starch
½ oz. (15 g) corn flour (made from finely
ground cornmeal)
1 slightly heaped teaspoon (6 g) baking
powder
1 teaspoon (5 g) sugar
½ teaspoon (3 g) salt

Basil Oil and Sauce

¾ cup (200 ml) basil oil, comprising
½ oz. (15 g) basil leaves and 2 ⅔ oz.
(75 g) grape-seed oil
2 egg yolks
1 tablespoon (15 ml) Dijon mustard
Salt and freshly ground pepper

For Garnish
*Sprigs of fresh thyme and small edible
flowers*

Open the oysters, remove them from
their shells, keeping some of their
water, and place them on paper towel.
Scratch out the shells and wash them
under cold running water. Set aside.
Use 1 sheet of gelatin per scant ¼ cup
(50 ml) seawater. Soften the gelatin in
cold water and then dip it in lukewarm
seawater. Heat the seawater, being
careful that it does not boil. Stir
until dissolved and cool down (but
not completely) in a cold water bain-
marie. The jelly will be used to cover
the oysters.

For the Tartare
Finely dice two-thirds of the porcini
and stew them lightly in butter with
a little of the oyster water. Add
the mayonnaise, salt, freshly ground
pepper, a drizzle of yellow wine vinegar
if required, a squeeze of lime juice,
the pureed fresh ginger. Set aside.
Place a spoonful of porcini tartare
in the oyster shells, top with an oyster,
and spoon a little of the jelled sea
water in.

Cut the frogs' legs in two so that
you have 40 pieces. Remove the lower
bone from each leg and with a small
kitchen knife, turn out the flesh

from the upper part to remove the
remaining bone.

For the Tempura Batter
Carefully combine all the ingredients
until you have a batter with a creamy
texture.

For the Basil Oil
In a mixing bowl, place the basil leaves
and grape-seed oil. Blend together
thoroughly, strain through cheesecloth,
and set aside.

For the Basil Sauce
Whisk together the egg yolks, the
mustard, salt, and freshly ground pepper
with the basil oil. Adjust the seasoning.
Continue to whisk until the mixture is
quite smooth and has the consistency of
thick cream.

Dampen the kosher salt and use a pastry
cutter to make a dome of salt on the
plates to hold the oysters. Season the
frogs' legs with salt and pepper. Heat
an oil bath to 325°F (160°C). Dip
the frogs' legs in the tempura batter
and fry until they are a nice golden
color. With a pastry bag, pipe out
small mounds of basil sauce on each
side of the plate and place a piece of
frogs' leg tempura on each mound.
For an attractive presentation,
garnish with a sprig of fresh thyme
and a small flower.

L'Auberge du Pont de Collonges p. 20–23

Red Mullet Dressed in Crisp Potato Scales (see photo p. 22)

Serves 4

2 red mullets, 11–12 oz. (320 g) each
2 big potatoes
1 egg yolk
Salt
2 tablespoons clarified butter
½ teaspoon potato starch
2 tablespoons olive oil
2 tablespoons veal jus
1 sprig chervil

Sauce

2 oranges
3 sprigs rosemary
3.3 oz. (100 ml) Noilly Prat
1 ½ cups (300 ml) crème fraîche
Salt and freshly ground pepper

Bone the fish with a thin knife or tweezers. Cut two rectangles of greaseproof paper, slightly bigger than the fish fillets. Place the fish on top with the skin facing up.

Wash and finely slice the potatoes, and carve tiny scales with an apple-corer. Put the potato scales in a pan and cover them with cold water. Bring to the boil for 1 minute and strain.

Thin the egg yolk with one teaspoon of water and a pinch of salt. Brush the fish skin with it.

Mix the potato scales with the clarified butter in a bowl. Carefully mix the potato starch. Place overlapped scales on top of the fish fillets starting from the head. Chill in the refrigerator for 15 minutes. Heat the olive oil in a frying pan. Take each rectangle with a fillet and flip it over the oil. Remove the paper. Salt the flesh side. Cook for about 6 minutes until the scales are brown. Flip the fillets and cook for a few seconds.

For the Sauce

Squeeze the oranges. Pour the juice and rosemary in a saucepan and reduce over a medium heat until dry. Add the Noilly Prat and reduce half the liquid. Add the crème and 2-3 pinches of salt and pepper. Reduce over a high heat until the sauce is thick, and strain.

To Serve

Coat the plate with the sauce and use a spoon to draw veal jus "scales". Place a fillet and add a little chervil.

Truffle Soup V.G.E. (see photo p. 21)

This dish was specially created for President Valéry Giscard D'Estaing when he awarded the Légion d'Honneur to Paul Bocuse at the Elysée, the presidential residence in Paris.

Serves 1

½ oz. (10 g) mixed carrots, onions, celery, and mushrooms in equal proportions
A little butter
⅓ oz. (10 g) cooked chicken breast

⅔ oz. (20 g) foie gras
⅔ oz. (20 g) black truffles
1 tablespoon Noilly Prat
2 cups (500 ml) double chicken consommé
One 2-oz. (60-g) disk puff pastry
1 egg yolk for basting
Sea salt and freshly ground pepper

Finely dice the vegetables and sauté them in butter. Cut the chicken breast into ¼ in. (5 mm) dice, cut the foie gras into pieces, and finely slice the truffles. Place these ingredients at the bottom of the soup dish. Add the Noilly Prat and the consommé. Season with salt and pepper. Place the disk of puff pastry over the soup dish, pressing it down well to seal it so that all the flavors of the soup remain concentrated inside.

Baste it with the egg yolk and place it in the oven at 425°F (220°C) for 18–20 minutes. Remove from the oven and serve immediately.

Bras p. 24–27

A Feast of Fall Vegetables (see photo p. 24)

Serves 4

2 Romaine or celtuce (stem) lettuce
4 carrots
4 turnips

1 celeriac
4 new leeks
4 leaves Swiss chard
2 parsnips
2 parsley roots (also known as root

parsley, turnip-rooted parsley, parsnip-rooted parsley)
1 Hubbard squash
1 oz. (25 g) muscovado sugar
Butter, for purees

Cream, for purees
14 oz. (400 g) white garden orache
and amaranth
16 baby spinach leaves
7 oz. (200 g) porcini (ceps)
7 oz. (200 g) chanterelles
7 oz. (200 g) black trumpet or horn of
plenty mushrooms
4 black figs
1 ½ tablespoons (25 ml) sweet wine
3 ½ tablespoons (50 ml) red wine
vinegar
5 juniper berries
4 slices ham
A little oil
A little hazelnut vinaigrette
12 groundnuts and hazelnuts

Separate the celtuce or Romaine leaves from the stems. Pare the stems and slice them lengthways using a knife or mandolin to a thickness of ⅛ in. (3 mm).

Cook the slices in salted boiling water. Peel the carrots, turnips, and celeriac, leaving a little of the leaves. Cut them in the same way as the lettuce stems; however, the celeriac should be cut into 8 slices. Cook them in salted boiling water. Peel and slice the leeks. Cook them in salted boiling water.

Wash the spinach and set aside.

Peel the parsnips and parsley roots, removing the hard core of the roots. Cook them in salted boiling water. Prepare a puree with these two vegetables, adding cream and butter as needed.
Peel the Hubbard squash and cook it in salted boiling water. Prepare it in a puree with the muscovado, butter, and cream. It should be smooth and soft.

Wash and set aside the orache and amaranth leaves.

Clean the mushrooms so that they are ready to be sautéed at the last minute.

Poach the figs for 1 minute in the wine and vinegar. Drain them, keeping the liquid, and set aside. Reduce the cooking liquid to a syrupy consistency. Add the juniper berries and set aside.

Just before serving, spoon the different purees in the plate, as well as the wine and vinegar reduction. Sauté the carrots, turnips, celeriac, Swiss chard, leeks, and Romaine or celtuce leaves in butter, and arrange them attractively on the plate with the slices of ham.
Dot the plate with the mushrooms and nuts. Scatter the salad leaves, seasoned with vinaigrette over.

Saddle of Allaiton Lamb Roasted on the Bone, Cow's Milk Curd Cheese, and Small Cabbage Leaves (see photo p. 26)

Serves 4

1 saddle of lamb
½ oz. (50 g) piece of cow's milk curd cheese
16 small cabbage leaves
1 egg
A little mustard
Garden cress, sorrel, bear's garlic, and dog's tooth violet flowers and leaves, the freshest you can find
Lemon juice
A little olive oil
Fleur de sel and freshly ground black pepper

Lamb Jus
Lamb trimmings
2 tablespoons (30 g) butter
2 oz. (60 g) onion
⅔ oz. (20 g) garlic
Aromatic garnish
¾ cup (200 ml) lamb consommé

Have your butcher prepare the saddle of lamb for cooking and reserve it in the refrigerator.
Select a curd cheese that is fresh and moist. Reserve it in the refrigerator.

For the Lamb Jus
Sauté the trimmings in butter, coloring them evenly. When they are done, add the vegetables and the aromatic garnish. Continue cooking, adding the consommé in several stages. It should reduce at each stage, except the last one. Leave it to infuse for a while. You may either keep the aromatic garnish or filter the jus. Set aside.

There is a wide variety of cabbage leaves, and we generally use those of the ordinary cabbage. Remove the hardest outer leaves. Use the tips of the leaves, which are more tender than the base. Remove the stems and fibers so that all that remains is the soft part of the leaf.

Cook the stems and soft leaves separately in boiling salted water. Refresh in ice water. Drain and chill.

Prepare a savory zabaglione (sabayon) according to the usual method, adding the mustard, ensuring that the egg is not overcooked.

Sort, wash, and dry the salad leaves and flowers. Prepare a vinaigrette with lemon juice and a little olive oil.

At the last moment cook the saddle of lamb to medium rare. Leave it to rest for an adequate time.
Spoon a little of the zabaglione into the plate with the cheese curds. Carve the saddle of lamb lengthways and season with fleur de sel and freshly ground pepper. Roll the cabbage leaves in a little butter and season the salad leaves with the vinaigrette.

Le Bristol *p. 28–31*

Sea Urchins in their Shells with Tongue and Foam, Delicate Egg Mousseline (see photo p. 29)

Serves 4

10 oz. (300 g) sea urchin tongues
⅓ cup (75 g) sea urchin jus
1 ¼ cup (300 ml) whipping cream
⅓ oz. (9 g) egg white powder
Lemon juice
Salt and pepper to taste

Scrambled Eggs
6 scrambled eggs

Butter
2 tablespoons (30 ml) cream
Salt and pepper to taste

Seaweed Butter
3 ½ oz. (100 g) seaweed
2 lb. (1 kg) salted butter

48 sea urchin tongues
Sprigs of dill
Toasted bread

Prepare the sea urchin siphon: blend all the ingredients and place them in a siphon with a gas canister over ice to chill.

Prepare the egg siphon: cook the scrambled eggs until well done. Blend in a food processor and add the butter, cream, salt, and pepper. It should have the consistency of a Béarnaise sauce. Place the mixture in a siphon with 1 gas canister and keep in a bain-marie.

Prepare the seaweed butter: blanch the seaweed and combine it with the butter.

Work it into a tube shape and leave it to harden in the refrigerator. Cut out 1 in. (2.5 cm) pieces and wrap them like candies.

Fill the sea urchin shells ¾ full with the contents of the egg siphon. Warm the urchin tongues a little and arrange 6 or 7 tongues, depending on the size, to form a flower. Prepare a nicely shaped scoop from the siphon with the urchin mixture. Garnish with the dill sprigs and serve with a seaweed butter "candy" and a slice of toast.

Litchi in Snowy Meringue (see photo p. 31)

Serves 4

Litchi Foam
7 oz. (¾ cup, 200 g) litchi juice
3 ½ oz. (scant ½ cup/100 g) pear juice
2 oz. (scant ¼ cup/50 g) lime juice
3 ½ tablespoons (40 g) sugar
3 sheets (6 g) gelatin

A few raspberries
A few litchis
A few pears
Rose syrup and crystallized rose petals

Combine the litchi, pear, and lime juices with the sugar. Dissolve the gelatin and incorporate it into the mixture. Pour it

into the siphon. Extrude the foam into a dome-shaped mold. Garnish it with pieces of raspberry, litchi, and pear, and a little rose syrup.

Freeze for 15 minutes, turn out of the molds, garnish with crystallized rose petals, and serve.

Carré des Feuillants *p. 32–35*

Wild Jumbo Prawns in "Crème de Tête" Melon Scoops in Chutney and Saffron-Scented Gazpacho (see photo p. 32)

Serves 6

3 firm, flavorful charentais (or cantaloupe) melons
6 jumbo prawns, 6–7 oz. (180–200 g) each

Melon Chutney
½ lb (250 g) remaining melon, finely diced (brunoise)
¼ cup (2 oz./50 g) sugar
Small pinch (0.5 g) curry powder
¼ clove
1 teaspoon (5 g) mustard seeds

Scant ½ teaspoon (2 g) crushed coriander seeds
1 heaped teaspoon (5 g) ground ginger
¼ preserved lemon
1 tablespoon plus 2 teaspoons (25 ml) white wine vinegar
¾ teaspoon (3 g) agar-agar
Scant ½ teaspoon (2 g) table salt

Melon Gazpacho

7 oz. (200 g) melon from remaining fruit
Scant ⅓ cup (75 ml) mild olive oil
2 tablespoons (30 ml) well-flavored white chicken stock
1 small pinch saffron threads
1 small slice (2 g) fresh ginger
1 pinch piment d'Espelette
Few drops lemon juice

Crème de Tête

The coral from the prawn heads
Scant ½ cup (100 g) whipping cream
Piment d'Espelette
Salt to taste

Garnish

Wasabi
Pureed garden peas
Mild paprika
2 or 3 scallions (young green onions)

Prepare 108 scoops from the halved, seeded melons using a melon baller and reserve the remaining flesh for the chutney and gazpacho.

For the Melon Chutney
Gently simmer all the ingredients with the exception of the agar-agar for 30 minutes. Then remove from the heat, add the agar-agar, and allow to cool.
Using 6 square frames, arrange 18 melon scoops mixed with the gelled chutney in each one. Chill to set.

For the Crème de Tête
Take the coral from the prawn heads and heat over high heat with the whipping cream. Season to taste and cook until the mixture is a lovely pink.

For the Melon Gazpacho
Liquidize the gazpacho ingredients together in a blender, adjust the seasoning with a few drops of lemon juice, and pour into small glasses as an accompaniment. Shell the prawn tails and make an incision lengthways to remove the gut. Season and steam for 3–4 minutes.

Slice and snip the scallions. Rinse in ice water.
Mix the pureed garden peas with a little wasabi.

For each individual plate, take a stencil and fill in a very thin square of the garden pea and wasabi mixture. Draw lines of mild paprika. On each plate, turn the squares of melon scoops out of their frames. Lastly, roll the still-warm prawn tails in the crème de tête and arrange them on the plate, garnished with snipped scallion.

Wild Turbot Fillet, Aquitaine Caviar, Rice in Squid Ink, Green Asparagus, and Girolles (see photo p. 34)

Serves 6

A little mild onion
Olive oil, for sautéing
Butter, for sautéing
3 ½–4 oz. (100–120 g) Arborio rice
Scant ¼ cup (50 ml) white wine
1 ¼ cup (300 ml) chicken broth
Squid ink
1 generous tablespoon Parmesan cheese, grated
12 small green asparagus
½ lb. (250 g) small girolles, apricot-colored chanterelle mushrooms
Dash of veal jus

Six 5-oz. (140-g) fillets of turbot, taken from the back of a large wild turbot
2 oz. (50 g) Aquitaine caviar
Salt and black pepper

For the Risotto
Chop the onion and sweat it in the olive oil and butter without allowing it to color. Add the rice and stir until it is translucent. Gradually pour in the white wine and a little chicken broth taking 20 minutes altogether, stirring all the time. Lastly add the squid ink and a generous spoonful of grated Parmesan. Adjust the seasoning with salt and black pepper.

Finely dice the green part of the asparagus stems and steam them. Clean the girolles and halve or quarter them. Sauté them at the last minute in a knob of butter with the veal jus to retain both their flavor and color. Lightly salt the turbot pieces and steam them for 8–10 minutes. Serve all the components of the dish hot, except for the caviar.

Arrange the black risotto and top it with the diced green asparagus. Place the cut chanterelles on the side, and set out the pieces of turbot with a line of caviar drawn across the top.

Alain Chapel p. 36–39

Mille-feuille of Chocolate Meringue and Crisp Praline (see photo p. 36)

Serves 8–10

Hazelnut Meringue
1 ¼ cups (9 oz./250 g) sugar
Scant ½ cup (110 ml) water
7 oz. (200 g) egg whites
5 ¼ oz. (150 g) hazelnuts, freshly ground
1 generous cup (5 ¼ oz./150 g) confectioners' sugar
3 ½ tablespoons (40 g) sugar

Nougatine Praline-Lemon Tuiles
¾ cup (5 ¼ oz./150 g) sugar
Generous ½ teaspoon (2.5 g) pectin NH
1 stick (4 ½ oz./125 g) butter
2 oz. (50 g) glucose syrup
2 ¾ oz. (80 g) Valrhona crunchy praline
Scant ½ cup (100 ml) milk
Grated zest of 1 lemon

Crisp Chocolate Meringue
10 oz. (300 g) egg white
¾ cup (5 ¼ oz./150 g) sugar
1 cup (5 oz./140 g) confectioners' sugar
6 tablespoons (1 ½ oz./40 g) unsweetened cocoa powder

Milk Chocolate Whipped Cream
1 ¾ cups (400 ml) whipping cream
10 oz. (280 g) Jivara milk couverture chocolate

Crisp Praline
1 lb. (480 g) crisp praline
5 ¼ oz. (150 g) milk chocolate
3 tablespoons (45 g) unsalted butter
10 oz. (300 g) feuillantine or crushed caramel waffle wafers

Cocoa Nib Marshmallow
2 cups (500 ml) milk
2 ¾ oz. (80 g) cocoa nibs
9 sheets gelatin (18 g)
7 ¾ oz. (220 g) pasteurized egg whites
3 ½ tablespoons (1 ½ oz./40 g) sugar

Chocolate Sauce
1 ¼ cups (300 ml) milk
2 ½ oz. (75 g) glucose syrup
½ lb. (250 g) Guanaja couverture chocolate, 70%

For the Hazelnut Meringue
To make an Italian meringue, cook the sugar with a little water to a temperature of 257°F (125°C). While it is cooking, beat the egg whites to stiff peaks. Pour the sugar over the whipped egg whites and continue beating until cooled. Incorporate the ground hazelnuts, confectioners' sugar, and smaller quantity of sugar into the cool meringue. Spoon into a pastry bag and pipe out 4 strips. Begin baking at 325°F (160°C) for a few minutes and finish at 200°F (100°C).

For the Tuiles
Combine the sugar and pectin and add the butter, milk, and glucose syrup. Cook all the ingredients together over low heat until combined. Add the praline and lemon zest.
Spread out over a silicone baking sheet and bake at 330°F (165°C) for 10–15 minutes.

For the Crisp Chocolate Meringue
Whisk the egg whites with half the sugar, starting slowly and then beating faster, and then add the remaining ingredients and incorporate either with the beater or by hand, being careful that the cocoa powder doesn't deflate the meringue. Pipe out 4 lines with a No. 6 tip onto a sheet of parchment paper. Bake at 200°F (100°C) for 2 hours.

For the Milk Chocolate Whipped Cream
Use a paddle or flat beater to prepare the ganache, process it, and chill, if possible overnight. Pipe it out through a square tip.

For the Crisp Praline
Place the praline in the food processor bowl with the paddle beater and process. In a round-bottomed mixing bowl, melt the chocolate with the butter. Pour it over the praline and add the feuillantine. Spread the mixture between two silicone sheets, with a ruler at each side so that it is ¼ in. (5 mm) thick. Chill until hardened and cut out into rectangles 2 ½ × 1 ¼ in. (6 × 3 cm).

For the Marshmallow
Bring the milk to the boil with the cocoa nibs. Remove from the heat and leave to infuse for a few minutes. Strain through a chinois and check that there is a total weight of 17 ½ oz. (500 g) of liquid. Add the gelatin and bring to the boil once again.

Slowly whisk the egg whites with the sugar. They should be foamy, not stiff.
Cool the milk to 77°F (25°C) and rapidly whisk in the egg whites. Be careful: this will set very quickly. Pour it into a pastry ring to about 1 in. (2–3 cm) depth. Chill, then cut and cover in plastic wrap.

For the Chocolate Sauce
Melt all the ingredients together to make a smooth sauce.

To plate: place a hazelnut meringue rectangle in the plate. Above that, place the chocolate meringue, the crisp praline, and then the marshmallow. Using a pastry bag with a square tip, pipe out a line of chocolate whipped cream. Top with a tuile and decorate with chocolate sauce.

Hen Pheasant with Foie Gras in Aspic, Hot Toasts (see photo p. 38)

Serves 8

2 hen pheasants
1 boiling fowl
1 ½ lb. (250 g) piece of raw foie gras cut lengthways, thickness . in ¾ (1.5 cm)
Gelatin, 7 sheets (14 g) per 4 cups (4 liters) liquid

Gratin Stuffing
⅔ oz. (20 g) fatback, in small dice
1 garlic clove, unpeeled
Thyme
3 ½ oz. (100 g) pork from the blade shoulder (US) or spare rib (UK), diced into pieces of approx. 1 in.(2.5 cm)
3 ½ oz. (100 g) chicken livers
Scant ½ cup (100 ml) red wine

Stuffing
½ lb. (250 g) meat from 1 of the hen pheasants
3 ½ oz. (100 g) fatback
Scant ¼ cup (50 ml) crème fraîche, 35% fat content
3 ½ oz. (100 g) raw foie gras, strained through a sieve
⅓ cup (75 ml) Madeira wine
Scant ¼ cup (50 ml) truffle jus
2 scant teaspoons salt per pound (18 g per kg)
3 turns of the pepper mill per pound (2 g per kg)

Aromatic Garnish for the Boiling Fowl
Carrots, turnips, celeriac (celery root), leeks, bouquet garni, etc.

Marinade
Foie gras,
Cognac,
Madeira,
Truffle jus
Salt and pepper

Garnish
Horn of plenty mushrooms
Girolles
Charbonnier mushrooms
Yellow knight mushrooms
Porcini (ceps)
Walnut oil vinaigrette

For the Gratin Stuffing
Melt the fatback over low heat. Add the unpeeled garlic clove, thyme, chicken livers, and diced pork. Cook for 1 minute and deglaze with red wine. Allow to reduce until dry. Remove the garlic clove and thyme. Place in the bowl of a food processor with a blade cutter and process until finely ground.

For the Stuffing
Cook the boiling fowl with the aromatic garnish and strain the cooking liquid. Keep this to cook the hen pheasants in. Bone 1 pheasant, reserving the meat for the stuffing and the carcass for the cooking liquid.
Finely mince the pheasant and the boiling fowl meat, together with the fatback and gratin stuffing. Add the Madeira, seasoning, truffle jus, cream, and foie gras. Chill overnight.
Bone the second pheasant carefully, starting from the back and leaving the meat intact. Do not tear the skin. Place the boned pheasant in a dish with the foie gras, salt, pepper, cognac, Madeira, and truffle jus, and marinate for 2–3 hours.
With the pheasant facing you, place a layer of stuffing in the cavity, then a piece of foie gras in the center, and cover with a layer of stuffing. Close up the pheasant, making sure that it looks whole. Truss it up at the back. Roll it up in a clean cloth, tying it up very tightly at each end and across the length of the bird.
Heat the chicken stock to 140–160°F (60–70°C) and add the carcass and the stuffed pheasant. Cook until the core temperature reaches 104°F (40°C). Dip into a bowl of ice water for 3–4 minutes, remove, and chill.
Take half the pheasant cooking liquid and remove the fat. Clarify it and set it with gelatin to set the liquid that you will pour over the slices. The other half should be more quivering (use 5 sheets (10 g) for every 4 cups (1 liter)) and should be spooned on to the plates next to the terrine.
Remove the cloth and string, and cut the pheasant in slices. Place the slices on a rack and slowly pour over the gelatine liquid.
Quickly sauté the mushrooms and season them with walnut oil vinaigrette.

Place a slice of pheasant hen on each plate with a few spoons of quivering jelly and the warm mushrooms. Accompany with hot toasted slices of bread.

La Bastide Saint-Antoine p. 40–43

Violet Asparagus with Foie-Gras Ice Cream and Truffle Coulis (see photo p. 41)

Serves 6

Foie-Gras Ice Cream
2 ¾ oz. (80 g) cooked mashed potato, pushed through a sieve
½ cup (120 ml) chicken stock
3 ½ tablespoons (50 ml) milk
1 tablespoon (15 ml) whipping cream
1 ½ oz. (40 g) foie gras terrine, fat removed
1 oz. (25 g) powdered milk
Salt and pepper to taste

Egg Cream
1 tablespoon plus 2 teaspoons (25 ml) whipping cream
1 ¾ tablespoons (1 oz./25 g) butter
2 egg yolks
Salt and pepper to taste

Truffle Coulis
½ oz. (15 g) truffle peel and trimmings
2 tablespoons (30 ml) olive oil
A few drops of balsamic vinegar
1 pinch of chicken stock powder
Salt and pepper to taste

Asparagus and Coulis
8 large asparagus, green or violet
1 tablespoon (15 ml) thick cream
1 teaspoon (5 ml) Noilly vermouth
1 teaspoon (5 ml) white wine
4 sprigs tarragon

Truffle Salad
2 large camus artichokes (large green variety from Brittany)
1 ½ oz. (40 g) white onion
Lemon juice
2 tablespoons (30 ml) olive oil
2 tablespoons (30 ml) white wine
2 tablespoons (30 ml) water
2 oz. (50 g) truffle
Salt and pepper to taste
24 baby beet or spinach leaves
⅓ cup (80 ml) pistachio oil
1 tablespoon paprika flakes

For the Foie-Gras Ice Cream
In a small saucepan, combine the strained mashed potato, chicken stock, milk, cream, and foie gras. Season with salt and pepper. Heat over low heat, stirring constantly with a whisk, until it reaches a temperature of 113°F (45°C), which you should check with a thermometer. Carefully incorporate the powdered milk and stir constantly with a rubber spatula for 5 to 6 minutes. Blend the mixture in a food processor. Check the seasoning, transfer to a small mixing bowl, and chill for 12 hours. Place the mixture in an ice-cream maker and leave until just a few minutes before serving.

For the Egg Cream
Use a saucepan with curved sides so that you can stir the egg yolks well, mixing them thoroughly as you would scrambled eggs. Melt the butter with the whipping cream. Season with salt and pepper and add the egg yolks. Cook over very low heat, stirring constantly until the desired consistency is reached: it must be as smooth as mayonnaise. Transfer to a small mixing bowl and leave at room temperature. (If you chill it, it will harden.)

For the Truffle Coulis
Place all the ingredients in the bowl of a food processor and process until the texture is perfectly smooth.

For the Asparagus and Coulis
Peel the asparagus carefully: make sure they are as regular as possible, and leave the tips unpeeled. Bring a pot of 4 cups (1 liter) water to boil with 4 teaspoons (20 g) salt and place the asparagus in the boiling water. In the meanwhile, prepare a bowl of cold water with ice cubes. Do not overcook the asparagus: they should retain a slight crunch. Remove from the water and cut to a length of approximately 5 in. (12 cm). Immediately refresh them in the ice water and drain on a clean cloth. Return the cut-off ends of the asparagus to the boiling water and cook them a little longer. Dip them briefly in the ice water; they should stay warm. Place these ends in the bowl of a food processor with the cream, the Noilly, white wine, 4 tablespoons (60 ml) water, salt, pepper, and tarragon. Process at high speed until the coulis is perfectly smooth. Transfer to a bowl and chill.

For the Truffle Salad
Finely slice the onion. Snap off the artichoke bracts and trim the base of the artichoke to obtain a nicely rounded bottom. Remove the choke (the hairy part) and squeeze with lemon juice. Cut the artichokes into slices just under ⅛ in. (2 mm) thick. Drizzle a little olive oil into a nonstick pan and sauté the artichoke bottom slices, seasoned with salt and pepper, over high heat until they turn a light golden color. Add the sliced onions and sauté them gently. Deglaze with a little white wine and water, cover with the lid, and cook over very low heat until all the liquid has evaporated. Chop ¼ oz. (5 g) of the truffles. Place the salad leaves attractively in a corner of the plate. Arrange the artichoke slices in a dome shape over the leaves. Use a mandolin to slice the remaining truffle very thinly. Arrange the slices attractively above the salad domes. Season with salt and pepper and drizzle with a little olive oil.

Place 2 asparagus tips on each plate opposite the truffle salad and garnish with a drizzle each of truffle coulis, asparagus coulis, and creamed egg. Then place an oval scoop of foie-gras ice cream on each plate, garnished with a few paprika flakes. Decorate with a few drips of pistachio oil. Drizzle a little balsamic vinegar over the asparagus.

Roasted Pears with Caramelized Honey Nougatine and Licorice Cream (see photo p. 43)

Serves 4

Roasted Pears
2 large pears, Williams or Bartlett
2 tablespoons (30 g) butter, softened
2 ½ teaspoons (10 g) sugar
2 teaspoons (15 g) honey
1 vanilla bean, split in two lengthways
1 pinch ground cinnamon

Roasted Figs
8 figs
1 tablespoon (20 g) honey
1 tablespoon plus 1 teaspoon (20 g) butter
1 teaspoon (5 ml) vanilla extract
1 tablespoon (15 ml) raspberry coulis
1 pinch ground cinnamon

Sautéed cherries
5–6 oz. (160 g) pitted Burlat cherries (net weight)
1 teaspoon (5 ml) vanilla extract
¼ cup (2 oz./50 g) sugar
1 tablespoon (15 ml) Amaretto
1 tablespoon (15 ml) kirsch
A little grated lemon zest

Salted Caramel Sauce
2 tablespoons (25 g) sugar
1 tablespoon plus 1 teaspoon (20 g) whipping cream
2 teaspoons (10 g) salted butter

Crisp Phyllo
2 sheets phyllo pastry
1 tablespoon plus 1 teaspoon (20 g) butter
2 teaspoons (15 g) honey

Cinnamon Cream
¾ cup (200 ml) milk
1 ½ sheets gelatin (3 g)
⅔ cup (180 ml) whipping cream
1 tablespoon plus 2 teaspoons (20 g) sugar
1 pinch ground cinnamon

Pistachio Crisp
2 tablespoons (30 g) butter, at room temperature and softened
1 tablespoon plus 2 teaspoons (20 g) sugar
⅓ oz. (10 g) pistachio paste
¾ oz. (20 g) egg white (this is about ⅔ of the white of one egg)
⅓ cup (1 oz./30 g) flour

For the Roasted Pears and Figs
Preheat the oven to 350°F (180°C). Peel and core the pears. Cut them in two and brush them with the softened butter. Slit the vanilla bean and place it at the bottom of an appropriately sized ovenproof dish. Sprinkle the pears with the sugar and honey and arrange them snugly over the vanilla bean. Sprinkle them with cinnamon. Bake for 20 to 30 minutes, pouring a little water over them every 5 minutes.
Repeat the procedure with the figs, adding the raspberry coulis. Bake them for about 10 minutes.

For the Sautéed Cherries
Spread 1 tablespoon plus 2 teaspoons (20 g) sugar evenly over a small nonstick pan over high heat. Leave until it forms a light caramel. Immediately add the cherries, the remaining sugar, the vanilla extract, and lemon zest. Cook, stirring continuously for 5 minutes. Then add the Amaretto and the kirsch and set aside.

For the Salted Caramel Sauce
Place the sugar and just a little water in a saucepan until it reaches the blond-brown caramel stage. Immediately pour in the whipping cream and butter and stir briskly with a spatula until you have a liquid caramel.

For the Crisp Phyllo
Preheat the oven to 350°C (180°F). Melt the butter. Carefully spread out 1 phyllo sheet and brush it, using a pastry brush, with the melted butter. Then brush it with the honey. Place the second phyllo sheet over it and cut out 8 triangles measuring 4 × 1 ¾ in. (10 × 4 cm). Place them on a baking tray and bake, keeping a careful eye on them. As soon as each triangle turns a light yellow, remove it with a spatula and place it on a cold baking tray. Set aside.

For the Cinnamon Cream
Warm the milk and place the gelatin sheets in it to dissolve. Whip the cream with the sugar and cinnamon until it reaches a firm Chantilly texture. Carefully fold the gelatin-milk mixture into the whipped cream and chill.

For the Pistachio Crisp
In a small round-bottomed mixing bowl, whisk the softened butter very energetically with the sugar for 2 minutes. Incorporate the pistachio paste, the egg whites, and the flour, and leave to rest for 1 hour at room temperature.
Preheat the oven to 325°F (160°C). Prepare a stencil: make a triangle 6 × 1 in. (15 cm × 2.5 cm). Place the stencil on a nonstick baking tray using a steel spatula. Place a little dough on the tip and fill the stencil to the same thickness as the plastic. Remove the surplus with the spatula. Bake as you would if you were preparing cigarette cookies. The pastry must not color. As soon as it is done, form it into a half-circle. It will then harden.

To Assemble
Spoon the cinnamon cream into a pastry bag and on each of 4 crisp phyllo triangles, pipe out small rounds of cream, no more than ½ in. (1 cm) thick, covering the entire surface. Top each one with a second triangle. Place the assembled pastry in the corner of the plate and than add a pear-half, still hot, wedging the pistachio crisp below. Draw two lines of hot caramel at the other corners of the plate and arrange the hot figs and warm cherries there.

Le Cinq p. 44–47

Lemongrass-Scented John Dory Cooked on the Bone with Green Melon (see photo p. 45)

Serves 2

1 John Dory weighing 2-lb. (1-kg)
3 tablespoons (40 g) olive oil
1 lime
3 sticks fresh lemongrass
1 bay leaf
Scant ½ cup (100 ml) water
2 tablespoons (30 ml) yellow wine
⅔ oz. (20 g) rhizome fresh turmeric, sliced
5 tablespoons (2 ½ oz., 70 g) butter, divided
3 ½ oz. (100 g) green melon
3 ½ oz. (100 g) cucumber
3 ½ oz. (100 g) Hubbard squash
1 sprig lemon thyme
2 oz. (50 g) fresh small calamari
1 ½ oz. (40 g) cuttlefish
Salt and white pepper to taste

Drizzle a little olive oil and the juice of half a lime over the John Dory. Wrap it in a parchment paper papillote with a stick of lemongrass and a bay leaf. Season with salt and white pepper. Place the papillote over a gas ring and heat for 1 minute, then cook for 20 minutes in a 325°F (160°C) oven until the flesh is translucent. Remove from the oven and leave to rest for 10 minutes. Then remove the skin. Prepare fillets and place them one on top of another.

Prepare the sauce. Take the fish bones and cooking liquid and add the water, 1 sliced stick of lemongrass, and the sliced turmeric.
Simmer for 15 minutes to infuse and strain through a fine sieve.
Add 3 tablespoons plus 1 teaspoon (50 g) butter, the juice of the other half of the lime, and whisk together to emulsify the sauce.
Using a melon baller, prepare large balls of green melon, cucumber, and Hubbard squash. Set aside the scoops of melon. Place the cucumber and Hubbard squash balls in a saucepan with a tablespoon of water, 1 tablespoon plus 1 teaspoon (20 g) butter, and the lemon thyme. Season with salt and pepper and cook with the lid on.

Spoon the lemongrass and turmeric sauce over the John Dory fillets. Brown the small calamari and cuttlefish pieces in olive oil and add them to the fish. Season to taste.
Glaze the scoops of raw melon, the Hubbard squash and cucumber with the cooking liquid and arrange them attractively around the plate. Serve the remaining John Dory sauce in a sauce dish.

Iced Coffee Viennetta with Piedmont Hazelnut Nougatine (see photo p. 47)

Serves 15

14 oz. (400 g) dark couverture chocolate
Whole, caramelized hazelnuts

Coffee Nougatine
14 oz. (400 g) glucose
2 cups (14 oz./400 g) sugar
8 ½ oz. (240 g) fresh almonds
5 ½ teaspoons (10 g) ground coffee
1 ¾ teaspoons (2 g) instant coffee

Light Hazelnut Coffee Cream
2 oz. (60 g) pastry cream (crème pâtissière)
⅔ oz. (18 g) hazelnut paste
¼ teaspoon (1 g) mocha paste
1 sheet gelatin (2 g)
Scant ¼ cup (40 g) cream, whipped

Coffee Ice Cream
2 cups plus ⅔ cup (700 ml) milk
¾ cup (200 ml) cream
1 ¼ oz. (36 g) atomized glucose
1 ½ oz. (40 g) roasted coffee beans
4 ¾ oz. (130 g) sugar
¼ oz. (8 g) Cremodan ice cream stabilizer
1 ¼ oz. (40 g) egg yolk
3 tablespoons (10 g) instant coffee

For the Coffee Nougatine
Combine all the ingredients and prepare strips of nougatine measuring ¾ × 6 ⅔ in. (2.5 × 17 cm).

For the Chocolate Strips
Melt the couverture chocolate and when it is at 104°F (40°C) spread it out onto a marble working surface to cool. Cut out strips measuring 1 × 7 in. (2.5 × 18 cm) and prepare decorations.

Combine the ingredients for the light hazelnut cream and set aside in the freezer.

For the Coffee Ice Cream
Put the milk, cream, and roasted coffee beans in a saucepan and bring to a boil. Separately, mix the sugar, egg yolk and instant coffee in a bowl, and whip until the mixture is pale and reaches a foamy texture.
Use a ladle to add a little boiling milk to the mixture in the bowl, and then pour the rest of the milk. Return the mixture to the saucepan and leave to cook on low heat. Stir constantly with a wooden spatula to obtain a thick crème anglaise at

176°F (80°C). Remove from the heat and chill over ice cubes. Put the coffee crème in an ice-cream maker until it is set.

To assemble, begin with the chocolate strip, follow with the nougatine, the coffee ice cream, another chocolate strip, nougatine, the light hazelnut cream piped out with a pastry bag and tip, the nougatine, coffee ice cream, the caramelized hazelnuts, and the chocolate decorations.

Les Crayères p. 48–51

Zebra-Striped Bresse Chicken Fillet, Rustici Pasta with Truffle Jus (see photo p. 51)

Serves 2

1 Bresse chicken weighing 3 ½ lb. (1.6 kg)
6 ⅓ pints (3 liters) chicken broth

Garnish
1 scallion
⅔ oz. (20 g) truffle
⅔ cup (150 ml) chicken broth
3 ½ oz. (100 g) new onions
Scant ½ cup (100 ml) chicken broth
¼ cup (60 ml) whipping cream
2 tablespoons (30 g) butter

2 teaspoons (10 ml) olive oil
5 oz. (140 g) Rustici (or any cylindrical pasta)
3 tablespoons (40 ml) truffle jus

⅓ oz. (10 g) bacon
2 tablespoons (30 g) butter
2 leaves Romaine lettuce
Raw foie gras for shavings

Gut the chicken and cut off the thighs, reserving them for another recipe. Place the remaining chicken in a pot and pour the broth over it. Bring to the boil and simmer for 25 minutes.

Cut the scallion and place it with half the truffle and the ⅔ cup (150 ml) chicken broth in a saucepan. Cover with the lid and cook for 10 minutes, then process to make a truffle puree. Set aside. Finely chop the new onions and place in a pot with a little olive oil. Sauté, ensuring that they do not brown. Add the pasta and the truffle jus and simmer for about 10 minutes on low heat. Finely dice the bacon and sauté the cubes in butter. Cut the Romaine lettuce leaves into half-circles and cut the remaining truffle into identical shapes. Reduce the ½ cup chicken broth, add the cream, and reduce again. Whisk in 2 tablespoons (30 g) butter.

Carve the chicken breasts and spoon over the sauce. Drizzle zebra stripes over them with the truffle puree. Arrange the pasta on one side of the place and top with truffle and lettuce half circles. Prepare fine shavings of foie gras and place them delicately over the pasta.

"Les Crayères" Pink Reims Lady Fingers, Grapefruit Sorbet, Sparkling Gelled Champagne (see photo p. 49)

Serves 4

French Meringue
2 ⅛ oz. (60 g) egg white
¾ oz. (20 g) sugar
1 ¾ oz. (50 g) confectioners' sugar

Pink Lady Finger Mousse
1 tablespoon plus 1 teaspoon (20 ml) milk
2 tablespoons plus 2 teaspoons (40 ml) whipping cream
1 oz. (25 g) egg yolk
1 ¾ oz. (50 g) ground pink ladyfingers (specialty of Reims)
½ cup (120 g) cream, whipped
¼ cup (30 g) sugar
1 gelatin paper

Champagne Sorbet
⅓ cup (70 g) water
2 ½ oz. (70 g) sugar
⅓ oz. (10 g) glucose
⅓ cup (120 g) champagne

Grapefruit Sorbet
⅓ cup (75 g) water
¾ oz. (20 g) sugar
1 ½ oz. (40 g) glucose
Generous ½ cup (140 g) grapefruit juice

Champagne Glaze
Scant ½ cup (100 g) rosé champagne
1 ⅛ oz. (30 g) sugar
¼ teaspoon (1 g) NH pectin

White Chocolate Tears
10 oz. (300 g) white chocolate

For the French Meringue
Begin beating the egg whites and pour in the sugar to finish whisking them to firm peaks. Using a flexible rubber or silicone spatula, gently fold in the confectioners' sugar. Spoon the mixture into a pastry bag and pipe out eight 2 ½-in. (7-cm) disks onto a baking tray. Bake for 2 hours at 200°F (100°C). Set aside in an airtight container.

For the Pink Lady Finger Mousse
Heat the milk and cream. Beat the egg yolks and sugar together, add to the

milk and cream, and cook to make a crème anglaise. Soften the gelatin and incorporate it into the mixture. Stir in the ground lady fingers. Fold in the whipped cream and chill.

For the Champagne Sorbet
Prepare a syrup with the water, sugar, and glucose. Allow to cool and pour it over the champagne. Prepare a sorbet in your ice-cream maker.

For the Grapefruit Sorbet
Prepare another syrup with the water,

sugar, and glucose. Allow to cool and pour it over the grapefruit juice. Prepare a sorbet in your ice-cream maker.

For the Champagne Glaze
Heat a scant ¼ cup (50 ml) champagne and add the sugar and pectin. Allow to boil for 5 minutes and cool down with the remaining champagne. Set aside.

For the White Chocolate Tears
Melt the white chocolate and spread it out to just under ¹⁄₁₀ in. (2 mm) on

a Rhodoid or acetate sheet. Fold the strips over to form tear-drop shapes.

Place a meringue in the center of each plate. Add the pink lady finger mousse and sprinkle with crushed pink lady fingers. Top with chocolate tear drops and fill them with grapefruit sorbet. Place a scoop of champagne sorbet on top. Then pour some drops of the champagne glaze over the plate for decoration.

Au Crocodile p. 52–55

Watercress Flan with Frogs' Legs (see photo p. 55)

Serves 8

2 bunches watercress
Olive oil
1 cup (250 ml) milk
1 cup (250 ml) cream
1 garlic clove
3 eggs
2 egg yolks
3 spoons pureed watercress
Nutmeg
Salt and pepper to taste
8 dariole molds or coffee cups

Frogs' Legs
2.2 lb. (1 kg) frogs' legs
1 ¼ cup (300 ml) Alsace Riesling
⅔ cup (150 ml) Noilly
1 ¼ cups (300 ml fish fumet)
3 shallots
1 ⅔ cups crème fraîche
Grey peppercorns

Garnish
Tomato
Chervil

For the Watercress Puree
Cook the watercress for 4 minutes in salted boiling water. Refresh, drain, and blend with ice cubes.

For the Watercress Chlorophyll
Blend the watercress stalks with a little water until the mixture is smooth. Strain through a fine chinois sieve lined with cheesecloth. Bring the juice to a simmer and skim the foam off. Drain the skimmed foam and whip up the liquid with olive oil. Set aside, and reserve 1 soupspoon for the sauce.
Beat the eggs. Combine the milk and cream and bring to the boil with the sliced garlic cloves. Pour the liquid over the beaten eggs and add the watercress puree and watercress chlorophyll. Whisk, season, and strain through a chinois. Butter the molds and fill them. Place them in a bain-marie and bake for 285°F (140°C) for 30 minutes.

For the Frogs' Legs
Gently cook the frogs' legs for two minutes with the Riesling, Noilly, fish

fumet, and chopped shallots. Drain and remove the meat from the bones.

For the Sauce
Reduce the cooking liquid used for the frogs' legs to one quarter its original volume. Stir in the crème fraîche and reduce again until you have 1 cup (250 ml) liquid.
Share the sauce equally between two bowls. Reserve one as it is (the white sauce). Add 1 soupspoon of watercress to one of the bowls and strain it (the green sauce).
Heat the frogs' legs in the white sauce. Turn the flans out onto plates. Surround them with frogs' legs, pour over first the white sauce, and then the green sauce. Garnish with a diamond-shaped slice of tomato and a sprig of chervil.

Black Forest Cake, Revisited (see photo p. 53)

Serves 8

Dried Fruit Crunch
2 sticks butter (240 g) butter
1 lb. (470 g) flour
½ lb. (240 g) confectioners' sugar
4 oz. (120 g) ground blanched almonds
1 scant teaspoon (4 g) salt
3 ½ oz. (100 g) eggs
1 lb. (460 g) Jivara Lactée couverture chocolate
2 ¾ oz. (80 g) extra bitter couverture chocolate (70% cocoa solids)
3 ½ oz. (100 g) plump raisins
3 ½ oz. (100 g) plump apricots
7 oz. (200 g) diced almonds, roasted

Griottine Chantilly
⅔ cup (150 g) cream
¾ cup (5 oz./150 g) granulated sugar
5 sheets (10 g) gelatin
⅔ cup (150 ml) griottine juice (from Morello cherries in liqueur)

Cocoa Sorbet
2 cups (500 ml) water
1 cup (7 oz./200 g) sugar
6 tablespoons (40 g) unsweetened cocoa powder
7 oz. (200 g) extra bitter couverture chocolate (70% cocoa solids)

Quivering Jelly
Scant ½ cup (100 ml) griottine juice
1 cup plus 1 scant cup (9 oz., 380 g) sugar

10 oz. (300 g) griotte (Morello cherries) puree
5 sheets (10 g) gelatin

Sauce
5 oz. (150 g) griotte puree
2 oz. (50 g) griottines
1 tablespoon plus 2 teaspoons (25 g) kirsch
1 tablespoon plus 2 teaspoons (25 g) griottine juice
⅛ oz. 0.5 g Xantana (thickening agent)

Garnish
Chocolate tuiles, caramelized cocoa nibs, and gold leaf

For the Dried Fruit Crunch
Using the paddle attachment of your stand-alone food mixer beat the butter and flour together until the mixture reaches the consistency of a powder. Incorporate the dry ingredients and the egg without over-mixing. Spread it out paper thin ¹⁄₁₆ in. (0.5mm) and bake until it begins to color. With the blade knife of a food processor, grind it to a fine powder and incorporate the melted couverture chocolates, dried fruits and nuts, using your hands. When it is thoroughly blended, mold and leave to set in the refrigerator.

For the Griottine Chantilly
Whip the cream with the sugar until it forms soft peaks. Soften the gelatin, melt it in the griottine juice and incorporate it into the whipped cream. Finish whisking—the cream should not be too stiff—and spoon into silicone molds to two-thirds of the height.

For the Cocoa Sorbet
Heat the water, add the sugar and cocoa, and bring to the boil.
Blend and pour it over the couverture chocolate. Process again and leave to mature for 4 hours. Process and place in the ice-cream maker. When done, pipe it directly into the silicone molds.

For the Quivering Jelly
Heat the griottine juice, add the sugar and pureed morello cherries. Soften the gelatin in cold water and add it to the liquid. Pour into molds and chill.

For the Sauce
Combine all the ingredients in a food processor and blend until quite smooth. Turn out the griottine Chantilly from the molds and chill. Place dried fruit crunch on each rectangle of Chantilly and freeze.

Arrange the chopped griottines and drizzle a line of sauce on the plate. Draw a line of chocolate sauce, place a bar of jelly on it, and a griottine. Place some cocoa sorbet on the side of the dish. To garnish, add a chocolate tuile, some caramelized cocoa nibs, and some gold leaf.

Alain Ducasse au Plaza Athénée p. 56–59

Turbot, Shellfish, and Swiss Chard (see photo p. 59)

Serves 4

3 ½ oz. (100 g) wakame
4 ½ oz. (120 g) dulse
3 ½ oz. (100 g) sea lettuce
7 oz. (200 g) royal kombu
1 turbot back, 4 ¼ lb. (2 kg)
1 bunch multicolored (rainbow)

Swiss chard
1 lb. 5 oz. (600 g) clams
1 lb. 5 oz. (600 g) cockles
11 oz. (300 g) periwinkles
6 razor clams
6 shallots
2 fennel bulbs
6 garlic cloves

Olive oil
3 cups (750 ml) white wine, divided
2 bay leaves
1 ½ oz. (40 g) salted butter
(2 teaspoons/10 g per slice of fish)
1 stick plus 6 tablespoons (200 g) unsalted butter
Fleur de sel

1 cup (250 ml) veal aspic
A few sprigs of parsley, leaves and stalks separated
10 peppercorns
A little lemon juice

Rinse the seaweed to remove any excess salt and dry it all on a clean cloth.

Trim the fish right to the fillets, reserve the barbels, and cut ½ lb (240 g) slices, keeping the skin. Set aside.

Pull off the ribs from the Swiss chard leaves. Strip off the fibrous strings and wash the ribs. Wash the leaves.

Rinse all the shellfish separately under running water and drain them. Open the razor clams and slice them finely into rounds. Set the slices aside, raw.

Finely chop the shallots and fennel and crush the garlic.
Take half the shallots, fennel, and garlic cloves and sweat them in olive oil. Open the cockles and clams by deglazing them separately with half the white wine. Remove the shellfish with a slotted spoon and place them immediately in a bowl over ice to stop the cooking process. Filter each type of cooking liquid separately through a fine-mesh sieve and chill over ice. Remove the shells of each of the shellfish and cut out the sand pouch. Keep the clams and cockles separate in their cooking liquid. Place the periwinkles in a large pot and cover them with cold water. Add 2 bay leaves and 1 ¼ cups (300 ml) white wine and bring to the boil. Cook them for 3 minutes and leave to cool in their cooking liquid for 30 minutes. Drain, remove the shells, and cut them up, reserving only the heads.

In a sauté pan, sweat the remaining shallots, fennel, and garlic in the 1 stick plus 6 tablespoons (200 g) unsalted butter. Deglaze with the remaining white wine. Bring to the boil and add half the cooking liquid used for each of the shellfish (cockles and clams). Add the aspic and simmer for about 20 minutes. Check that it is beginning to thicken and add the parsley stalks and peppercorns. Leave to infuse for 10 minutes then strain through a fine-mesh chinois. Set aside.

In a large pot with 2 tablespoons of olive oil, sweat the Swiss chard ribs. Season them with salt and cover with the lid for 10 minutes. Add 2 ladlefuls of white chicken stock and cook for another ten minutes or so, until they have softened. Brush each turbot slice with 2 teaspoons (10 g) salted butter and wrap them tightly in the various types of seaweed. Cook them over steam until the core temperature reaches 104°F (40°C). Transfer them to a warm dish and leave to rest. The final core temperature should be 126°F (52°C).
Brown some butter in a sauté pan and wilt the Swiss chard leaves. Use the same pan to sear the turbot barbels. Cut the parsley leaves into julienne strips. Deglaze with lemon juice and add the julienned parsley leaves.

To serve
Remove the turbot slices from the seaweed, keeping a few of the leaves. Remove the skin and clean the fish of all impurities. Brush it with melted salted butter. Combine the four types of shellfish and the sauce in a sauté pan and heat, ensuring that it does not come to the boil. Heat the Swiss chard ribs and place them at the bottom of four plates. Place the fish pieces above the Swiss chard and pour over generous servings of the shellfish and jus. Arrange the turbot barbels and the Swiss chard leaves in small cups.

Fruit and Vegetables (see photo p. 58)

Serves 4

1 celery stick
4 carrots
½ black radish
1 quince
4 beets (beetroot)
4 Reinette apples or other autumn variety
2 pears, preferably Martin Sec, or other cooking variety
4 chestnuts
1 cup (250 ml) olive oil
Scant ½ cup (100 ml) cider vinegar, divided
2 cups (500 ml) white stock
7 tablespoons (100 g) butter, divided
Fine table salt
Freshly ground pepper
2 handfuls kosher salt

Peel and wash the celery stick, the carrots, the black radish, the quince, and the beets. Wash the apples and pears and peel the chestnuts.
Use approximately 5 in. (12 cm) of the base of the celery stick. Cut it into 4 slices. Remove the fibers from each piece and set aside. Remove the fibers from the remaining piece of celery and cut half of it into fine dice (brunoise). Place the remaining celery into the blender and process.
Cut the carrots into half lengthways and remove the hard central part. Cut the pieces so that they are 5 in. (12 cm) long. Place the trimmings in the blender and process.
Cut the black radish into 4 disks, each ⅓ in. (1 cm) thick. Cut the quince into quarters and round off the angles with a knife.
Cut the pears into halves and remove the cores.
Peel and core 2 of the 4 apples and cut them into fine dice (brunoise).

In a large heavy-bottomed pot, heat 1 cup (250 ml) oil and add the 4 pieces of celery, carrots, quince quarters, the radish slices, the pear halves, and the chestnuts. Add a little salt and put the lid on. Cook for 5 minutes, until the fruit and vegetables are lightly colored. Add half the cider vinegar (scant ¼ cup/50 ml) and then the blended carrot and celery juice, and white stock. Leave the fruit and vegetables to cook gently, testing them frequently so that you remove them as soon as they are soft. When they are all removed from the pot, reduce the juice, adjust the seasoning with salt and vinegar,

and whip in half the butter (3 ½ tablespoons/50 g). Set aside.

Arrange the beets in a small pot and cover them with the kosher salt. Bake at 325°F (160°C) for about 30 minutes, until the tip of a knife goes in easily. Remove from the oven and pour over half a tablespoon of cider vinegar and olive oil. Melt the remaining butter (3 ½ tablespoons/50 g) in a medium-sized pot and add the diced celery and apple brunoise. Season lightly with salt and

cook for 12 minutes. Set aside half the diced mix and mash the rest with a fork.

To Serve
Heat 4 soup plates. Attractively arrange the condiment and diced celery and apple, the carrots, celery, and radish pieces, with the chestnuts, quince quarters, pears, and beets.
Serve the dish. Pour the juice into each plate at the table and grate apple shavings from the remaining apples over each plate.

Pierre Gagnaire p. 60–63

Prat-Ar-Coum Oysters from Brittany and Simple Scallops, Grated Pink Radishes with Horseradish, Watercress Disk, and Smoked Parsley Water (see photo p. 61)

Serves 6

6 cups (1.5 liters) spring water
1 ½ oz. (40 g) smoked bacon, finely diced and 1 ½ oz. (40 g) smoked eel, finely diced
7 oz. (200 g) flat-leaf parsley
Water collected after opening
18 oysters
6 sheets (12 g) gelatin
3 ½ oz. (100 g) watercress leaves
18 Prat-ar-Coum No. 2 Breton oysters
2 ½ oz. (70 g) pink radishes, grated
⅓ oz. (10 g) fresh horseradish, grated
3 tablespoons (45 ml) grape-seed oil
6 scallops, cut into thick slices
Salt to taste

Prepare the smoked parsley water: pour the spring water into a pot with the smoked bacon and eel and bring to the boil.
Remove from the heat and cover with

plastic wrap so that it is airtight. Leave to infuse until quite cold. Filter the infusion. Cook the parsley in salted boiling water. Refresh and drain without pressing it dry. Carefully process the parsley and strain the puree through cheesecloth to obtain green parsley water. Combine the parsley water, the smoked spring water, and the water from the oysters. Prepare this cocktail so that the flavor is well balanced. Soak 3 sheets of gelatin thoroughly in cold water. Heat a little of the smoke-scented liquid and dissolve the gelatin in it. Remove from the heat and add the rest of the water. Pour the parsley water into soup plates and chill to set.

Prepare the watercress disks: blanch the watercress well in salted boiling water. Refresh it and drain without pressing it to remove excess liquid.
Soften the 3 remaining sheets of gelatin.

Process it until it reaches a smooth consistency. Place the softened gelatin sheets in some of the watercress puree and heat it to dissolve them. Remove from the heat and add the remaining puree. Adjust the seasoning.
Line a baking tray with plastic wrap and spread the puree over to a thickness of about ⅕ in. (5 mm). Chill in the refrigerator until set.

Cut out 18 rectangles measuring 2 × 1 ⅕ in. (5 × 3 cm) and reserve in the refrigerator.

To plate, arrange 3 jelled watercress rectangles on each plate and top each one with an oyster. Season each oyster with a teaspoon of grated pink radish mixed with grated fresh horseradish and grape-seed oil. On each oyster, place a slice of scallop.

Poached Fattened Hen in a Pouch (see photo p. 63)

Serves 4

1 Bresse fattened hen (about 5 ¼ lb. or 2.4 kg)
7 oz. (200 g) fresh truffle

5 oz. (150 g) duck or goose foie gras
1 pork bladder, thoroughly washed, rinsed, and dried just before use
1 scant cup (200 ml) red port wine
1 scant cup (200 ml) truffle jus

Spring water
1 cup (250 ml) crème fraîche
1 ⅓ stick (5 oz., 150 g) butter
Dash of balsamic vinegar
4 Belgian endives

Sugar
Maple syrup
Salt and freshly ground pepper

Ask your butcher or poultry specialist to remove the innards and skin of the fattened hen, and cut off the thighs and fillets.
Prepare a broth with the thighs, trimmings, and carcass. This broth should be very tasty but barely salty. Slit three-quarters way through the two breasts so that you can open them out. Pound them and season with just a little salt.

Cut a little of the truffle into fine dice (brunoise) and place the cubes on the breasts. Cut the foie gras into large cubes and place them on the chicken.
Fold the breasts over, truss them carefully, and chill overnight.
Place them inside the bladder with a little of the broth to which you have added the port and truffle jus.

The next day, place the bladder in a large pot of simmering spring water to cook for 50 minutes. When it is done, remove the bladder from the water and bring it to the table. Open it and place the breasts in a deep dish, keeping the broth. Return to the kitchen with it to complete the preparation.

Reduce the broth that was used in the bladder together with the remaining broth. Add the cream and remaining truffles, and whip in the butter. Check the seasoning and add freshly ground pepper and balsamic vinegar.

The Belgian endives should be cooked in the traditional manner, and then warmed in butter with a little sugar and maple syrup to give them a nice color.

To serve: in each of four soup plates, place a Belgian endive and 3 generous slices of the hen ballotine. Spoon a generous serving of sauce into each plate.

Les Prés d'Eugénie p. 64–69

Soft Marquis de Béchamel Cake

Serves 8

Caramel Sauce
1 ⅓ cups (330 g) water
2 cups (500 g) hot water
2 lb. (1 kg) sugar

Sweet Béchamel
3 tablespoons (1 ½ oz./40 g) butter
6 ½ tablespoons (1 ½ oz./40 g) flour
2 cups (500 g) milk
1 vanilla bean
⅓ cup (2 ½ oz./70 g) sugar
2 ½ oz. (70 g) egg yolks
4 ¼ oz. (120 g) egg whites

Rhubarb Ice Cream
3 cups (750 g) rhubarb juice
1 vanilla bean
1 cup plus 3 tablespoons (½ lb./230 g) sugar
5 ¼ oz. (150 g) egg yolks

24 raspberries
A few mint leaves
A coulis of your choice

For the Caramel Sauce
Prepare a caramel with 1 cup (250 g) sugar, 2 oz (60 g) water, and 4 1/2 oz. (125 g) hot water at 400°F (200°C) until it has a dark brown color.
Deglaze with 2 cups (500 g) hot water and bring to the boil for 1 minute. Allow to cool.

For the Sweet Béchamel
Prepare the béchamel: make a roux with the butter and flour. Add the milk and vanilla and bring to the boil. Cook the béchamel for 7 minutes, stirring constantly. Then add ¼ cup (1 ¾ oz./50 g) sugar. Transfer and chill. When it has cooled, combine the béchamel with the egg yolks. Whip the egg whites and beat them to firm peaks, adding the remaining 1 ½ tablespoons (20 g) sugar. Carefully fold it into the béchamel base.

Take 8 round dariole molds with a diameter of 2 ¾ in. (7 cm). Spoon in 1 spoonful of caramel sauce and then fill with the béchamel mixture.

Place the molds in a roasting pan with just under 1 in. (2 cm) water and bake at 400°F (200°C) for 14 minutes. Chill.

For the Rhubarb Ice Cream
Bring the rhubarb juice to boil with the vanilla and ¾ cup (5 ¼ oz./150 g) sugar. Beat the egg yolks with the remaining sugar until pale and thick. Pour some of the hot rhubarb juice over the egg yolks, beating constantly, and then return the mixture to the saucepan. Cook as you would for a custard. Prepare in the ice-cream maker.

To plate, place 3 raspberries at the lower end of the plate, pour a little coulis over them, and garnish with a small sprig of mint.
Turn the béchamel cakes out of their molds onto the upper part of the plate and surround with rhubarb ice cream. Drizzle a little caramel sauce over the béchamel cake and ice cream.

Moon-Fishermen's Drunken Lobster (see photo p. 67)

Serves 4

*2 lobsters, each 1 lb 2 oz.–1 lb 5 oz.
(500–600 g)*
½ bottle Fine blanche or other Armagnac
*3 ½ oz. (100 g) mesclun (mixed salad
leaves)*
Olive oil

Cocktail Sauce
2 oz. (60 g) mayonnaise
*Scant ½ teaspoon (2 g) Fine blanche or
other Armagnac*
⅓ oz. (10 g) ketchup
Juice of ½ lemon

Baroque Vinaigrette
*2 tablespoons (30 g) distilled vinegar
(white vinegar)*
½ cup (120 mg) water
1 tablespoon (½ oz./12 g) sugar
⅓ oz. (10 g) lime zest
⅓ oz. (10 g) lemon zest
¼ oz. (7 g) ginger
*1 oz. (30 g) red bell pepper, peeled and
finely diced (brunoise)*
1 bird's eye chili, chopped
⅔ oz. (20 g) olive oil

Shrimp Egg Rolls
2 oz. (60 g) shelled shrimp, diced
½ oz. (12 g) mango, diced
⅓ oz. (8 g) sesame oil
⅔ teaspoon (3 g) neutral oil

*2–3 sprigs of fresh cilantro (coriander),
chopped*
8 sheets phyllo pastry
Salt and pepper to taste

Marinade
*7 oz. (200 g) Noilly Prat, reduced to a
glaze*
Scant tablespoon (12 g) lemon juice
3 tablespoons (40 g) extra virgin olive oil
*A few drops of Fine blanche or other
Armagnac*
Scant ½ teaspoon (2 g) table salt
A few sprigs chervil, for garnish

Place the 2 lobsters in a deep pot and cover them fully in Fine blanche for 6 hours. They will die of drunkenness. Then drop them in well-salted boiling water for 1 minute and remove immediately. Cut off the claws and return them to the pot for 2–3 minutes. Shell the lobster tails and claws. Place the tails in the deep freeze so that they are easy to cut into fine slices.

For the Cocktail Sauce
Combine the mayonnaise, Fine blanche or Armagnac, ketchup, and lemon juice.

For the Baroque Vinaigrette
Bring the vinegar to the boil with the water and sugar. Add the lime and lemon, ginger, and finely diced red bell pepper. Boil for 2 minutes and remove from the heat. Add the bird's eye chili and cover with plastic wrap. Leave to infuse for 2–3 hours and use as a marinade for the lobster claws. Incorporate the olive oil: for every 2 oz. (50 g) of the mixture, use ⅔ oz. (20 g) olive oil.

Prepare the stuffing for the 8 egg rolls. Combine the shrimp, mango, two types of oil, and chopped cilantro. Cut the phyllo pastry into 3 ½ in. (9 cm) rolls with a diameter of ⅓ in. (1 cm). Place ⅓ oz. (10 g) of the shrimp mixture on each piece and roll up.

Using a square stencil just smaller than the length of the phyllo rectangle (3 ⅓ in. or 8.5 cm), spread out a very thin layer of cocktail sauce. Slice the lobster medallions very finely into a carpaccio and arrange them, slightly overlapping, over the cocktail sauce.
Arrange the mesclun, seasoned with olive oil, attractively to the right of the carpaccio. Top with a lobster claw marinated in the baroque vinaigrette. Fry the egg rolls, brush the carpaccio with the Noilly marinade and garnish with a few sprigs of chervil. Place the lobster head on the right-hand side of the plate.

L'Auberge de l'Ill p. 70–73

Mousseline of Frogs' Legs (see photo p. 72)

Serves 6

7 tablespoons (100g) butter, divided
4 shallots, chopped
2 lb. (1 kg) frogs' legs
½ bottle Riesling
*10 oz. (300 g) fillets freshwater pike
perch*
2 eggs

2 cups (500 ml) cream, divided
1 lb. (500 g) spinach
1 unpeeled garlic clove
A few sprigs of chives
1 tablespoon roux
*3 ½ tablespoons (50 g) very cold butter,
cubed*
Juice of ½ lemon
Salt and pepper to taste

For Garnish
A few sprigs of chervil
1 tomato, peeled and diced

In a sauté pan, melt 3 ½ tablespoons (50 g) butter and sweat the chopped shallots. Add the frogs' legs and pour in the half-bottle of Riesling. Season with salt and pepper and simmer, covered, for 10 minutes. Then transfer the frogs' legs into a colander placed over a bowl to catch the cooking liquid. Strain the liquid through a chinois and return it to the sauté pan to reduce it by half.

For the Mousse
Finely mince the pike perch fillets and place in a food processor. Season with salt and pepper and add the eggs. Begin to process and gradually pour in 1 ¼ cups (300 ml) of the cream. As soon as the mixture is thoroughly blended, remove it from the processor bowl and transfer it to a terrine placed over ice.

Preparing the Spinach
Blanch the spinach in boiling salted water for 5 minutes. Drain in a colander, pressing with your hands to remove the water. Place 3 ½ tablespoons (50 g) butter and the unpeeled garlic clove in a sauté pan. As soon as the butter begins to sizzle, add the spinach. Season with salt and pepper and heat for 5 minutes.

Remove the bones from the frogs' legs and set aside the meat (you will have the 2 muscles).

For the Sauce
Thicken the reduced cooking liquid with the roux and bring to the boil. Add the remaining cream and, using an immersion blender, incorporate the 3 ½ tablespoons (50 g) of cold, cubed butter. Add the lemon juice, salt, and pepper. Adjust the seasoning.

Butter 6 ramekins. Spoon the mousse into a piping bag with a round tip and cover the sides of the ramekins. Fill the hollows with the frogs' legs meat and cover with a layer of mousse. Top with a tablespoon of sauce and some chives. Preheat the oven to 400°F (200°C). Place the ramekins in a bain-marie and cook for 15 to 20 minutes.

Arrange the spinach leaves in soup plates and turn the ramekins out onto the spinach.
Pour the remaining sauce over the mousselines and scatter finely snipped chives over them. Garnish with a sprig of chervil and a cube of tomato.

Peaches Haeberlin

Serves 8

8 peaches poached in vanilla-scented syrup

Pistachio Ice Cream
2 cups (500 ml) milk
2 cups (500 ml) cream
1 Tahiti vanilla bean, slit lengthways
1 ¼ cups (8 ¾ oz./250 g) sugar, divided
10 egg yolks
3 ½ oz. (100 g) pistachio paste
1 tablespoon (15 ml) kirsch

Champagne Zabaglione (Sabayon)
8 egg yolks
¾ cup (5 ¼ oz./150 g) sugar
½ bottle champagne

For Garnish
Chantilly cream

For the Pistachio Ice Cream
Bring the milk and cream to the boil with the vanilla bean and half the sugar. In a mixing bowl, beat the egg yolks with the remaining sugar until the mixture thickens and becomes pale. Pour the boiling milk mixture over it, beating constantly. Return the mixture to the saucepan and cook over low heat, or in a bain-marie, stirring constantly, until it coats the back of a spoon. Remove from the heat and incorporate the pistachio paste and kirsch. Strain the mixture through a chinois and place in the ice-cream maker, following directions.

For the Champagne Zabaglione
In a saucepan, beat the egg yolks with the sugar until the mixture becomes pale. Pour in the champagne. Place the mixture in a bain-marie set over low heat and whip until the mixture thickens. Remove from the heat and continue to whip until it cools.

Place a peach on a large soup plate together with a scoop of pistachio ice cream. Pour over the champagne zabaglione and garnish with a little Chantilly cream.

À l'Huîtrière p. 74–77

Poached Turbot Steak, Potatoes Mashed with Flat-Leaf Parsley

Serves 1

1 turbot steak, 12–14 oz. (350–400 g)
1 bouquet garni
Flat-leaf parsley, chopped
Juice of ½ lemon
3 oz. (100 g) potatoes cooked in their jackets
Butter
Salt and pepper to taste

Sauce Hollandaise
2 egg yolks
1 tablespoon plus 1 teaspoon (20 ml) brown vinegar
A little mignonette pepper
7 tablespoons (3 ½ oz./100 g) unsalted butter, melted

Poach the turbot steak in water with the bouquet garni and aromatic garnish. Prepare 3 oval scoops of the mashed potatoes.

Remove the black skin and the central bone from the piece of fish.

For the Sauce Hollandaise
Reduce the vinegar with the mignonette pepper. Prepare an emulsion with the egg yolks and the reduction and add the melted butter. Adjust the seasoning and spoon the sauce into a sauce dish.

Spicy Roasted Monkfish, Leek Open Sandwich with Brown Shrimp (see photo p. 75)

Serves 1

Scant ¼ cup (50 ml) fish fumet
Scant ¼ cup (50 ml) orange juice
Pinch of ginger
Drizzle of olive oil
Snipped chives
1 large piece of monkfish, 7 oz. (200 g)
Mignonette pepper

3 slices of leek, cooked in water with salt and pepper
1 oz. (30 g) brown shrimp, shelled
3 rings fried onion
Salt and pepper to taste

Prepare an orange sauce: reduce the fumet and orange juice by half. Add a pinch of ginger and whisk together with a drizzle of olive oil. Add a few snipped chives.

Roll the monkfish up with the mignonette pepper and cook it in a nonstick pan or on a plancha cooking surface. Arrange the leek slices and cover them with the shrimp and the three onion rings. Dab the monkfish dry and cut it into 3 medallions. Draw a line of orange sauce around the leek.

La Côte Saint-Jacques p. 78–81

Medallions of Ginger-Scented Sweetbreads, Pearl Onions, Rhubarb, and Pink Radishes (see photo p. 80)

Serves 4

4 veal sweetbreads weighing 5–6 oz. (160 g) each
¾ lb. (350 g) rhubarb
30° syrup, for poaching rhubarb
3 ½ oz. (100 g) pearl onions
3 tablespoons (1 ½ oz./40 g) butter
2 ⅔ oz. (70 g) fresh ginger
32 radishes
¼ teaspoon (1 g) Jamaica pepper (allspice)
2 tablespoons (40 g) honey
3 tablespoons (40 g) cane vinegar
1 ¼ cups (300 ml) chicken jus

2 ½ cups (600 ml) veal jus
Salt, crushed pepper, and sugar

Rapidly blanch the sweetbreads, clean them, and chill them, pressed, in a clean cloth.
Peel 5 oz. (150 g) rhubarb. Cut a third of it into 12 thin strips ½ in. wide and 4 in. long (1.5 × 10 cm). Poach them rapidly in a 30° syrup and drain.
Braid them on a baking tray and bake for 4 minutes in a hot oven. Cut the braid into 4 triangles and leave them to dry in a dry place.
Cut another third of the rhubarb into

sticks 1 ¼ × ¼ in. (3 cm × 5 mm). Poach them in the 30° syrup and drain, reserving the liquid.
Slice the onions and sauté them gently in 2 teaspoons (10 g) butter. Candy ⅔ oz. (20 g) of the ginger in the rhubarb syrup. Combine the remaining third of this rhubarb in sticks with the pearl onions and add the candied ginger.
Turn the radishes and boil them in salted water. Refresh and glaze them in the rhubarb poaching syrup to which the Jamaica pepper has been added.
Cook the honey with the crushed pepper until it is a blond caramel. Deglaze with

the cane vinegar, add the renaining 7 oz. (200 g) rhubarb and 2 oz. (50 g) roughly chopped ginger. Leave to stew gently until the water has evaporated.
Divide this preparation into halves. Pour the chicken jus over the first half and simmer to reduce by half. Strain through a chinois and whip in the butter.
Pour the veal jus over the second half and reduce to a glaze. Then strain it through a chinois.

Cook the veal sweetbreads in a sauté pan over high heat and finish the cooking in the oven. Remove the fat from the sauté pan by deglazing with a little water. Add the brown sauce to glaze the sweetbreads. Heat the radishes, rhubarb, and onions. Gently sauté the tops of the radish leaves in butter.
Check the seasoning of all the components.

On a large plate, prepare a bed of onions and rhubarb and place the sweetbread on this. Arrange 5 radishes and their leaves around the sweetbread. Drizzle little drops of the brown sauce around the sweetbread. Spoon the second sauce into the middle of the plate.
Spear 3 radishes onto a small wooden skewer and stick it into the sweetbread. Lastly, garnish with a triangle of braided rhubarb.

Variations on an Oyster Theme (see photo p. 79)

Serves 4

Rye Porridge
2 ½ oz. (75 g) rye flakes
2 cups (500 ml) milk

Crêpe Batter
2 eggs
2 egg yolks
½ cup (50 g) flour
½ cup (50 g) rye flour
1 cup (250 ml) milk
3 tablespoons plus 1 teaspoon (50 g) browned butter
Salt to taste

Creamed Lettuce
2 lettuces
2 ½ oz. (80 g) red onion
1 tablespoon (15 g) butter
Scant ¼ cup (50 ml) whipping cream

28 large oysters, approx. 2 ¾–3 oz. each (80–90 g)
⅔ oz. (20 g) broccoli floret tips
⅔ oz. (20 g) cauliflower tips
2 tablespoons dried pink peppercorns (dried fruit of baies roses)
⅓ oz. (10 g) rye flakes

For the Porridge
Gently cook the rye flakes in the milk, process, and season to taste. Set aside.

For the Crêpe Batter
Beat the eggs and egg yolks with the two types of flour. Beat the mixture well and add the milk. Lastly, add the browned butter and a pinch of salt. Set the batter aside to rest.
Make thin crêpes and cut some of them into 24 small triangles measuring ½ in. × 1 ¼ in. (1.5 × 3 cm). Dry them out in an oven heated to 105°F (40°C). Take more crêpes and cut 8 strips with a width of ⅛ in. (3 mm) from their widest section. Roll the strips around skewers to make small spirals. Leave them to dry out with the triangles.

For the Creamed Lettuce
Separate the leaves of the lettuces, wash them, and cook them in salted boiling water to remove their crunch. Refresh them in ice water and drain them, pressing hard to remove all the excess water. Peel the red onion and chop it. Stew it gently in butter before processing it.
Heat the cream and add the lettuce leaves. Process and add the pureed red onions. Process once again and season with salt and pepper.

Open the oysters and remove them from their shells, making sure you retain all their water. Trim them, clean them in their own water, and drain. Keep the trimmings to use to season the porridge. Finely chop the broccoli and cauliflower

florets and mix them with a teaspoon of dried pink peppercorns. Dip 20 oysters in this mixture and fry them gently. Transfer them to a plate with the raw oysters. Cover the plate with plastic film so that it is airtight.

Heat the porridge and add the oyster trimmings. Adjust the consistency and seasoning by adding the liquid from the oysters, salt, and pepper.

Heat the creamed lettuce and adjust the consistency and seasoning in the same way.

Heat the oysters for about 20 seconds in the microwave oven.

Spoon the porridge into 4 small bowls in the following way: place porridge only in the first bowl; in the second bowl place some porridge and cover it with creamed lettuce; in the third bowl, place a layer of porridge, cover it with creamed lettuce, and top it with an unfried oyster; in the fourth bowl, place a layer of porridge covered with creamed lettuce, 1 oyster, and a triangle of dried crêpe.

To plate: place a spoonful of porridge on the plate and cover it with creamed lettuce, then place 5 fried oysters overlapping it. Garnish with 5 crêpe triangles, 2 small spirals, and 1 pinch of pink peppercorns, and scatter with rye flakes.

Lasserre *Paris* p. 82–85

Citrus-Scented Sea Bass (see photo p. 84)

Serves 4

4 slices sea bass, each 5 oz. (150 g)
3 oranges
3 blood oranges
1 grapefruit
4 tangerines
2 limes
*1 tablespoon black Sarawak
pepper*
*1 tablespoon black Malabar
pepper*
1 tablespoon soy sauce
1 tablespoon bonito flakes
¼ teaspoon (1 g) agar-agar
¼ teaspoon (1 g) pectin
2 fine Swiss chard leaves
Oil, butter, and white stock as needed

For the Citrus Fruits
Wash and dry the fruits. Zest one of each and dry the zest in a 175°F (80°C) oven. They should dry out enough to be ground into a powder and mixed with the Sarawak and Malabar peppers.

Take one fruit of each variety and cut out segments. Cut the segments into ¼ in. (5 mm) dice.

Arrange them on a baking tray and partially dry them in an oven. Squeeze the juice from the remaining fruit and marinate the dried bonito flakes in it with the soy sauce. Leave to infuse for 12 minutes and filter. Divide the juice into two parts. Heat one half with the pectin and the agar-agar. As soon as it boils, remove from the heat and add the remaining juice to cool it down. Transfer the juice to a flat-bottomed dish, pouring it out to a depth of ¼ in. (5 mm). When it has cooled down, prepare 10 citrus-juice cubes per person. The remaining juice should be dissolved and served separately in a sauce bowl.

Cook the pieces of sea bass, ensuring they do not brown too much.

For the Garnish
Separate the white ribs from the green part of the Swiss chard leaves. Peel the white part and cook it in a sauté pan with a little oil, butter, and white stock. When the whites have softened, remove from the heat and leave to cool. Cut them out into 2 in. (5 cm) diamond shapes.

Remove the hard fibers from the green parts, wash the greens, and cut them into strips just under 1 in. (2 cm) wide. Wilt them lightly in a sauté pan with a little olive oil, making sure they retain their crunch.

To Serve
Warm the dried pieces of fruits and divide them equally between each warmed plate with the jelled cubes and the diamond-shaped Swiss chard whites glazed in their cooking liquid. Place the piece of sea bass in the center of the wilted Swiss chard greens. Serve the sauce separately.

Crisp Chocolate with Raspberries and Soft Manjari Ganache (see photo p. 83)

Serves 10

A few fresh raspberries

Capucine Sponge
2 ½ oz. (70 g) ground blanched almonds
3 ⅓ oz. (generous ⅔ cup/90 g) confectioners' sugar
3 tablespoons (⅔ oz./20 g) cocoa powder, unsweetened
4 oz. (110 g) egg whites
1 oz. (30 g) sugar

Chocolate Raspberry Ganache
6 ½ oz. (175 g) pureed raspberries
1 oz. (30 g) trimoline (inverted sugar)
7 oz. (190 g) Manjari chocolate
3 tablespoons (45 g) butter, cubed

Manjari Mousse
7 oz. (200 g) Manjari chocolate
⅔ cup (150 g) milk
3 g (1 ½ sheets) gelatin
10 oz. (300 g) whipped cream

Chocolate Shortcrust Pastry
1 stick (4 ½ oz./120 g) butter
¼ cup (35 g) confectioners' sugar
1 oz. (30 g) egg yolk

Scant 1 oz. (25 g) ground blanched almonds
1 pinch salt
1 ¼ cups (4 ½ oz./120 g) flour
3 tablespoons (1 oz./30 g) cocoa powder, unsweetened
Generous ½ teaspoon (3 g) baking powder

Raspberry Sorbet
⅔ cup (150 g) water
⅓ cup (2 ½ oz./75 g) granulated sugar
½ oz. (15 g) trimoline (inverted sugar)
9 ¼ oz. (250 g) pureed raspberries
1 tablespoon plus 2 teaspoons (25 g) lemon juice

For the Capucine Sponge
Sift together the ground almonds, confectioners' sugar, and cocoa powder. Whip the egg whites with the sugar. Fold the sifted ingredients into the egg whites. Spread out over a baking tray and bake at 350°F (180°C). Cut out into 3 in. (8 cm) disks.

For the Chocolate Raspberry Ganache
Bring the pureed raspberries to the boil with the trimoline. Melt the Manjari chocolate. Gradually pour the boiling puree over the chocolate, whisking to create an emulsion. When the mixture reaches a temperature of 95–104°F (35°–40°C), whisk in the cubed butter.

For the Manjari Mousse
Melt the chocolate. Bring the milk to the boil. Add the softened gelatin and pour it over the melted chocolate in several stages until the mixture is elastic, smooth, and shiny. When it reaches a temperature of 95–104°F (35–40°C), fold in the whipped cream. Pour the mixture into 1 ½-in. (4-cm) diameter cylinders.

For the Chocolate Shortcrust Pastry
Beat the softened butter well with the sifted confectioners' sugar, egg yolks, ground almonds, and salt until the mixture is thick and smooth. Sift together the flour, cocoa powder, and baking powder. Fold the dry ingredients into the mixture until just combined. Be careful not to overmix. Spread the batter out and cut it into cubes. Bake at 325°F (160°C) for 12 minutes.

For the Raspberry Sorbet
Prepare a syrup with the water, sugar, and trimoline and pour it over the pureed raspberries. Stir in the lemon juice. Leave to mature for 24 hours in the deep freeze.

To Assemble
Place the Manjari mousse over the disks of capucine sponge. Carefully spoon a little ganache over the mousse. Arrange the raspberries around the ganache. Top with a scoop of raspberry sorbet and scatter with chocolate shortcrust cubes.

Ledoyen p. 86–89

Kumquat Aperitif Snacks

Serves 10

Candied Kumquats
20 kumquats
2 cups (500 ml) water
¾ cup (150 g) sugar

Kumquat Juice
20 kumquats

Garnish
1 tablespoon (15 ml) sesame oil

Maldon salt as needed
⅓ oz. (10 g) white sesame seeds, toasted

For the Candied Kumquats
Remove the green part and make a small hole with a kitchen knife.
Prepare a syrup: bring the water and sugar to the boil. Place the kumquats in the syrup and leave to boil for 1 to 2 minutes before removing. Chill the candied kumquats as quickly as possible.

Gently scoop out the flesh with tongs.

For the Kumquat Juice
Cut the kumquats into quarters and remove the seeds. Process them in a blender just before serving.

To Serve
Fill the candied kumquats with kumquat juice. Drizzle with sesame oil, then sprinkle with Maldon salt and toasted white sesame seeds.

Peppered Tuna Belly Cooked with Watermelon (see photo p. 87)

Serves 4

4 slices tuna belly, 5 oz. (140 g) each
½ watermelon
4 tomatoes
1 bunch basil
Olive oil
12 fresh almonds
12 pistachios
4 green onion stalks
Soy glaze
Szechuan pepper
Paprika salt

Tuna Sauce Base
1.1 lb. (500 g) sea bass bones
½ carrot
2 tomatoes
1 stalk celery
2 shallots
½ onion

Vinegar Reduction
7 oz. (200 g) wine vinegar
3 ½ oz. (100 g) glucose

Peel the watermelon and cut out four rectangles using a pastry cutter. Dice the remaining watermelon flesh into ¼ in. (1 cm) cubes.
Peel and dice the tomatoes.

Prepare the tuna sauce: reduce the tuna base slightly.

Prepare a pistou using the basil and a little olive oil, reserving the small leaves. Color the watermelon rectangles in the olive oil, discard the fat, and pour in the tuna sauce.

Cook for 10 minutes, ensuring the watermelon is well glazed. Then deglaze with a drizzle of wine vinegar.

Sauté the tomato and melon cubes and deglaze with the tuna sauce. Season well with pepper.
Separately, reduce the wine vinegar with the glucose until it reaches a syrupy consistency. Slowly integrate it to the reduced tuna base.
Drain the watermelon slice, cover it with pistou, and top it with the watermelon and tomato cubes.
Garnish with the almonds, pistachios, onion greens, and small basil leaves.

Cook the tuna: cut it into pieces the same size as the watermelon slices. Sprinkle them with Szechuan pepper, salt, and paprika. Pan-fry them evenly. When they are cooked, trim them and drizzle with pistou and soy glaze. Arrange them on the plate with the watermelon and sprinkle the sauce.

Le Louis XV p. 90–93

Full-Cream Milk Ice Cream with Fleur de Sel, Caramel Crunch, and Ewe's Milk Curd Cheese (see photo p. 91)

Serves 10

Full-Cream Milk Ice Cream
4 ¼ pints (2 liters) full-cream milk
½ cup (3 ½ oz./100 g) light brown sugar
2 ½ teaspoons (10 g) granulated sugar
1 ⅓ teaspoons (5 g) stabilizer
⅓ cup whipped cream
1 teaspoon (4 g) fleur de sel

Homemade Cream
5 ¼ pints (2.5 liters) full-cream milk

Arlettes
1 quantity puff pastry, confectioner's sugar

Tuiles with Homemade cream
⅔ cup (150 g) homemade cream

2 ¾ tablespoons (1 ¼ oz./35 g) light brown sugar
2 tablespoons (½ oz./13 g) flour
1 egg white

Walnut Nougatine
½ cup (3 ½ oz./100 g) sugar
3 ½ oz. (100 g) glucose
1 ¾ tablespoons (1 oz./25 g) butter
3 ½ oz. (100 g) chopped walnuts

Sweet Shortcrust Pastry Nougatines
7 oz. (200 g) sweet shortcrust pastry
1 cup (7 oz./200 g) sugar

Caramel Chantilly Cream
1 scant cup (6 oz./175 g) sugar
2 ¼ cups (560 g) whipping cream

Dulce de Leche Sauce
½ cup (3 ½ oz./100 g) sugar

Scant ½ cup (100 ml) whipping cream
Scant ¼ cup (50 ml) milk
1 oz. (25 g) milk chocolate
1 tablespoon plus 2 teaspoons (25 g) butter

Ewe's Milk Curd Cheese
1 lb. (500 g) ewe's milk curd cheese

For the Full Cream Milk Ice Cream
Reduce the milk by half. Pour in the brown sugar and heat to a temperature of 167°F (75°C). Combine the granulated sugar with the stabilizer and incorporate into the milk. Bring to the boil and allow to cool. Place in the ice-cream maker and incorporate the whipped cream when the process is almost finished. Then incorporate the fleur de sel. Turn into 1 ½ × 2 ⅓-in. (4 × 6-cm) molds and reserve in the freezer.

For the Homemade Cream
Bring the full cream milk to the boil. Leave it for 5 minutes in the saucepan without allowing it to continue to boil. Chill for 24 hours. Scoop off the cream that forms on the surface with a spoon and return it to the refrigerator.

For the Arlettes
To prepare the Arlettes, cut out 10 rectangles measuring 2 ½ × 3 in.- (7 × 8 cm) of puff pastry sprinkled with confectioners' sugar. Leave them to dry for 12 hours. Bake them on a nonstick tray at 400°F (200°C). When you remove them from the oven, roll them round a ½ in. (1.5 cm) tube to make a cigarette shape. Remove from the tube and store in an airtight container.

For the Tuiles with Homemade Cream
Combine the homemade cream, light brown sugar, and flour. Carefully fold in the unbeaten egg white.
Pipe out thirty 1 ½-in. (4-cm) diameter tuiles onto a nonstick baking tray. Bake in a ventilated oven 300°F (150°C) for 5 minutes. Turn them out onto a tuile mold sheet. Store in an airtight container.

For the Walnut Nougatines
Cook the sugar, glucose, and butter together. Incorporate the walnuts before the sugar begins to change color and mix well. Spread the mixture out onto a silicone sheet and bake for 350°F (170°C) until it is nicely colored. Cut out ten 1 ½-in. (4-cm) squares. Store in an airtight container.

For the Sweet Shortcrust Pastry Nougatines
Prepare the sweet shortcrust pastry and roll it out to a thickness of ⅛ in. (3 mm).

Bake at 300°F (150°C) for 20 minutes. Allow to cool. Crush the pastry to a fine powder. Caramelize the sugar, add the ground pastry, and mix well. Spread onto a silicone sheet to cool. When it has cooled, crush again to a fine powder. Place 30 chablon stencils, each ¾ × 6 in. (2 × 15 cm) on a silicone baking sheet. With a small strainer, sprinkle this powder into them. Bake again at 350°F (170°C) for 6 minutes. Set aside in the warming oven.

For the Caramel Chantilly Cream
Prepare a caramel using the dry method. When it is dark, pour in 2 cups (500 g) cream and allow to cool. Then pour in the remaining ¼ cup (60 g) cream. Pour the mixture into a siphon with two gas chargers and chill.

For the Dulce de Leche Sauce
Prepare a light caramel with the sugar. Pour in the cream and milk, and add the chocolate, then the butter. Mix well and allow to cool. Store in the refrigerator.

For the Ewe's Milk Curd Cheese
Place the cheese in a strainer for 1 hour and allow to drain until firm. Spread it out to a thickness of ⅛ in. (3 mm). Cut out twenty ½ × 5 ½-in. (1.5 × 14-cm) strips and chill them.

To Finish and Serve
Fill the Arlette cigarettes with Caramel Chantilly cream.
Assemble 10 mille-feuille as follows: one strip of nougatine, one strip of curd cheese, another strip of nougatine, another strip of curd cheese, and lastly, a third strip of nougatine.
On each plate, place a square of walnut nougatine. Turn the milk ice cream out of the molds and place above the mille-feuille. Add a cigarette filled with caramel Chantilly cream and three cream tuiles. Place a mille-feuille on the side and finish with a line of dulce de leche sauce.

Mesclun and Black Truffles Seasoned with New Olive Oil, Tuber Melanosporum Sandwich (see photo p. 92)

Serves 4

3 ½ oz. (100 g) mesclun
4 large black truffles
1 garlic clove
Herbs
3 ½ oz. (100 g) riquette (or arugula)
A few sprigs chervil
1 bunch barbes de capucin (forced chicory leaves)
3 ½ oz. (100g) purslane
2–3 green dandelions
12 radicchio leaves
A few sprigs chives
12 leaves yellow celery
3 ½ oz. (100 g) mâche (lambs' lettuce)
2 oz. (50 g) doucette (wild lambs' lettuce)

Sandwich
8 slices country bread, ¼ in. (0.5 cm) thick
Salted butter

Vinaigrette
2 oz. (50 g) sherry vinegar
2 oz. (50 g) balsamic vinegar
10 oz. (300 g) new mountain olives
2 ½ teaspoons (12 g) ground Maldon salt, and a little whole Maldon salt for seasoning
6 grinds of the pepper mill

Using a slicer and rubbing it every 10 slices with a clove of garlic, slice the truffles to ⅛ in. (3 mm). Use the best slices for the salad and the others for the sandwiches and to chop.
Line a tray with parchment paper and spread out all the truffle slices on it. Chill.

Cut 8 slices of bread using the slicing machine and spread the salted butter on one side of each.
Carefully arrange the truffle trimmings on the bread and sandwich them together. Wrap them separately in plastic film and chill for 6 hours.

Combine the vinaigrette ingredients and chop the remaining pieces of truffle. Wash and dry the salad leaves. Prepare the aromatic herbs and reserve them wrapped in damp paper towel.

To serve, season the salad with just a little vinaigrette. Use a pastry brush to season the best truffle slices on one side only. Weigh the truffle sandwiches down so that they are nice and flat, and toast them on both sides on a grill surface. Arrange the mesclun in a 5-in. (12-cm) steel ring, counting about 1 oz. (25 g) per person.

Arrange the truffle slices around the salad, seasoned side facing inside. Make 2 layers so that they form a dome. Place the mixed herbs at the top.
Grind the pepper mill over the salad and sprinkle it with Maldon salt. Combine 1 tablespoon of chopped truffles with 3 tablespoons of vinaigrette and serve it in a sauce dish.
Cut the sandwiches lengthways and serve hot.

Le Relais Bernard Loiseau p. 94–99

Frogs' Legs with Garlic Puree and Parsley Jus (see photo p. 94)

Serves 4

14 oz. (400 g) garlic
½ cup (125 ml) milk
7 oz. (200 g) flat parsley leaves
48 frogs' legs (2 lb./1 kg)
Scant ¼ cup (50 ml) duck fat
4 tablespoons (60 g) butter
A little flour
Table salt, kosher salt
Freshly ground pepper

For the Garlic Puree
Crush the heads of garlic with the palm of your hand, then blanch them 3 times in boiling water. Remove the skin and shoot from each garlic clove. Blanch the cloves again as many times as necessary to diminish the strength and reduce the bitterness, and for them to cook. When they are thoroughly cooked, drain them well. Process with a blender to make a puree. Add milk to make the consistency slightly more liquid. Set aside.

For the Parsley Jus
Wash and drain the parsley. Prepare a pot of boiling salted water and boil the leaves for 4 to 5 minutes. Refresh in ice water. Drain well in a colander and then process in a blender to make a puree. Thin it slightly with a little water: it should have the consistency of a coulis. Set aside.

For the Frogs' Legs
Cut the tips of the frogs' legs and remove the two lower muscles so that you are left with only the upper muscle.
Season the meat with table salt and freshly ground pepper and dust it with flour. Heat the duck fat and butter in a sauté pan. When the fat is hot (it will be lightly browned), place the frogs' leg meat in to cook. Color it for 3 minutes on one side, turn over, and cook for 1 minute on the other side. As soon as the meat is cooked, transfer it to sheets of paper towel.

While the frogs' legs are cooking, heat and season the garlic puree and parsley jus. Pour the parsley jus into the bottom of the plates and place a spoonful of garlic puree in the middle. Arrange the frogs' legs around the puree.

Restaurant Régis et Jacques Marcon p. 100–103

Porcini in Chestnut Leaves, Grill-Scented Zabaglione (Sabayon) (see photo p. 103)

Serves 10

4 large porcini (ceps)
4 dried porcini
4 thin slices of bacon soaked in salt water (lard demi-sel)
8 chestnut leaves

Zabaglione
2 sticks (8 oz./250 g) butter
2 oz. (50 g) porcini
3 eggs
⅔ oz. (20 g) egg yolk (this is roughly equivalent to one egg yolk)
1 teaspoon (5 g) salt
1 teaspoon (5 g) sherry vinegar

Wash the mushrooms and cut them into halves. Using a knife, make an incision in the stems and insert a strip of bacon. Wrap the porcini in a chestnut leaf and fasten with a wooden skewer. Set aside in a pot with a little water.

For the Zabaglione
In a heavy-bottomed sauté pan, heat the butter. Add the dried porcini and fry gently. The butter will brown slightly and absorb the taste of the porcini. Keep the pan with the butter and porcini in a warm place.
You will need a warmed siphon to make this sabayon. In a mixing bowl, whisk the egg yolks, eggs, salt, and vinegar. Remove the dried porcini from the pan and keep them for another use. Slowly pour the warm melted butter into the egg mixture, whisking constantly. Pour the mixture into the warm siphon. Close the siphon and shake vertically. The contents should be at a temperature of 140°–150°F (60°–65°C). Insert 2 gas canisters and place in a bain-marie at 150°F (65°C) until needed.

Cook the porcini wrapped in leaves in a cast-iron pot in a 400°F (200°C) oven for 10 minutes.
Arrange the wrapped porcini on the plates with the liquid they have rendered. Serve the zabaglione separately.

Jelled Garden Peas with Mousserons (see photo p. 101)

Serves 4

6 tomatoes
Basil
A drizzle of sherry vinegar
Scant ¼ cup (50 ml) olive oil
2 onions
1 garlic clove
1 bouquet garni
2 sheets (4 g) gelatin
10 oz. (300 g) fresh garden peas
Mixed salad leaves, such as Boston,
Batavian, and frizzy lettuce
1 cup (250 ml) milk
6 mint leaves
Tabasco sauce
7 oz. (200 g) mousserons, also known as
fairy ring mushrooms
A few shoots of maidenstears (Silene
vulgaris), also known as bladder campion
Salt and pepper to taste

Cut 2 tomatoes in two, remove the seeds, and dice finely. Chop the basil and add it to the diced tomato, season with salt and pepper, and drizzle in a little vinegar and olive oil.

For the Jelled Tomatoes
Quarter the remaining tomatoes. Heat some olive oil in a pot and add a sliced onion. Sauté one of the onions and add the tomato quarters, garlic, and bouquet garni. Cover with water and bring to the boil. Allow to simmer for 10 minutes, skimming frequently. Set aside and leave to infuse for 10 minutes before filtering through cheesecloth. Soften the gelatin sheets in cold water. Bring the tomato liquid to the boil, add enough tomato juice to make 1 cup (250 ml). Drain the gelatin sheets and place them in the hot liquid.

Creamed Garden Peas
Cook the peas in salted boiling water.

Refresh them under cold water and drain them. Set aside 3 ½ oz. (100 g) for garnish. Sauté the other sliced onion in a pot with a little olive oil. Add the shredded salad leaves and peas. Pour in a little water and the milk and season with salt. Leave to cook, uncovered, for about 10 minutes. Then process the vegetables with the chopped mint until the consistency is very smooth. Strain through a chinois and season with salt. Add a little Tabasco sauce and set aside.

Arrange the chopped tomatoes at the bottom of the glasses and pour in the jelled tomatoes to about 1 ½ in. (4 cm). Chill until set, then pour in the creamed peas and return to the refrigerator. Just before serving, quickly sauté the fairy ring mushrooms in a little oil and add the remaining peas. Arrange while still warm in the center of each glass. Garnish with a few shoots of maidenstears and the reserved peas.

L'Espérance p. 104–107

Marie-Antoinette Strawberries (see photo p. 107)

This dessert was created for Sofia Coppola's film, Marie-Antoinette.

Serves 4

Mousse
3 ⅙ oz. (90 g) egg whites
3 ½ tablespoons (1 ½ oz./40 g) sugar
½ cup (125 g) cream
2 tablespoons (30 ml) raspberry eau-de-vie

Mixed Berry Coulis
2 lb. 2 oz. (1 kg) mixed red berries
¼ cup (¾ oz./50 g) granulated sugar

Italian Meringue Scoops
3 ½ oz. (100 g) egg whites
½ cup (3 ½ oz./100 g) superfine sugar
¾ cup (3 ½ oz./100 g) confectioners' sugar

Strawberry and Raspberry Brunoise
5 oz. (150 g) strawberries
5 oz. (150 g) raspberries
Grated lime zest
1 tablespoon sugar

Ginger Emulsion
Scant ½ cup (100 g) milk
Scant ¼ cup (50 g) cream
3 ½ oz. (100 g) 30° syrup
2 tablespoons (30 g) orange juice
¾ oz. (20 g) fresh ginger

Hibiscus Flower Granita
4 cups (1 liter) water
1 cup plus 1 scant cup (¾ lb. or 350 g) sugar
1 ⅓ oz. (37.5 g) hibiscus flowers

For the Mousse
Whip the egg whites, add the sugar, and whip to firm peak stage. Whip the cream and fold the egg whites into the cream. Stir in the raspberry eau-de-vie. Set aside.

For the Mixed Berry Coulis
Process the red berries with the sugar and strain through a chinois to prepare the coulis.

For the Italian Meringue Scoops
Whip the egg whites until they form stiff peaks and then finish by incorporating the superfine sugar and the confectioners' sugar. Spoon into a pastry bag and pipe out 40 small balls, diameter ¼ in. (5 mm), onto a baking tray.

Bake for 1 minute 30 seconds at 175°F (80°C). Set aside.

For the Strawberry and Raspberry Brunoise

Cut the strawberries and raspberries into ½ in. (1 cm) dice and add the sugar and grated lime zest.

For the Ginger Emulsion

Heat all the ingredients together, process, and strain through a fine-meshed chinois. Allow to cool.

For the Hibiscus Flower Granita

Bring the water and sugar to the boil and add the hibiscus flowers. Remove from the heat and allow to cool. Strain through a chinois and freeze for 2 hours, scratching with a fork for the granita texture.

Prepare the dessert in cocktail glasses: place the mousse to a height of just under 1 in. (2 cm), spoon in a thin layer of coulis, cover with 10 meringue scoops, and place 1 tablespoon of fruit brunoise in the center of the glass. Fill with the ginger emulsion and top with 1 spoonful of hibiscus granita.

Lobster with Arugula Jus (see photo p. 104)

Serves 4

1 lb. 1 oz. (500 g) fine Breton lobster (homard bleu)

Arugula Jus

7 oz. (200 g) arugula (rocket)
7 oz. (200 g) spinach
⅔ cups (150 ml) fish fumet
1 cup (250 ml) white wine
1 teaspoon potato starch
1 cup (250 ml) Jordan olive oil
⅔ cup (150 ml) olive oil
2 cups (500 ml) sunflower seed oil
Scant ½ cup (100 ml) lemon juice
15 drops Tabasco sauce

Polenta

2 cups (500 ml) milk
3 ½ oz. (100 g) polenta

Truffle Sauce

⅓ oz. (10 g) truffle
⅓ oz. (10 g) shallot
Scant ¼ cup (50 ml) Madeira wine
1 tablespoon plus 2 teaspoons (25 ml) white port wine
¾ cup (200 ml) chicken jus
2 tablespoons (30 ml) truffle jus
4 tablespoons (60 g) butter

Piquant Oil

1 oz. (25 g) red bell pepper
1 oz. (30 g) leek greens
2 teaspoons (5 g) niora chili flakes
Scant ¼ cup (50 ml) whipping cream
Mignonette pepper, fleur de sel, sherry vinegar, olive oil, nutmeg

For the Arugula Jus

Process the arugula and spinach leaves in a blender. Heat the fish fumet and white wine with a little potato starch. Whisk in the olive and sunflower seed oils. Season with salt, pepper, lemon juice, and Tabasco sauce. Incorporate the blended arugula and spinach leaves at the last moment.

Cook the lobsters in a court bouillon, the tails for 1 minute and the claws for 6 minutes. Cool and cut the tails into two.

For the Polenta

To prepare the polenta, heat the milk with a little nutmeg. Pour in the polenta, cook, and season.

For the Truffle Sauce

To prepare the truffle sauce, sweat the chopped truffle and chopped shallots.

Deglaze twice with Madeira, and then again twice with the white port wine. Reduce by two-thirds.
Add the chicken jus, reduce by one-third, and add the truffle jus.
Whisk in the butter and season with salt, pepper, and lemon juice.

For the Piquant Oil

To prepare the piquant oil, peel the bell pepper and cut it into fine dice (brunoise). Cut the leek greens into fine dice. Mix the vegetable brunoise with the niora chili, Tabasco sauce, and olive oil, adding a pinch of salt.

To Finish the Lobsters

Color the lobsters in the piquant oil, pouring butter over as you cook. Season with fleur de sel and mignonette pepper. On the plate, place a spoonful of polenta, and draw a line of truffle sauce and another of arugula emulsion around. Place half a roast lobster on each spoonful of polenta. Garnish with a bunch of arugula and season with sherry vinaigrette.

La Mère Brazier p. 108–111

Apple Chabraninof (see photo p. 108)

Chabraninof is a contraction of the three names of the Brazier family and chef.

Serves 4

4 apples
5 ½ tablespoons (80 g) butter
3 ½ tablespoons (40 g) sugar
Rum
4 scoops vanilla ice cream

Prepare the apples: peel and core them and cut them into 8 pieces. Preheat the oven to 400°F (200°C). Melt the butter and sauté the pieces of apple in it, 10 minutes on each side.

Place them, with the melted butter, in an oven- and flameproof dish. Sprinkle with sugar and bake for 10 minutes. As soon as you remove the dish from the oven, place it over the gas ring and pour in some rum. Flambé it, taking care to move away quickly to a safe distance.

Arrange the apple pieces in a rose shape around the plates. Place a scoop of ice cream in the center and pour over a little of the sauce.

Bresse Chicken in "Half Mourning" (see photo p. 110)

Serves 4

1 Bresse chicken weighing around
3 ½ lb. (1.7 kg)
12 truffle slices
6 ¼ pints (3 liters) white chicken stock
8 baby carrots
8 baby turnips
8 baby leeks
4 small leaves of green cabbage
2 cups (500 ml) whipping cream
1 ⅓ stick (5 ¼ oz./150 g) unsalted butter
Salt and fleur de sel

Condiment Jars
Pickled cherries
Gherkins
Truffle vinaigrette

For the Chicken
Slip the slices of truffle under the chicken skin and roll up the chicken well in plastic wrap. Poach in the chicken stock at 160°F (70°C) for 3 hours. Unwrap and keep in a warm place. Cook the vegetables.

For the Sauce Supreme
Reduce the cooking liquid by two-thirds, add the cream, and simmer until it reaches the desired consistency. Whip in the butter, strain through a chinois, and set aside.

Place the chicken and the cooked vegetables in a very hot cast-iron pot. Sprinkle with fleur de sel.
Serve the sauce separately and accompany with the jars of condiments.

Le Meurice p. 112–115

Tarte Fine of Scallops, Whipped Cream with Condiments (see photo p. 115)

Serves 4

Tart
4 scallops
⅓ oz. (10 g) tetragonia (summer spinach) leaves
4 slices of white sandwich loaf
2 ½ oz. (70 g) osetra caviar

Condiments
2 eggs
½ shallot
2 scallions
1 ¼ cup (300 g) whipping cream

1 tablespoon plus 1 teaspoon (20 g) lemon juice
30 small capers
Gold leaf
Salt and pepper to taste

Prepare the hardboiled eggs. Separate the white from the yolk and carefully cut the white into extremely fine dice (1/16 in. or 2 mm). Chop the ½ shallot into dice of the same size. Finely slice the scallions at an angle.

Beat the cream to fairly firm peaks, adding the lemon juice. This should be formed into quenelles and served on the side.

Cut the scallops into ⅛ in. (4 mm) slices. Spread them out onto a sheet of parchment paper and season them with salt and pepper. Heat under the salamander for 1 minute and allow to cool.

Cover a baking tray with plastic wrap and spread the tetragonia leaves on it. Place in a steam oven at 195°F (90°C) for 3 minutes, remove and allow to cool. When they have cooled, spread the leaves over the scallops and cut them into tart slice shaped pieces.

Use a rolling pin to flatten the bread slices and cut them into triangles. Grease a sheet of parchment paper and place the triangles on it. Using a vertical piece of metal, fold the edges of the bread up to form the side of the tart and bake at 325°F (160°C) for 12 minutes.

When the triangles are baked, place the sliced scallops and tetragonia leaves on them. Cover it all with the osetra caviar and arrange the condiments on top.

Cristalline with Unctuous Coffee-Chocolate Cream and Soft Meringue (see photo p. 114)

Serves 4

Coffee Cristalline
1 lb. (450 g) white fondant
11 oz. (300 g) glucose
3 ½ tablespoons (12 g) instant coffee
1 ½ tablespoons (8 g) finely ground coffee

Nyambo Chocolate Cream
1 cup (250 g) whipping cream
1 cup (250 g) milk
3 ½ oz. (100 g) egg yolks
¼ cup (2 oz./50 g) sugar
8 ¼ oz. (235 g) Nyambo couverture chocolate

Whipped Ivory-Coffee Ganache
1 cup plus 1 scant cup (450 g) whipping cream, plus a little extra
2 ¾ oz. (80 g) Arabica coffee beans
1 ¼ cups (300 g) whipping cream
3 tablespoons (10 g) instant coffee
1 oz. (30 g) inverted sugar
1 oz. (30 g) glucose
3 ½ oz. (100 g) ivory couverture chocolate
1 ⅕ oz. (35 g) cocoa butter

Meringue
5 ¼ oz. (150 g) egg whites
⅓ cup (2.6 oz., 75 g) sugar

Chocolate Hazelnut Sauce
½ cup (125 g) full cream milk
¼ cup (62.5 g) whipping cream
3 tablespoons (35 g) sugar
5 ¼ oz. (150 g) Pur Caraïbes couverture chocolate
½ oz. (12.5 g) cocoa paste
1 tablespoon (15 g) butter
1 ½ oz. (40 g) hazelnut paste

Speculoos Paste
1 stick plus 6 tablespoons (7 oz./200 g) butter
1 cup (7 oz./200 g) brown sugar, preferably vergoise
⅓ cup (2.1 oz./60 g) white sugar
1 ½ oz. (40 g) egg
1 tablespoon (16 g) milk
4 cups (14 oz./400 g) flour
1 generous tablespoon (10 g) ground cinnamon
½ teaspoon (2 g) baking powder
Scant ½ teaspoon (2 g) salt
7 oz. (200 g) hazelnuts

For the Coffee Cristalline
Cook the fondant and glucose together in a saucepan to 325°F (160°C). Dissolve the instant coffee in just enough water to form a paste and add it to the fondant and glucose. Then add the ground coffee. Allow the mixture to cool down and solidify, and grind it finely. Sift the powder onto a silicone sheet using rectangular stencils of 1 × 4 in. (2.5 × 10 cm) and 1 × 3 ¼ in. (2.5 × 8 cm). Preheat the oven to 350°F (180°C) and bake the rectangles. When you remove them from the oven, shape them by placing the large rectangles in two ¾-in. (7-cm) diameter tuile molds and the smaller rectangles in 2-in. (5-cm) diameter tuile molds. Store them in an airtight container.

For the Nyambo Chocolate Cream
In a saucepan, bring the cream and milk to the boil. Beat the egg yolks and sugar together until thick and prepare a crème anglaise (custard) with the milk and cream. Slowly pour the mixture over the chopped chocolate, blend together, and chill overnight.

For the Whipped Ivory-Coffee Ganache
Leave the coffee beans to infuse overnight in 1 cup plus 1 scant cup (450 g) whipping cream. Strain through a chinois and add enough cream to bring it back to the original volume. Bring the 1 ¼ cups (300 g) whipping cream to the boil with the instant coffee, inverted sugar, and glucose. Melt the couverture chocolate and cocoa butter and prepare an emulsion with the cream mixture. Incorporate the coffee-bean-infused cream using an immersion blender.

For the Meringue
Prepare the meringue: in the bowl of a stand-alone food processor, beating the egg whites as you pour in the sugar. Spread the mixture out in a layer ½ in.–⅔ in. (1.5 cm) thick on baking parchment on a baking sheet. Bake at 195°F (90°C) for 8 minutes.

For the Chocolate Hazelnut Sauce
Bring the milk, cream, and sugar to the boil in a saucepan. Pour it slowly over the couverture chocolate and cocoa paste. Incorporate the butter and hazelnut paste.

For the Speculoos Pastry
Rub the butter, vergeoise sugar, and white sugar together until the mixture forms crumbs. Add the eggs and milk. Sift the flour with the cinnamon, salt, and baking powder and incorporate into the dough. Chill and roll out to less than ⅛ in. (2 mm). Cut out 8 × 1 ½ in. (20 × 4 cm) strips. Sprinkle roasted chopped hazelnuts over the rest of the pastry and cut out 1 ½ in. (4 cm) disks. Bake at 325°F (160°C) for about 12 minutes.

To Plate

Place 2 round dabs of ivory-coffee ganache on the plate.
Take 2 meringue circles, and put each one between 2 speculoos disks. Set them on top of the ganache dabs. Assemble the cristalline tuiles by filling them with the nyambo chocolate cream piped through a pastry bag.
Cut the assembled cristalline in two halves and place them on the plate. Decorate the plate with 2 round dabs of chocolate hazelnut sauce, and place a speculoos band on top of the crystalline halves.

Le Château de Beaulieu p. 116–119

Puff Pastry Case of Prawns with Gently Cooked Eggplant, Herb Marinade, and Aquitaine Caviar (see photo p. 116)

Serves 6

4 squares of puff pastry measuring
3 × 2 ½ in. (8 × 6 cm)
12 prawns, total weight of 2 lb. (1 kg)

Carrot Syrup
2 carrots
1 ½ tablespoons (20 g) heavy cream
3 ½ tablespoons (50 g) mayonnaise
1 tablespoon plus 1 teaspoon (20 ml) white vinegar
A few drops of lemon juice
Salt and white pepper to taste

Eggplant Caviar
2 tablespoons (30 ml) olive oil
1 eggplant (aubergine)
1 small white onion
1 garlic clove
1 sprig thyme
Scant ½ cup (100 ml) whipping cream
20 green olives, pitted
2 sheets gelatin (4 g)
A few drops of lemon juice
Tabasco sauce
Salt and white pepper to taste

Herb Marinade
Juice of 1 lime
A few drops Tabasco sauce
1 tomato

½ cucumber
2 unblemished white button mushrooms
½ fennel bulb, blanched
2 tablespoons (30 ml) olive oil
A few leaves cilantro (coriander), flat-leaf parsley, marjoram, all finely chopped
Salt, white pepper, Szechuan pepper

Garnish
⅔ oz. (20 g) Aquitaine caviar
Shiso leaves
1 pinch sesame seeds, toasted

For the Carrot Syrup
Peel the carrots and place them in a blender. When liquidized, filter the puree to keep the juice. Add the heavy cream and mayonnaise. Adjust the seasoning with white vinegar and lemon juice. Season with salt and pepper and set aside.

For the Eggplant Caviar
In a saucepan, heat the olive oil. Cut the eggplant into chunks and chop the onion and garlic clove. Place the onion, eggplant, garlic, and thyme in the saucepan and cook over low heat with the lid on. The vegetables should not brown. When cooked through, add the whipping cream and olives, and stew a little until the mixture reaches the texture of a compote. Blend together.

Soften the gelatin leaves and add them to the mixture. Adjust the seasoning with salt, pepper, and Tabasco sauce. Fill a mold to a height of ½ in. (1 cm) and chill.
Flatten 3 prawns between 2 sheets of parchment paper. They should be the same size as each puff pastry rectangle. Repeat the procedure for the other pastry rectangles.

For the Herb Marinade
In a mixing bowl, place the lime juice, salt, pepper, and a few drops of Tabasco sauce. Blanch the fennel. Cut the tomato, cucumber, mushrooms, and blanched fennel into fine dice. Place the vegetables in the bowl, add the herbs and the olive oil, and mix.

To Plate
Place the eggplant caviar on the puff pastry rectangle and then arrange the flattened langoustines above that. Heat for 30 seconds under a salamander. Season the prawns with the carrot syrup. Just before serving, add the herb marinade with the vegetable brunoise. Top with a little Aquitaine caviar and shiso leaves for garnish. Sprinkle with a few toasted sesame seeds and a little ground Szechuan pepper.

Milk-Fed Veal with Seasonal Vegetables (see photo p. 119)

Serves 2

2 oz. (50 g) fresh garden peas

10 snow peas
2 freshly picked carrots
2 salsify roots

4 vitelot potatoes
1 ½ lb. (700 g) veal chop on the bone, trimmed

3 tablespoons (40 ml) olive oil
1 tablespoon plus 1 teaspoon (20 ml) white wine
1 tomato
¾ cup (200 ml) veal stock
7 tablespoons (3 ½ oz./100 g) butter
1 bunch chives, snipped
3 ½ oz. (100 g) morel mushrooms

Vegetable Mirepoix
½ carrot
½ onion
1 stalk celery
1 garlic clove
1 sprig thyme

Nutmeg
Salt and white pepper

Peel, turn, and cook the seasonal vegetables. Reserve, ready for reheating.

Prepare the veal chop. Drizzle a little olive oil in a sauté pan and color the veal. Add the mirepoix (½ carrot, ½ onion, and celery stalk), the garlic, thyme, and seasoning, and cook in a 400°F (200°C) oven for 8 minutes. Remove from the oven and set aside.

Return the sauté pan to the heat, deglaze with a little white wine, and leave to reduce. Quarter the tomatoes and add the pieces to the pot. Then pour in the veal stock and cook over low heat. Filter the liquid: you should have approximately one scant ½ cup (100 ml) sauce.

When you are ready to serve, reheat the seasonal vegetables quickly in the butter with the snipped chives, slice the veal thickly, and arrange the vegetables around the slices. At the last minute, sauté a few morel mushrooms, add them, and finish by drizzling the jus over the meat. Serve immediately.

L'Ambroisie Paris p. 120–123

Braised Medallions of Veal Sweetbreads with Fresh Almonds and Parsley Puree (see photo p. 123)

Serves 4

4 medallions of veal sweetbreads, each weighing 5 oz.
(150 g)
10 oz. (300 g) flat-leaf parsley
1 oz. (30 g) Meaux mustard
7 tablespoons (3 ½ oz./100 g) butter
Scant ½ cup (100 ml) veal jus
1 celery stalk
3 ½ oz. fresh almonds, blanched
Juice of 1 lemon
1 tablespoon (15 ml) almond oil
Salt and pepper to taste

A Day Ahead
Blanch the sweetbreads, press them (for 24 hours), and reserve in the refrigerator.

To Prepare for Serving
Remove the parsley leaves from the stalks, wash them, and blanch them briefly in a large pot of boiling salted water. Refresh, drain, and dry them, pressing the moisture out using a clean cloth. Process the leaves.
Add the Meaux mustard and keep in a warm place.

Season the sweetbreads with salt and pepper. Sauté them in butter until lightly colored and then deglaze with the veal jus. Set aside in a warm place.

Peel the celery stalk and slice very finely. Slice the fresh blanched almonds finely. Squeeze most of the lemon juice over the sliced almonds and sliced celery and stir in the almond oil.

Heat the serving plates well. Reduce the veal jus and add the remaining lemon juice to it. Place the sweetbreads in the center of the plates, scatter the almond and celery salad over, and draw an attractive circle of jus around it. To accompany the sweetbreads, serve a scoop of parsley puree.

Chocolate Tart (see photo p. 121)

Serves 4

Pastry Base
2 cups (7 oz./200 g) cake flour
1 ½ sticks (6 ⅓ oz./180 g) unsalted butter
¾ cup (3 ½ oz./100 g) confectioners' sugar
1 egg

1 pinch salt
1 tablespoon (15 ml) coffee extract

Chocolate Filling
5 oz. (150 g) couverture chocolate, 70% cocoa
2 egg yolks plus 1 whole egg
⅓ cup (2 ⅛ oz./60 g) granulated sugar

A Day Ahead
Prepare the pastry base, using the method required for a sweet short pastry. Chill the dough.

To Prepare the Chocolate Tart
Roll out the pastry dough to a thickness of just under ⅛ in. (2 mm) and line an 8-in. (20 cm) tart circle with it.

Chill for 1 hour. Preheat the oven to 350°F (180°C). Bake the pastry for 12 minutes.

Lower the temperature to 325°F (160°C). Melt the chocolate in a bain-marie.

Whip the egg yolks, the whole egg, and the sugar with an electric hand beater until the mixture is pale and thick. Combine this mixture with the melted chocolate and fill the pastry base. Bake the tart for 8 minutes.

L'Arpège p. 124–127

Delicate Ravioles from the Vegetable Patch in Amber Consommé (see photo p. 127)

Serves 4

Red Ravioles
3 ½ oz. (100 g) mild onions
2 oz. (50 g) red cabbage
3 tablespoons plus 1 teaspoon
2 oz. (50 g) salted butter
⅓ oz. (10 g) roasted almonds
3 sprigs thyme
1 pinch quatre épices (a 4-spice blend including pepper, nutmeg, cloves, and cinnamon)
Juice of ½ lime
16 sheets of Chinese ravioli dough
1 dried fig
Fleur de sel

Green Ravioles
3 ½ oz. (100 g) mild onions
A few sprigs cilantro (coriander)
A few sprigs fresh mint
3 tablespoons plus 1 teaspoon (2 oz./50 g) salted butter
⅓ oz. (10 g) roasted pistachios

1 pinch curry powder
1 pinch ground cumin
Juice of ½ lime
16 sheets of Chinese ravioli dough
2 dried dates
Fleur de sel

Consommé
1 lb. (500 g) celeriac (celery root)
2 cups (500 ml) water
Aged Shoyu (Japanese soy sauce)

For the Red Ravioles
Finely slice the onions and cabbage and sauté in the salted butter, adding the almonds, a few thyme leaves, the spices, lime juice, and fleur de sel. Allow to cool and set aside.

For the Green Ravioles
Finely slice the onions and sauté them with the cilantro and mint leaves in the salted butter, adding the pistachios, curry, cumin, lime juice, and fleur de sel.

To Assemble
Spread out the sheets of ravioli dough and cut them into disks no bigger than 1 ¼–1 ½ in. (3–4 cm) in diameter. In the center of each one, place a small amount (4 g, about 1 teaspoonful), adding a sliver of fig for the red raviole and a sliver of date for the green ravioles. Close the ravioles.

For the Consommé
Process the celeriac with the water. Cook the mixture over low heat for about 15 minutes and strain it through cheesecloth. Season to taste with the aged Shoyu.

Cook the ravioles in simmering water for 20 seconds and serve them in the consommé.

Apple Mille-Feuille (see photo p. 125)

Serves 6

2 pre-rolled sheets of puff pastry
Confectioners' sugar for caramelizing the pastry
2 tablespoons (30 g) butter
1 tablespoon (15 g) sugar
4 apples, Reinette Clochard variety or similar

Preheat the oven to 300°F (150°C). Bake the 2 sheets of puff pastry until golden. Sprinkle them with confectioners' sugar and bake further until just slightly caramelized.

While they are baking, melt the butter in a saucepan with the sugar. Peel and

finely slice the apples. If you have the necessary equipment, you may prepare wafer slices.

Caramelize the apples in the butter and sugar and then arrange them regularly on the first layer of puff pastry. Top with the second layer of pastry, and serve with praline ice cream.

Le Petit Nice p. 128–131

Mediterranean Langouste with Bay Leaf Souplesse, Pear, and Cucumber (see photo p. 131)

Serves 4

1 Mediterranean langouste,
3 lb. 5 oz.–4 lb. 6 oz. (1.5–2 kg)
⅔ cup (150 g) partially skimmed milk
3 bay leaves
2 cucumbers
¾ sheet (1 ½ g) gelatin
1 pear, Williams or Bartlett
Olive oil
Salt and pepper to taste

Cider Ice Cubes

1 pear, Williams or Bartlett
1 cup (250 ml) hard apple cider,
preferably Éric Bordelet's "sydre"
1 cup (250 ml) poiré, hard cider made
from pears, preferably Éric Bordelet's
"sydre"

Kill the langouste quickly by slitting its head in two with a precise, rapid movement. If it is a female, retrieve the eggs to use when you plate the dish. You will need to process them through a vegetable mill, add a drizzle of olive oil, and season with salt and pepper.
Cut the langouste tail into 4 identical pieces, leaving the rings of the shell (they will be removed later).
Set aside in the refrigerator, making sure you keep the liquid, which you can use for another recipe such as a vinaigrette.

Bring the milk to the boil and add the bay leaves. Leave, covered, to infuse for 3 hours.

In the meantime, wash and peel 1 cucumber and cut it in 2 lengthways. Remove the seeds. Blanch it and refresh it in ice.

Process it in the bowl of a food processor and drain it through cheesecloth. Adjust the seasoning of this puree with salt and pepper.
Peel the second cucumber and cut fine strips lengthways using a vegetable peeler. Blanch the strips and refresh them. Drain and cut into ¾ × 5 in. (2 × 12 cm) strips. Set aside in the refrigerator.

For the Cider Ice Cubes

Peel the pear and remove the seeds. Bring the hard apple cider to the boil in a sauté pan. Quarter the pear, place it in the sauté pan, and simmer. When it is done, process the pear with the cider in the food processor and strain through cheesecloth.
Pour the mixture into small round silicone molds and freeze for 3 hours. Take the poiré and pour it, uncooked, into silicone molds of the same shape as those used for the pear mixture. Freeze for 3 hours.

Soften the gelatin in cold water. Strain the infused milk and incorporate the gelatin. Bring to room temperature. Whip the mixture over ice using an electric hand beater. The final consistency should be similar to a lightly whipped Chantilly and this is the bayleaf-scented souplesse.

Leave it in the bowl over ice and set aside.

To cook the langouste: season the medallions with olive oil, salt, and pepper and cook them in a steam oven at 160°F (70°C) for 3–8 minutes, depending on the thickness.
When cooked, remove the shells and trim to remove the outside skin, ensuring that you leave most of the flesh of the medallion.
Cut the pieces into 16 regular medallions and heat them very, very gently in a steam oven at 140°F (60°C) until they are served.

Turn the cider ice cubes out of the molds and insert cucumber strips between them. Arrange them attractively in an iced plate.

Wash the second pear, leaving the skin. Cut it into thin strips. Use a pastry cutter to cut out perfectly shaped half spheres from the center of the pear.

Use a long, flat plate for the main dish. Divide this plate into three with 3 oval scoops of cold cucumber puree.
Place 4 langouste medallions per person on each plate. Place an oval scoop of bay leaf souplesse on each medallion and top with a thin curved slice of raw pear. If the langouste was female and you have eggs, arrange them lengthways on the cucumber scoops. Serve the two plates simultaneously.

Sea Bass, As Lucie Passédat Liked It (see photo p. 129)

Serves 4

Garnish for the fish fumet

1 sea bass weighing 3 lb. 5 oz. (1.5 kg)
1 shallot
1 carrot

½ leek
1 bouquet garni
1 cup (250 ml) olive oil
6 cups (1.5 liters) water

Lucie's Base

6 cups (1.5 liters) fish fumet
14 oz. (400 g) tomatoes
1 teaspoon (5 ml) tomato paste
1 teaspoon (8 g) coriander seeds
½ teaspoon (2.5 g) sugar

Garnish

3 lemons
4 ripe vine tomatoes
2 stalks (20 g) basil
2 stalks (20 g) cilantro (coriander)
1 truffle weighing ⅔ oz. (20 g)
1 cucumber
2 zucchini (courgettes)
3 tablespoons (50 ml) clarified butter
1 green tomato
2 pinches (2 g) wild fennel seeds
1 cup (250 ml) extra virgin olive oil,
preferably Galiga e Vetrice
Cuve Monte Gualberto Grati
Scant ½ cup (100 ml) truffle jus
Fleur de sel (preferably from the
Camargue)
Mignonette pepper

Remove the scales of the fish, gut it, and wash it. Prepare the fillets, removing the bones. Set them aside to use for the fish fumet. Slice the two fillets to make four equal servings of 5 ½ oz. (160 g). Make shallow, regular incisions in the skin.

For the Fumet

Begin with the aromatic garnish. Wash, peel, and chop the shallot, carrot, and leek half.

For the Bouquet Garni

Crush the fish bones and sauté them with 1 cup (250 ml) olive oil. Add the garnish and pour in 6 cups (1.5 liters) water. Add the bouquet garni. Cook for 20 minutes, strain through a chinois, and set aside. You should have 4 ¾ cups (1.2 liters) clear fumet; keep 4 cups (1 liter) for Lucie's Base and the remainder to cook the fish.

For Lucie's Base

Place the 4 cups (1 liter) fish fumet in a pot with the chopped tomatoes, tomato paste, coriander seeds, and sugar, and reduce by half. Strain through a chinois and set aside.

While it is reducing, prepare the lemon zest: dice it very finely (brunoise), blanch it 3 times, and refresh. Set the diced zest aside.
Peel 4 vine tomatoes and dice them finely to make a brunoise. Prepare the leaves of the basil and cilantro (fresh coriander). Wash and chop the leaves.
Prepare the truffle shavings and cut them into round disks with a small pastry cutter. Dice the trimmings into a brunoise. Set aside.
Peel the cucumber and use a mandolin or peeler to form tagliatelle shapes around the seeds. Do the same with the zucchini skin. Work carefully so that they are all nicely shaped and the same size.
Blanch them and refresh. Line a pan with parchment paper and arrange the vegetable tagliatelle on it, alternating 7 zucchini skins with 6 cucumber strips.

Brush a stainless steel ovenproof dish with clarified butter and season it with salt and pepper.

Arrange the slices of green tomato and sea bass fillets in the dish and season with the wild fennel seeds, olive oil, Camargue salt and mignonette pepper. Pour the fish fumet over and cook for 12 minutes in a steam oven at 140°F (60°C), or use a steam cooker. When done, allow it to rest.

Take Lucie's Base and add the chopped cilantro (coriander) and basil, diced lemon zest, tomato cubes, truffle brunoise, olive oil, juice of 2 lemons, and scant ½ cup (100 ml) truffle jus. Adjust the seasoning with salt and pepper. Reheat slightly but do not allow to boil.

Place the vegetable tagliatelle on the cooked fish. Reheat slightly over steam. Take 4 truffle shavings, brush them with olive oil, and season them with salt and pepper. Reheat them in the oven at 300°F (150°C) and then place them carefully on the fish pieces just before serving.

Pour the base into soup plates, place the fish in this, and drizzle the vegetable tagliatelle and base with a little olive oil. Sprinkle with a little Camargue salt or fleur de sel.

Maison Pic p. 132–137

Sea Bass Fillet with Caviar by Jacques Pic (see photo p. 136)

Serves 4

1 sea bass, between 3 ½–6 lb. (2–3 kg)
⅓ oz. (10 g) fennel, sliced
1 shallot, chopped
1 button mushroom, peeled and sliced
Butter
1 ¼ cups (300 ml) champagne
2 ½ cups (600 ml) sea bass fumet
2 cups (500 ml) whipping cream

4 oz. (120 g) royal osetra caviar (1 oz. or 30 g per person)
Salt and freshly ground white pepper

Sweat the sliced fennel, chopped shallot, and mushroom in butter. Pour in 1 cup (250 ml) champagne and ⅔ cup (150 ml) sea bass fumet. Reduce by half. Add the cream and bring to the boil for 2 minutes. Leave to infuse for about 15 minutes. Strain through a fine-mesh chinois and season with salt and freshly ground white pepper.

Fillet the sea bass and remove the bones. Cut the fillets into slices. Season and steam for 3 minutes. Pour over the sauce and top with 1 oz. (30 g) caviar just before serving.

Timeless Warm Grand Marnier Soufflé (see photo p. 133)

Serves 4

Hot Soufflé
½ cup (130 g) milk
1 tablespoon (13 g) sugar
Scant tablespoon (⅓ oz./9 g) cornstarch
or potato starch
1 ¼ oz. (36 g) egg yolks
2 teaspoons (10 g) Grand Marnier
Zest of ½ orange
6 ⅓ oz. (180 g) egg whites
Generous ½ cup (4 oz./110 g) sugar

Iced Soufflé
Scant ½ cup (3 ¾ oz./105 g) orange juice
3 oz. (81 g) sugar
Zest of 1 orange
3 oz. (90 g) egg yolks
½ cup (120 g) cream, whipped
2 tablespoons (30 g) Grand Marnier
2 tablespoons (30 g) Mandarin Napoléon
liqueur

Orange Jelly
7 oz. (200 g) orange juice
Zest of ½ orange
¼ cup (50 g) granulated sugar
½ teaspoon (2 g) agar-agar
1 sheet (2 g) gelatin

Creamed Rice Foam
1 ¾ cups (450 g) milk
Scant ¼ cup (1 ½ oz./45 g) sugar
Knife tip (0.3 g) salt
Zest of ½ orange
½ vanilla bean
⅓ cup (2 ⅔ oz./75 g) rice
¾ oz. (23 g) egg yolk
¾ oz. (23 g) butter
¾ oz. (23 g) milk
¾ oz. (23 g) cream

For the Hot Soufflé
Heat the milk and prepare a pastry cream with the sugar, starch, and egg yolks. Cool down the mixture with a beater and when almost cooled add the Grand Marnier and grated zest. Measure out 7 oz. (200 g) of pastry cream. Whip the egg whites and sugar and combine with the pastry cream.
Butter the molds and sprinkle them with sugar. Fill the molds with the mixture and bake at 350°C (180°F) for 4 minutes, rotating them halfway through.

For the Iced Soufflé
Cook the juice, sugar, and zest to 221°F (105°C). Pour the mixture over the yolks, beating constantly, and cool down by beating. Add the whipped cream and then incorporate the liqueurs. Pour into molds and freeze.

For the Orange Jelly
Heat the juice with the zest. Add the sugar and mix in the agar-agar. Bring the juice to the boil and incorporate the gelatin. Pour out to a thin layer and, when set, cut out with pastry cutter.

For the Creamed Rice Foam
Bring the milk to the boil with the sugar, salt, orange zest, and vanilla. Add the rice and simmer over low heat. Remove from the heat and incorporate the egg yolks and butter. Process and strain the mixture. Then add the same weight of a mixture of half milk, half cream. Use a siphon to serve the foam.

On a plate, place the bowl of hot soufflé. Hollow out the center of the iced soufflé and fill it with creamed rice foam. Place the bowl of iced soufflé next to the hot soufflé. Top the iced soufflé with a disk of orange jelly. Flambé the hot soufflé with warm Grand Marnier.

Le Pré Catelan p. 138–143

Soy Glazed Prawns with Avocado (see photo p. 142)

Serves 4

8 large prawns
1 green, firm avocado pear
¾ cup (150 ml) Kikkoman soy sauce
1 scant teaspoon (3 g) cornstarch
⅔ cup (150 ml) extra virgin olive oil
1 tablespoon (10 g) sesame seeds, toasted
12 small wooden skewers

Shell the prawns and remove the gut. Place them, two by two, and skewer the pairs together with 3 skewers.
Peel the avocado pear, making sure not to damage the flesh, and slice it finely. Bring a scant ½ cup (100 ml) of the Kikkoman sauce to the boil and thicken it with the cornstarch. Place half the thickened sauce in a paper decorating cone. Combine the other half with the olive oil and roasted sesame seeds and prepare a vinaigrette.

Just before serving, sauté the prawns and deglaze them with the remaining Kikkoman sauce. Drizzle the 4 largest slices of avocado pear with the vinaigrette and arrange them over the prawns. Use the decorating cone to dot the plate with sauce.

Crisp Souffléed Apple, Caramel Ice Cream, Hard Cider, and Sparkling Sugar

Serves 4

Garnish

⅓ oz. (10 g) bits of shortcrust pastry
⅓ oz. (10 g) caramelized puffed rice
1 teaspoon (5 g) popping sugar
4 disks of génoise sponge, diameter
1 ¼ in. (3 cm)
4 silver leaves
Apple syrup
Silver powder

Carambar Ice Cream

⅔ cup (180 g) milk
⅔ cup (180 g) whipping cream
4 Carambars (French toffees)
4 egg yolks
Scant ½ cup (2 ¾ oz./80 g) sugar

Sugar Balls

5 ½ oz. (160 g) cube sugar
⅓ cup (80 g) water
2 oz. (50 g) glucose
¼ teaspoon (1 g) green coloring

Light Cream

Scant ⅔ cup (170 g) milk
1 vanilla bean
2 egg yolks
¼ cup (1 ¾ oz./50 g) granulated sugar
⅓ oz. (8 g) flour
⅓ oz. (8 g) "poudre à crème" or
cornstarch

Scant teaspoon (4 g) butter
⅓ cup (80 g) whipping cream
1 scant tablespoon (8 g) confectioners'
sugar
1 Granny Smith apple

A Whiff of Cider

14 oz. (400 g) hard apple cider
3 ½ tablespoons (40 g) sugar
⅔ cup (180 g) cream
1 sheet (2 g) gelatin

For the Carambar Ice Cream

Bring the milk and cream to the boil and melt the Carambar toffees in the mixture. Beat the egg yolks with the sugar until pale and thick. Pour the milk and cream over the egg yolk mixture, return to the saucepan, and cook until it reaches a temperature of 181°F (83°C). Place in the ice-cream maker and freeze.

For the Sugar Balls

Bring the sugar and water to the boil, skimming carefully. Add the glucose and heat to 311°F (155°C). Incorporate the green food coloring and spread the syrup over a silicone baking sheet. Smooth the mixture out. Take a piece and hold it under a hot sugar-heating lamp. Prepare a bubble the size of an apple using a sugar pump. Store in an airtight container.

For the Light Cream

Slit the vanilla bean lengthways and scrape the seeds. Bring the milk to the boil with the vanilla bean. Beat the egg yolks with the sugar until pale and thick and add the flour and the thickening agent, such as cornstarch or French poudre à crème. Pour a little hot milk over the egg mixture, then return it to the saucepan and cook. Whisk in the butter and allow to cool. Whip the cream with the confectioners' sugar. Take ⅓ oz. (10 g) of the Granny Smith apple and cut it into fine dice (brunoise). Combine the pastry cream with the Chantilly cream and chill.

For the Whiff of Cider

Bring the hard cider to the boil and pour in the sugar and cream. Bring to the boil again and incorporate the softened gelatin. Allow to cool and pour into a siphon. Add 3 gas canisters.

Take a ball of sugar and turn it upside down. Fill it with the cider mixture and add the bits of pastry, the puffed rice, and the popping sugar, as well as a scoop of Carambar ice cream. Cover with light cream and diced Granny Smith apple and close with a disk of genoise sponge. Turn the sugar ball the other way round and top it with a sheet of silver. Using a paper decorating cone, dot a mixture of apple syrup and silver powder around the ball. Serve immediately.

Guy Savoy p. 144–147

Coco (see photo p. 146)

Serves 2

2 Thai coconuts, liquid and flesh separated

Tapioca

1 ¼ oz. (35 g) tapioca
Scant ¼ cup (50 ml) water

2 tablespoons plus 2 teaspoons (40 ml)
full cream milk
1 ⅔ cups (400 ml) coconut milk

Coconut Tuiles

⅓ cup (2 oz./50 g) confectioners' sugar
2 ½ tablespoons (15 g) flour

½ oz. (15 g) unsweetened shredded
coconut
1 tablespoon plus 2 teaspoons (25 ml)
coconut milk
2 tablespoons (30 g) butter, melted

A Day Ahead

To make the granita, place the coconut liquid in a container and place it in the freezer. Scratch it regularly with a fork.

For the Tapioca

Cook the tapioca in the water and drain in a fine chinois sieve. Pour the milk and coconut milk into a saucepan and add the tapioca. Simmer over low heat for 10 minutes and cool.

For the Coconut tuiles

In a mixing bowl, whisk together the confectioners' sugar, flour, and shredded coconut. Stir in the coconut milk and melted butter.

Spread the batter over a nonstick baking tray and bake at 325°F (160°C) for 10 minutes. Allow to cool and then crush the tuiles. Store the crushed tuiles in an airtight container.

Cut out the flesh of the coconut and shred it finely. Place a tablespoon of tapioca in each bowl and cover with the crushed coconut tuiles. Top with the julienned coconut and granita.

Jellied Summer Tomatoes with Seaweed and Lemon Granita (see photo p. 145)

Serves 10

Seaweed and Lemon Granita
2 cups (½ liter) water
¾ cup (5 oz./150 g) sugar
1 oz. (30 g) anti-crystallizing agent
1 teaspoon (2 g) dried seaweed
(at Japanese grocery stores)
⅔ oz. (20 g) chopped nori
(at Japanese grocery stores)
2 cups (500 ml) lemon juice

Tomato Chips
2 beefheart tomatoes

Jellied Tomatoes
3 cups (750 ml) water
4 cups (1 liter) tomato juice
Trimmings of 2 tomatoes used for chips
8 sheets (16 g) gelatin
Celery salt
Pepper

Tomato Tartare
2 eggs
⅓ oz. (10 g) capers
⅓ oz. (10 g) gherkins
2 oz. (50 g) new onions
A few sprigs flat-leaf parsley
2 lb. (1 kg) beef-heart tomatoes
8 tablespoons (½ cup/120 ml) extra virgin olive oil

Green Vegetables
2 lb. (1 kg) fava beans, unshelled
1 lb. (500 g) peas, unshelled
3 oz. (100) snow peas
5 oz. (150 g) string beans
Scant ¼ cup (50 ml) lemon-scented olive oil

Salad
7 oz. (200 g) mixed salad greens, such as tatsoi or flat pak choy, mizuna, winter cress, arugula (rocket), and baby spinach leaves
1 bunch chives
¾ cup (200 ml) extra virgin olive oil
1 lb. (500 g) fresh almonds, unblanched

A Day Ahead

Prepare the granita: heat the water to 122°F (50°C). Add the sugar and stir in the anti-crystallizing agent. Combine with the seaweed and lemon juice and freeze.
Using a meat-slicing machine set at ¹⁄₁₆ in. (1.5 mm), and cut the tomatoes. Dry the slices in a ventilated oven at 175°F (80°C) for about three hours. Peel the tomatoes for the tartare, cut them in half, and remove the seeds. Chill until needed.

For the Jellied Tomatoes

Simmer together the tomato juice, water, and tomato trimmings over low heat for 1 hour 45 minutes. Soften the gelatin and dissolve in the mixture. Season with salt and pepper. Strain the jellied tomatoes through cheesecloth. Season with celery salt and pepper.
Pour the jellied tomatoes into deep plates to a height of ¼ in. (5 mm) and chill.

For the Tartare

Hard boil the eggs. Chop the capers, gherkins, and hardboiled eggs. Chop the new onions and the parsley. Cut the tomatoes into large dice. Season with olive oil and add the tartare garnish (capers, gherkins, eggs, onions, and parsley).

For the Green Vegetables

Top and tail and shell the green vegetables. Cook them and refresh. Season with the lemon-scented oil and salt.

Using a fork, scratch the seaweed granita and return it to the freezer.

For the Salad

Remove the hard stems from the salad leaves and wash and dry them.
Puree the chives with the ¾ cup (200 ml) of olive oil and strain through a fine-mesh chinois. Chop the salad greens and shell and chop the almonds. Stir the chopped salad greens and chopped almonds into the pureed chives and season.

To plate, place the tomato tartare in a pastry ring in the center of the plate over the jellied tomato. Arrange the green vegetables and tomato chips attractively on the plate. Drizzle a line of chive vinaigrette over and top the tomato tartare with a spoonful of granita. If you wish, serve this starter with a tomato and basil puff pastry tart.

Dill-Scented Crab Rémoulade, Light Lemon Cream (see photo p. 149)

Serves 1

1 crab weighing approx. 1 ¼ lb. (600 g)
1 egg
⅓ oz. (10 g) Dijon mustard
Scant ½ cup (100 g) peanut oil
1 oz. (30 g) carrot
1 oz. (30 g) celery stalk
1 oz. (30 g) zucchini (courgette)
⅓ oz. (10 g) dill leaves
1 tablespoon plus 1 teaspoon (20 ml)
whipping cream
Juice of 1 lemon
2 oz. (50 g) spinach
3 red radishes, sliced with a mandolin
Piment d'Espelette
Ground Guérande salt
Freshly ground pepper

Cook the crab in salted boiling water and shell it.
Prepare a mayonnaise with the egg, mustard, and peanut oil.
Finely dice the carrot, celery, and zucchini. Blanch the vegetables, drain, and refresh.

Pick the dill leaves off the stalks and chop them.
To make the light lemon cream, take 1 tablespoon (15 ml) mayonnaise and add the whipping cream and lemon juice to it. Adjust the seasoning.

Blanch the spinach leaves and process them until they form a smooth, green puree. Combine the crab, diced vegetables, a little mayonnaise, and dill.
Stir some pureed spinach into some more mayonnaise to give it a nice color and spoon it into a paper decorating cone.

Draw a line of light lemon cream around the plate. Dot the green mayonnaise around the lemon cream. Place a pastry circle in the center of the plate and fill it with crab. Smooth it over with a spatula and arrange the radish slices in a rosette shape over it. Brush with olive oil and sprinkle with piment d'Espelette.

Upside-Down Chocolate and Coffee Cake (see photo p. 151)

Serves 10

Soft Ganache
1 ¼ cups (300 g) cream
10 oz. (300 g) dark chocolate
2 eggs
4 tablespoons (60 g) butter, room temperature

Chocolate Sponge
1 ½ oz. (45 g) dark chocolate
2 oz. (60 g) egg yolks
Scant ⅔ cup (4 ¼ oz./120 g) sugar, divided
6 ⅓ oz. (180 g) egg whites

Coffee Crème Brûlèe
1 ½ cups (13 oz./375 g) cream
½ cup (125 g) milk
4.4 oz. (125 g) egg yolks
¼ cup (1 ¾ oz./50 g) sugar
2 tablespoons plus 1 teaspoon
(¼ oz./8 g) instant coffee
1 sheet (2 g) gelatin

Chocolate Decoration
13 oz. (375 g) dark chocolate,
70% cocoa
Light brown sugar

For the Soft Ganache
Bring the cream to the boil and pour it over the chocolate. Incorporate the eggs, followed by the butter.

For the Chocolate Sponge
Melt the chocolate. Beat the egg yolks with half the sugar until thick and pale. Whip the egg whites with the remaining sugar. Incorporate the egg yolks into the chocolate. Carefully fold in half the egg whites, and then fold in the remaining half. Pour the batter onto a baking tray to a thickness of just under ⅛ in. (2 mm) and bake at 350°C (180°F) for 8 minutes.

For the Coffee Crème Brûlée
Bring the cream and milk to the boil. Beat the egg yolks with the sugar and instant coffee until thick. Pour the cream-milk liquid over the egg yolks, and stir in the softened gelatin sheet.

Line a pastry ring smaller than the sponge with plastic wrap and fill it with the crème brûlée mixture. Freeze.

When the cream has set, bake at 175°F (80°C) for 25 minutes. Allow to cool for at least 1 hour in the refrigerator.

To Assemble the Cake
Top the chocolate sponge with the soft ganache. Place in a 350°F (175°C) oven and switch the oven off. Leave it for 4 minutes.
Allow to cool in the refrigerator for at least 15 minutes.

For the Chocolate Decoration
Melt the dark chocolate in a bain-marie until it reaches 113°F (45°C). Place it over ice until the temperature is lowered to 75–77°F (24°–25°C). Put it back in the bain-marie until it reaches a temperature of 88–90°F (31°–32°C). Spread the chocolate onto a sheet of silicone paper. Cut out circles using a 1 ½ in. (3.5 cm) diameter pastry cutter. Then cut them into halves and chill.

To Plate

Turn the chocolate tart upside down into the center of the plate.
Sprinkle the top of the crème brûlée with brown sugar and brush off any excess.

Remove the plastic wrap from beneath the pastry ring of the crème brûlée and place it carefully in the center of the sponge. Remove the ring.

Using a salamander, caramelize it regularly and neatly.
Take the half-circles of chocolate off the paper and insert them at a slight angle all the way round the crème brûlée.

Auberge des Templiers p. 152–155

Tanariva Chocolate Cannelloni, Whole Raspberry Sorbet (see photo p. 155)

Serves 4

Cannelloni
3 ½ oz. (100 g) chocolate for tempering
1 stainless steel cylinder, 5 in. (12 cm) long, diameter 1 ¼ in. (3 cm)

Chocolate Mousse
Scant ½ cup (100 ml) water
Scant ¼ cup (1 ½ oz./45 g) sugar
2 egg yolks
3 ½ oz. (100 g) Tanariva chocolate
2 tablespoons (½ oz./15 g) unsweetened cocoa powder
¾ cup (200 ml) whipping cream

3 ½ oz. (100 g) raspberry bits
⅔ pint (⅓ liter) raspberry sorbet

For the Canelloni
Melt the chocolate until it reaches a temperature of 90°F (32°C). Using a brush, criss-cross lines of chocolate around the cylinder so that you have an open-work "cannelloni." Allow to cool and detach from the cylinder. Repeat the procedure 3 times.

For the Chocolate Mousse
Bring the water and sugar to the boil, to a temperature of 243°F (117°C).

Pour it steadily into the bowl of a mixer over the egg yolks. Beat until the volume has tripled.
Melt the chocolate with the cocoa powder. Whip the cream and incorporate the melted chocolate. Carefully fold the chocolate cream into the egg yolk mixture with the raspberry bits.

Spoon it into a pastry bag and pipe it into the chocolate cylinders. Chill.
Serve a scoop of whole raspberry sorbet with the Tanariva cannelloni.

Venison Medallions *en Poivrade*, Juniper-Scented Brussels Sprouts (see photo p. 153)

Serves 4

14 oz. (400 g) Brussels sprouts
2 tablespoons (30 g) butter
8 juniper berries, crushed
12 venison medallions, each 1 ½ oz. (40 g)
Butter
1 shallot, chopped
1 tablespoon (15 ml) cognac
¾ cup (200 ml) red wine, preferably a Rhône red
Salt and pepper to taste

Cook the Brussels sprouts in salted boiling water and drain them.
Melt the butter in a sauté pan, add the Brussels sprouts, and sauté until slightly colored. Sprinkle with the crushed juniper berries. Keep in a warm place.

Season the venison medallions and brown them in a pan with a little butter, 1 minute on each side. Transfer to a dish and keep in a warm place.

Sweat the shallot in the same pan, flambé with the cognac, and pour in the red wine. Reduce until thick. Whisk in a knob of unsalted butter and grind the pepper mill over 4 or 5 times.

Arrange the Brussels sprouts and venison medallions in the plates, accompanied by the sauce.

La Tour d'Argent p. 156–159

Duck Tour d'Argent (see photo p. 157)

Serves 4

2 large ducks, each weighing 3 ½ lb. (1.6 kg)
Livers of the 2 ducks, finely minced
1 shot glass of aged Madeira wine
1 small glass of cognac
A little lemon juice
1 glass well-spiced consommé
Salt and pepper to taste

Roast the duck over a strong fire for 25–30 minutes.

Place the chopped livers in a deep silver dish. Add the Madeira wine, cognac, and lemon juice.

Cut off the thighs and grill them while you prepare the fillets.

Remove the skin from the fillets and slice them, making your slices as thin and wide as possible. Place the slices in the silver dish with the other ingredients. Crush the carcass to extract the blood. While it is exuding, pour in the glass of consommé.

Pour this juice over the fillets. Place the dish over a plate warmer and cook for 25 minutes, ensuring that you stir the sauce constantly. The reduction should be very creamy.

Arrange the fillets on a heated plate and serve with a generous helping of sauce, accompanied by pommes soufflées (thinly sliced double-fried potatoes). The grilled thighs are served as the following course, accompanied by a small salad.

Pike Quenelles in the Style of André Terrail (see photo p. 159)

Serves 6 to 8

2 lb. (1 kg) fillets freshwater pike perch
4 egg whites
3 ⅔ pints (7 cups/1.75 liters) crème fraîche
1 stick (110 g) butter
1 lb. 10 oz. (750 g) button mushrooms
Juice of 1 lemon
4 shallots
4 ¼ pints (2 liters) water
3 ½ oz. (100 g) grated cheese, such as Gruyère
Salt and pepper to taste, kosher salt

Sauce Mornay

3 ½ tablespoons (2 oz./50 g) butter
½ cup (2 oz./50 g) flour
2 cups (500 ml) milk
1 generous pinch grated nutmeg
2 ⅔ oz. (75 g) grated cheese
Salt and pepper to taste

For the Quenelles

Ensure that there are no bones in the pike and press the fish through a fine sieve or process it to make a smooth puree. Place the puree in a mixing bowl, and then place the mixing bowl in a large bowl filled with crushed ice. Incorporate the egg whites one by one using a wooden spoon to mix them in. Season with salt and pepper. Leave to rest over the ice for 2 hours.

Then gradually pour in all the crème fraîche, stirring constantly, until the mixture is thoroughly blended. Preheat the oven to 400°F (200°C). Grease a large ovenproof dish with 2 tablespoons (25 g butter). Use a soupspoon to scoop out the quenelle mixture and place them in the buttered dish.

Salt the 4 ¼ pints (2 liters) water and bring to the boil. Pour the water into the dish. Place the dish in the oven and cook for about 35 minutes, ensuring that the liquid does not boil. If necessary, reduce the oven temperature.

For the Garnish

While the quenelles are cooking, remove the sandy base from the button mushrooms. Wash them quickly, dab dry, and mince them very finely. Immediately mix in the lemon juice. Peel and finely chop the shallots. Heat 4 tablespoons (60 g) butter in a heavy bottomed pan and add the shallots. Sauté for 2 minutes without allowing them to color. Then add the mushrooms and cook for 4–5 minutes over high heat, stirring constantly so that the liquid evaporates. When the vegetables are dry, season with salt and pepper and incorporate the remaining cream. Lower the heat and cook for a further 5 minutes. Remove from the heat.

For the Sauce Mornay

Melt the butter in a heavy bottomed saucepan and add the flour. Stir for 2–3 minutes over low heat, then pour in all the milk, whisking as you do so. Season with the nutmeg, salt, and pepper. Stir for 5 minutes as the sauce thickens and then remove it from the heat. Incorporate the grated cheese and set aside.

Remove the dish with the quenelles from the oven. Remove them from the dish with a slotted spoon and place them on paper towel to absorb their liquid.

Turn the oven to "broil."

Grease a large gratin dish with 2 tablespoons (25 g) butter. Spread out the minced mushrooms on the bottom of the dish and place the quenelles above.

Pour over the sauce Mornay and sprinkle with 3 ½ oz. (100 g) grated cheese. Place the dish under the broiler and grill for 7–8 minutes. Serve immediately.

L'Aubergade p. 160–163

Lamb Club Sandwich (see photo p. 163)

Serves 4

1 shoulder of milk-fed lamb weighing between 1 lb. 5 oz. and 1 ¾ lb. (600–800 g)
2 tablespoons (1 oz./30 g) salt
Freshly ground black pepper
1 lb. 5 oz. (600 g) spunta potatoes or other floury variety
¾ cup (200 ml) milk
1 ⅔ cups (400 ml) cream
Nutmeg to taste
2 cloves garlic
1 sprig thyme

Herb Pesto

2 oz. (60 g) parsley leaves
2 oz. (60 g) cilantro (coriander) leaves
2 oz. (60 g) mint leaves
2 garlic cloves
½ teaspoon ground ginger
¼ teaspoon ground cumin
¾ cup (200 ml) olive oil

Crisp Potatoes

14 oz. (400 g) spunta potatoes or other floury variety
7 tablespoons (3 ½ oz./100 g) clarified butter

Two Days Ahead
Bone the shoulder of lamb and season it. For every pound, use 1 teaspoon plus one heaped ½ teaspoon salt and 6 turns of the pepper mill (17 g salt and 2 g pepper per 2.2 lb./1 kg). Rub the seasoning in and chill for 12 hours.
Preheat the oven to 285°F (140°C). Roll the lamb shoulder in aluminum foil as you would for a roast beef. Cover the bottom of the roasting pan with kosher salt and cook the meat for 4 hours. Chill for 24 hours.

One Day Ahead
Preheat the oven to 300°F (150°C). Combine the milk, cream, nutmeg, garlic, and thyme in a large pot or an ovenproof dish.
Peel and dry the potatoes, and with a mandolin slice them into rounds about ⅛ in. (4 mm) thick. Place the slices in the milk mixture, stir carefully, and bring to the boil. Place the dish in the oven for 40 minutes. Then drain the potato slices and overlap them in two rows in a terrine.

For the Herb Pesto
Wash the green herbs and combine them in a mixer with the garlic, ginger, cumin and oil to create a pesto. Brush the slices of potato with pesto. Cut the lamb into slices ⅒–⅛ in. (3–4 mm) thick and arrange them over the layer of pesto. Brush the lamb with pesto. Repeat with two rows of potato slices covered in pesto and continue until all the ingredients are used, finishing with a layer of potato slices.

Preheat the oven to 250°F (120°C). Weigh down the contents of the terrine and place it in a bain-marie. Cook for 30 minutes. Remove from the oven, leaving the weight, and chill for 24 hours.

For the Crisp Potatoes
Preheat the oven to 285°F (140°C). Peel and dry the potatoes. Using a mandolin, slice them into disks under ⅛ in. (1.5–2 mm) thick. Line an ovenproof dish with parchment paper and carefully arrange the potato slices on it, overlapping them like scales. Ensure that your rectangle of potato slices measures 12 × 10 in. (30 × 40 cm). Using a pastry brush, baste them with clarified butter. Cover with another sheet of parchment paper and place a baking tray over this.
Cook for 40 minutes and remove from the oven. Season with salt while still hot and cut triangles that fit the diagonal of the terrine. Turn the potato and lamb terrine out of the mold, cut it into slices 1 ½ in. (4 cm) thick, and heat them in the oven or under the grill for 5 minutes. Cut them on the diagonal and stand them on their sides on the plates. Cover with potato triangles and serve with additional pesto.

Vegetable Risotto

Serves 4

1 lb. 5 oz. (600 g) vegetables, such as
Carrots
Celeriac (celery root)
Zucchini (courgette), or your choice of
vegetables
¼ cup (60 g) vegetable jus
2 oz. (60 g) Parmesan cheese

⅓ cup (80 g) mascarpone
5 ½ tablespoons or ¾ stick (80 g) butter
Salt and pepper

Peel and cut the vegetables into a brunoise (very fine dice).
Bring a pot of salted water to the boil and briefly boil the diced vegetables. Refresh immediately in ice water, drain, and dry by pressing the dice between two dishcloths.
Bring the vegetable jus to the boil in a saucepan, add the diced vegetables, and bring to the boil again. Add the grated Parmesan and the mascarpone. Bring to boiling point and whisk in the butter. Season to taste with salt and pepper.

La Maison Troisgros p. 164–167

Truffle and Parmesan Mezzaluna (see photo p. 167)

Serves 4

2 large potatoes, each 14 oz. (400 g)
Olive oil
40 girolle mushrooms
1 stick (120 g) butter
Scant ½ cup (100 ml) white chicken stock
White Orléans vinegar
20 fresh truffle shavings
Salt and pepper to taste

Stuffing
3 tablespoons (50 g) butter
½ cup (2 oz./50 g) flour
1 cup (250 g) full-cream milk
1 oz. (30 g) pureed truffle
2 oz. (60 g) Parmesan

To prepare the stuffing, cook the roux (butter and flour) for a few minutes over low heat. Add the milk and cook for a further 5 minutes.
Remove from the heat, add the pureed truffle and grated Parmesan, and adjust the seasoning. Set aside.

Peel the potatoes. Using a mandolin, slice them very thinly lengthways. You will need 40 slices. Place them in a sous vide bag with a drizzle of olive oil. Vacuum seal the bag and cook at 195°F (90°C) in a steam oven for 12 minutes. Open the bag. Place a little stuffing in the center of each potato slice. Fold over as you would for ravioles and trim with a pastry cutter so that it is neat and perfectly sealed. Repeat the procedure with the remaining potato slices. Sauté the girolle mushrooms with 1 tablespoon plus 1 teaspoon (20 g) butter. Adjust the seasoning.

Place the mezzaluna individually on the dish, leaning them on the mushrooms to give them a little height. Cover the dish with plastic wrap and heat in a 175°F (80°C) oven for 10–15 minutes.

While the mezzaluna are baking, heat the white chicken stock and whip in the butter. Season with salt, pepper, and a few drops of vinegar.
Remove the plastic. Dot the truffle shavings around the dish and surround with the hot butter sauce. Serve immediately.

Piquant Red Mullet and Tart Red Belgian Endives (see photo p. 167)

Serves 8

4 red Belgian endives
⅓ oz. (10 g) fleur de sel
Juice of 3 lemons
⅓ oz. (10 g) fresh ginger
4 red mullet, weighing 8 oz. (250 g) each
Olive oil
Cherry tomatoes

For the Spiced Butter
2 lb. (1 kg) beefheart tomatoes
1 ⅓ stick (5 ¼ oz./150 g) butter, softened
1 teaspoon (5 g) ground chili pepper
1 tablespoon (15 g) yuzu juice
Table salt

Three Days Ahead
Pick off the leaves of the red Belgian endives. Blanch them briefly in boiling water, no more than 30 seconds, and drain. Arrange them, separated, in a dish and sprinkle with fleur de sel. Set aside for 3 hours. Add the lemon juice and chopped ginger, cover with plastic wrap, and leave to marinate for at least 3 days.

Spiced Butter
Wash the tomatoes and remove the stems. Cut them up roughly and process. Leave them to stew over low heat until all the liquid has evaporated. Then strain

the pulp through a sieve. Return it to the stove to reduce further until you have a dense, concentrated paste. You will need just over 5 oz. (150 g).

In the bowl of a food processor, use the blade knife to combine the butter, chili pepper, yuzu juice, and tomato paste. Season with salt.

Prepare the mullet fillets. Season them with salt and pepper and brush the skin with olive oil. Rinse some parchment paper and cut into an 8 in. (20 cm) square and wrap each mullet fillet up. Set aside in the refrigerator.

Spread the tomato butter over a chablon silicone stencil sheet in the shape of the mullet fillet. Make as many shapes as you have fillets. Chill them to set.

Just before serving, cook the mullet fillets on a perforated tray over steam for a few minutes.

On each plate, arrange 3 red leaves, 3 slivers of cherry tomato, the red Belgian endive juice, and a few drops of olive oil. Unwrap the mullet fillets. Place a piece of butter on the skin.

Place them under the broiler so that the butter melts slightly and arrange the fillets on the plates.

Le Grand Véfour p. 168–171

Manjari Chocolate Cubes, Spiced Pineapple, Shiso Foam, Tonka Bean Sorbet (see photo p. 171)

Serves 10

10 molded cubes of Manjari couverture chocolate, each 3 ½ × 2 ¼ × 2 ¼ in. (9 × 5.5 × 5.5 cm)

Spiced Pineapple
2 lb. (1 kg) pineapple
Scant ½ cup (80 g) sugar
Small pinch (0.5 g) ground ginger
Small piece (0.5 g) star anise
Small pinch (0.5 g) green anise
Small piece (0.5 g) cinnamon stick
Sliver (0.3 g) tonka bean

Spiced Pineapple Sauce
1 lb. (500 g) pureed pineapple
3 ½ oz. (100 g) spiced pineapple juice
¾ teaspoon (2 g) Xantana (thickening agent)
Scant ¼ cup (50 ml) lime juice
Grated zest of 1 lime

Creamed Shiso
1 cup (250 ml) milk
⅓ oz. (10 g) green shiso, finely chopped
2 egg yolks
3 tablespoons (1 ¼ oz./35 g) granulated sugar
3 tablespoons (½ oz./15 g) flour
1 tablespoon plus 1 teaspoon (⅓ oz./10 g) powdered milk
5 tablespoons plus 1 teaspoon (2 ½ oz./75 g) butter

Shiso Foam
1 cup (250 ml) full-cream milk
1 scant cup (200 ml) whipping cream
Scant ¼ cup (1 ½ oz./45 g) sugar
⅓ oz. (10 g) green shiso, finely chopped
2 sheets (4 g) gelatin

Tonka Shortbread
1 ⅔ sticks (6 ½ oz./185 g) butter
1 cup plus 1 scant cup (6 ½ oz./185 g) flour
½ cup (3 ½ oz./100 g) white sugar
¼ cup (2 oz./50 g) light brown sugar, preferably vergeoise
¾ teaspoon (3 g) fleur de sel
1 oz. (30 g) beaten egg, the equivalent of half a beaten egg
1 ½ teaspoons (6 g) baking powder
½ vanilla bean
½ tonka bean, grated

Tonka Ice Cream
2 cups (500 ml) full cream milk
3 egg yolks
Scant ⅓ cup (1 ⅕ oz./35 g) powdered milk
½ cup (125 ml) whipping cream
1 tonka bean
⅓ cup (2 ½ oz./75 g) granulated sugar

Green Flakes
7 oz. (200 g) cocoa butter
7 oz. (200 g) ivory couverture chocolate
¼ teaspoon (1 g) green food coloring

Yellow Flakes
7 oz. (200 g) cocoa butter
7 oz. (200 g) ivory couverture chocolate
Few drops (3 g) yellow food coloring

For the Spiced Pineapple
Grind the spices to a fine powder. Prepare a dry caramel with the sugar. Cut the pineapple into ⅓ in. (1 cm) dice and add to the caramel. Add the spices. Simmer for about 10 minutes, until the pineapple is cooked but retains a slight crunch. Drain, reserving the juices separately.

For the Spiced Pineapple Sauce
Process all the ingredients and chill.

For the Shiso Cream
Bring the milk to the boil and place ¼ oz. (8 g) shiso to infuse for 10 minutes. Beat the egg yolks with the sugar until pale and thick. Incorporate the flour and powdered milk. Strain the milk into the egg yolk mixture, pressing down well, and return the liquid to the heat. Bring to the boil and simmer for 3 minutes. Transfer to a dish to cool. When it has reached 95°F–104°F (35°C–40°C), whisk in the butter. Add the remaining teaspoon (2 g) of chopped shiso with a flexible spatula and chill.

For the Shiso Foam

Bring the milk to the boil with the cream and sugar and then add ¼ oz. (8 g) shiso to infuse for 8 minutes. Blend the mixture, soften the gelatin, and incorporate it into the liquid. Strain through a chinois, pressing down well, and leave to cool. Pour into a siphon.

For the Tonka Shortbread

Combine all the ingredients in the bowl of a food processor using a paddle beater. Leave the dough to rest for 4 hours. Roll it out to a thickness of ¹⁄₁₀ in. (3 mm) and bake at 325°F (160°C) for 15 minutes. Cut out ten 1 ¾ in. (4.5 cm) squares.

For the Tonka Ice Cream

Combine the milk, cream, powdered milk, and finely crushed tonka bean and bring to the boil. Beat the egg yolks and sugar together until pale and thick and pour the hot milk mixture over. Return to the saucepan and heat to 185°F (85°C). Remove from the heat, allow to cool, and leave to rest for 4 hours. Strain the custard through a chinois and freeze in an ice-cream maker.

Colored Flakes

Melt the cocoa butter in a bain-marie. Add the food colorings and then the ivory couverture chocolate.

Cover the 10 cubes of Manjari chocolate with the green and yellow flakes and leave to harden in the refrigerator.

To serve, carefully turn the cubes upside down and fill them with pineapple, spiced pineapple sauce, shiso cream and foam, and a small scoop of tonka ice cream. Use a tonka shortbread square to make a lid to close. Turn the cubes with the shortbread square on the bottom onto the plates and decorate attractively.

Lamb Fillet and Salsify au Jus and au Vinaigre, Delicately Pureed Hubbard Squash, Preserved Lemon Zest, and Chervil (see photo p. 169)

Serves 10

5 racks of lamb, 6 chops each

Salsify au Jus
Twenty 5-in. (12-cm)-long salsify, peeled
3 tablespoons (40 g) olive oil
½ teaspoon (2 g) kosher salt
1 sprig thyme
1 bay leaf

Salsify au Vinaigre
Twenty 5-in. (12-cl) long salsify, peeled
⅓ cup (4 ½ oz./125 g) multifloral honey
4 ½ oz. (125 g) white distilled vinegar
½ cup (125 ml) water
12 coriander seeds
6 cardamom pods

Pureed Hubbard Squash
7 oz. (200 g) peeled Hubbard squash
1 ½ cups (350 ml) water
1 tablespoon plus 1 teaspoon (20 ml) Hubbard squash cooking liquid
1 tablespoon (15 g) butter
Salt

Preserved Lemon
1 lemon
2 cups (500 ml) water

⅔ cup (4 ½ oz./125 g) sugar

Jus
1 tablespoon plus 1 teaspoon (20 ml) cooking liquid used for the lemon
Approximately 1 teaspoon (5 g) finely chopped preserved lemon
½ teaspoon (2 g) chopped chervil
Salt and freshly ground pepper

Chervil Puree
1 ½ oz. (40 g) chervil stalks
Salt

Lemon Scoops
5 oz. (150 g) good quality plain yoghurt
Approximately ½ teaspoon (2.5 g) lemon zest, grated
Salt and freshly ground pepper

Algin Bath
2 cups (500 ml) water
½ teaspoon (2.5 g) alginic acid

For the Salsify au Jus

The salsify should all be of the same diameter, about ½ in. (1 cm). Place them in a pot large enough to hold them side by side. Pour the olive oil over, add the other ingredients, and cover with a parchment paper lid. Bring the pot to the boil and cook for 10 minutes over medium heat.

For the Salsify au Vinaigre

The salsify should all be of the same diameter, about ½ in. (1 cm). Caramelize the honey until brown. Deglaze it with the vinegar and water. Add the spices and the salsify. Cover with the lid, bring to the boil, and simmer over low heat for 20 minutes.

For the Pureed Hubbard Squash

Cut the squash into chunks and place them in a pot. Cover with water and add salt. Bring to the boil and cook. Drain, reserving the cooking liquid.

Process the squash with some of the cooking liquid. Pour the puree into a saucepan and whip in the butter. Adjust the seasoning.

For the Preserved Lemon

Bring the water to the boil with the sugar. Quarter the lemon lengthways and put the pieces into the boiling water. Cover with a parchment paper lid and simmer for 1 hour. Leave to cool in the syrup.

For the Jus
Combine the ingredients, heat, and adjust the seasoning.

For the Chervil Puree
Cook the chervil for 5 minutes in salted boiling water. Refresh and drain. Blend into a fine puree.

For the Lemon Scoops
Combine the ingredients and season with salt and pepper. Strain through a sieve.

For the Algin Bath
Combine the water with the alginic acid. Using a half-teaspoon (2.5 ml) melon baller, prepare 30 scoops of lemon yoghurt. Soak them for 2–3 minutes in the alginic acid bath. Rinse them under clear water. Set aside.

Prepare the lamb fillets, making sure that no sinews or skin remain. Cut the meat fillets into 10 × 4 ½ oz. (130 g) portions and push a salsify au vinaigre lengthways through them. Set aside.

Season the lamb fillets with salt and pepper. Brown them in olive oil and leave to rest on a rack for 10 minutes. When necessary, cook them for 4 to 5 minutes in a 480°F (250°C) oven. Heat 2 salsify au jus and 1 au vinaigre per person in a saucepan with a little of the salsify cooking liquid.

Heat the pureed squash in a saucepan and adjust the texture by adding a little water.

At the left of the plate, arrange the salsify (dabbed dry) with a line of squash puree drawn between each one.
At the right, draw out an attractive teardrop shape of squash puree, from the top to the bottom, and draw a thin line of chervil puree in the squash puree, following the shape.
Cut the lamb fillet in 2 and arrange the two halves over the salsify. Drizzle over with jus.
To finish, place 2 lemon scoops at each side of the lamb and another on the tail end of the teardrop of pureed squash.

Index of Recipes

Index of Restaurants and Chefs